Constructing Invisibility

Publishers of Architecture, Art, and Design
Gordon Goff: Publisher

www.oroeditions.com
info@oroeditions.com

Published by ORO Editions

Editor: Jeffrey S. Nesbit
Foreword: Kate Wingert-Playdon
Contributors: Pedro Ignacio Alonso, Ryan Bishop, Keaton Bruce, Randy Crandon, Lindsey Freeman, Philip Glahn, Gretchen Heefner, Ghazal Jafari, Eliyahu Keller, May Khalife, César Lopez, Jeffrey S. Nesbit, Hugo Palmarola, Victoria Sanger, Malkit Shoshan, Mark Stanley, Charles Waldheim, Dongwoo Yim
Graphic Design: Michael Ray and Keaton Bruce
Copyeditor: Elizabeth Kugler
ORO Managing Editor: Kirby Anderson

10 9 8 7 6 5 4 3 2 1 First Edition

Library of Congress data available upon request. World Rights: Available

ISBN: 978-1-935935-57-5

Color Separations and Printing: ORO Editions, Inc.
Printed in China.

International Distribution: www.oroeditions.com/distribution

ORO Editions makes a continuous effort to minimize the overall carbon footprint of its publications. As part of this goal, ORO Editions, in association with Global ReLeaf, arranges to plant trees to replace those used in the manufacturing of the paper produced for its books. Global ReLeaf is an international campaign run by American Forests, one of the world's oldest nonprofit conservation organizations. Global ReLeaf is American Forests' education and action program that helps individuals, organizations, agencies, and corporations improve the local and global environment by planting and caring for trees.

Temple University
Tyler School of Art and Architecture
2001 N. 13th St. Philadelphia, PA 19122

https://tyler.temple.edu

Constructing Invisibility

Infrastructure, Militarization, and the Extreme Environment

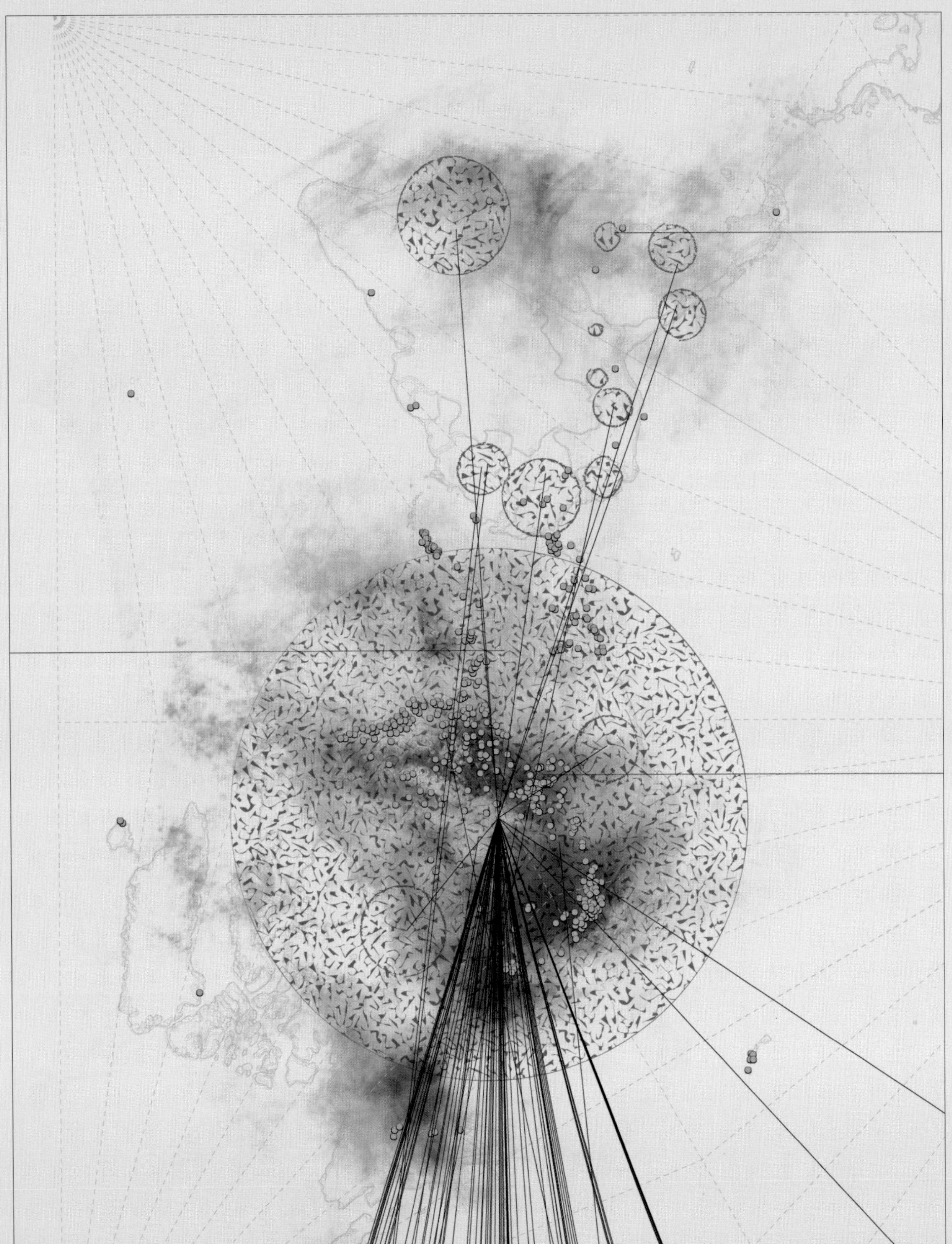

Camels,
Cables,
Bombs.

0.1 A network of infrastructure [detail]. Global port densities, telecommunication cables, commercial flight paths, and per capita infrastructure spending.

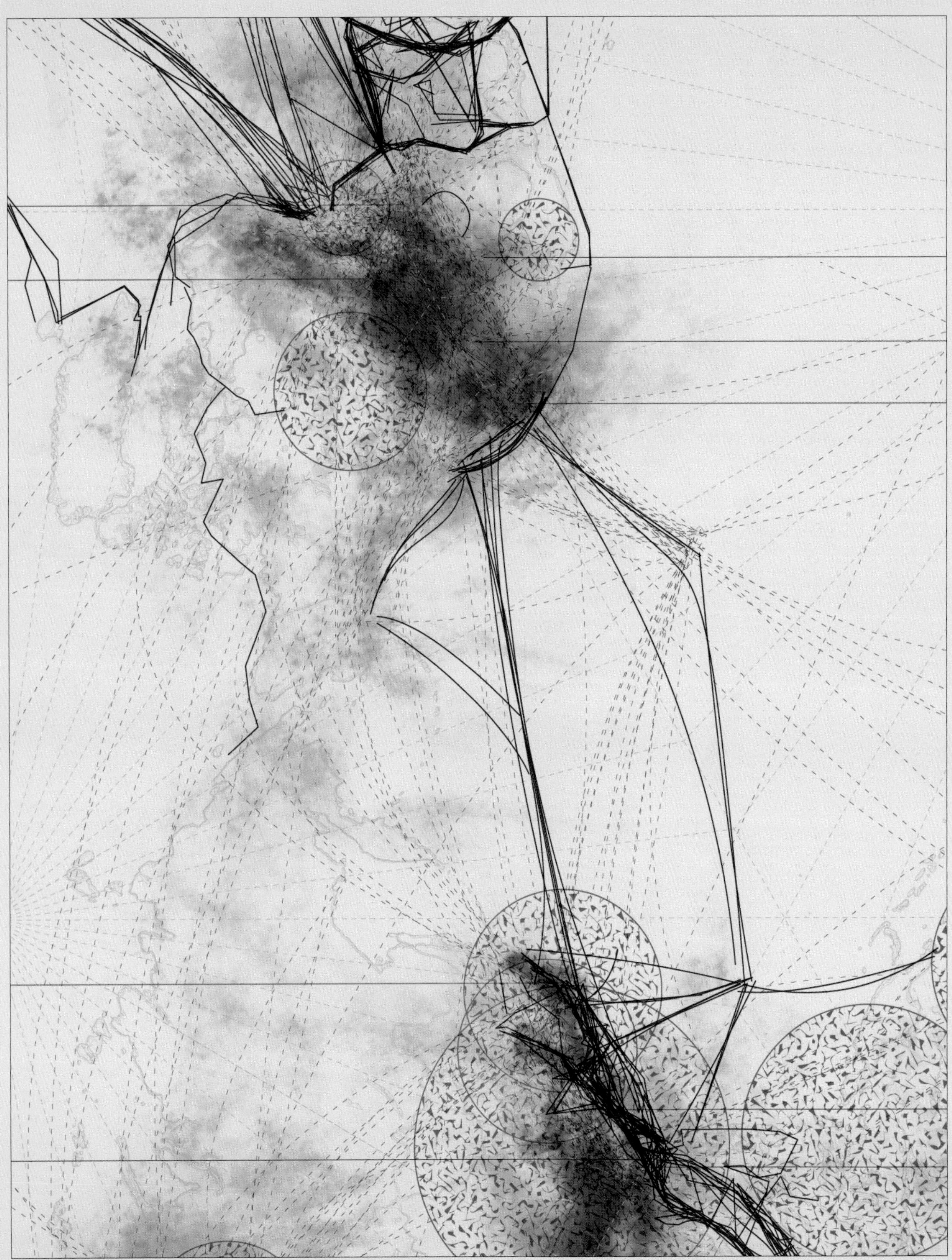

Atomic **Territories** and Nuclear Theory. Cold War **Imaginaries** and Critical Infrastructure.

0.2 A Territory of militarization [detail]. Global Military Index values, U.S. military occupation, global arms trading, and per capita military spending.

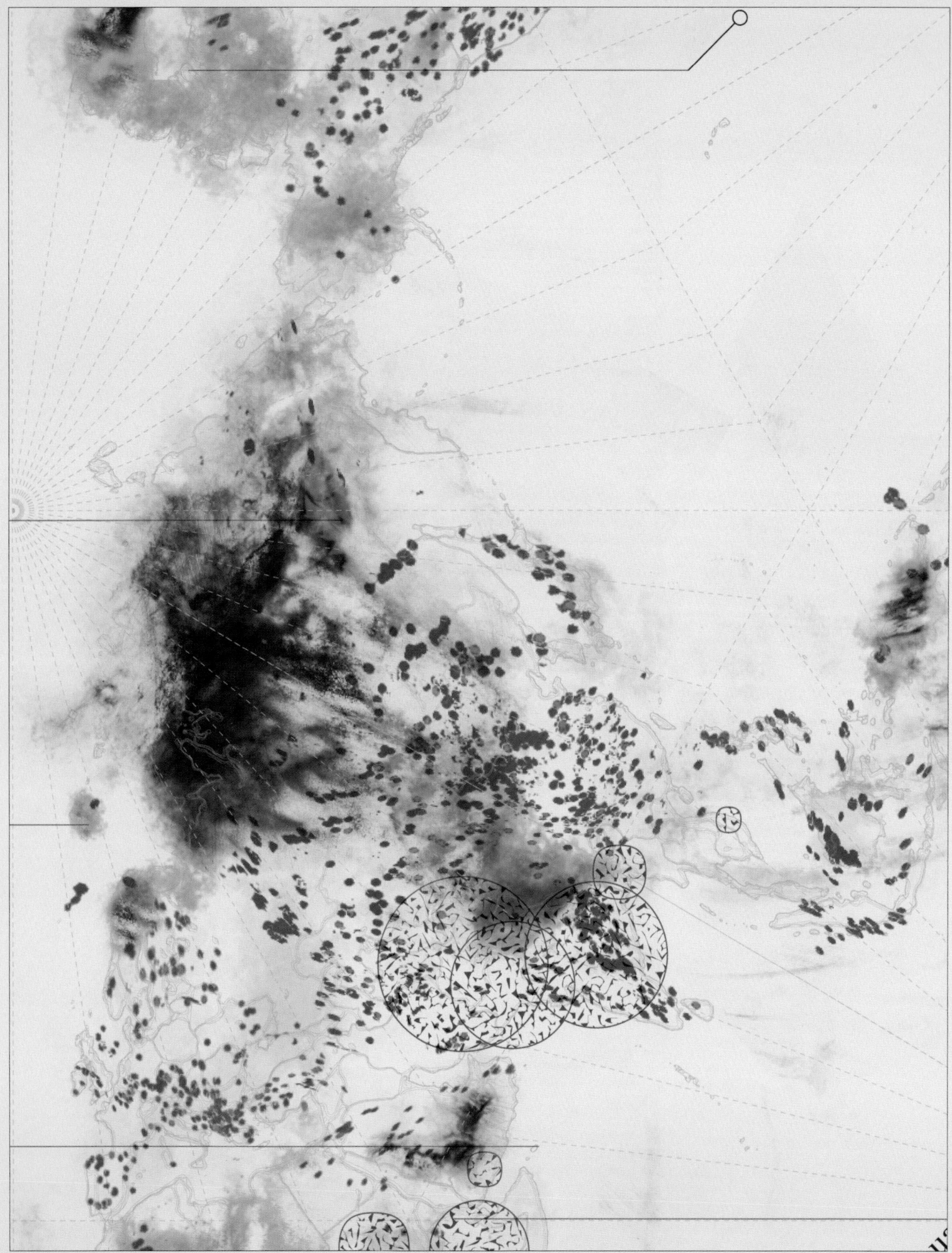

Honed Islands and
Hidden **Edges**.
Borders and **Space**.
A new planet.
Unseen.

0.3 A Geography of Extreme Environments [detail]. Physical and chemical land disturbance, climate refugee migrations, and national index of remoteness values.

Contents

PART 3
URBANISMS AND DEFENSES

Coda

Foreword

Kate Wingert-Playdon

This edited volume *Constructing Invisibility* follows the 2023 Architecture and Environmental Design (AED) symposium establishing a design and research series focused on the inherent interdisciplinary nature of Tyler School of Art and Architecture's built environment disciplines, specifically including architecture, landscape architecture, city planning, and connecting with school wide lenses such as history, aesthetics, and critical studies, to name a few. Integrated into a bi-annual symposium, this volume is the first of a multi-year research effort centered on forward-focused topics related to the advancement of research initiated by the AED faculty and include speakers and scholars whose research and creative work branches out from, and overlaps with, pressing challenges and current practices in the design fields. A primary goal of each symposium is to reach scholars and researchers from within the Tyler School of Art and Architecture and Temple University, and to engage topics that are trending across allied fields and diverse disciplines, more broadly. The series success relies on the collaborative dialogue with invited speakers from multiple universities, institutions, and cultural organizations who can catalyze and inspire the Tyler community—faculty and graduate students alike—to continue to address the role of cross disciplinary engagement as a part of increasing design praxis and elevating design research. The topics are not pre-established, rather they come from the relationship between faculty areas of research and urgent issues affecting the built environment.

The interdisciplinary dialogue that comes with each symposium is expected to push at areas of research about the built environment that will impact the future of design practice.

Constructing Invisibility is in part a record of the dialogue from the 2023 symposium, a segment in a stream of design research activities at Tyler and stands on its own merits for increasing the production of knowledge.

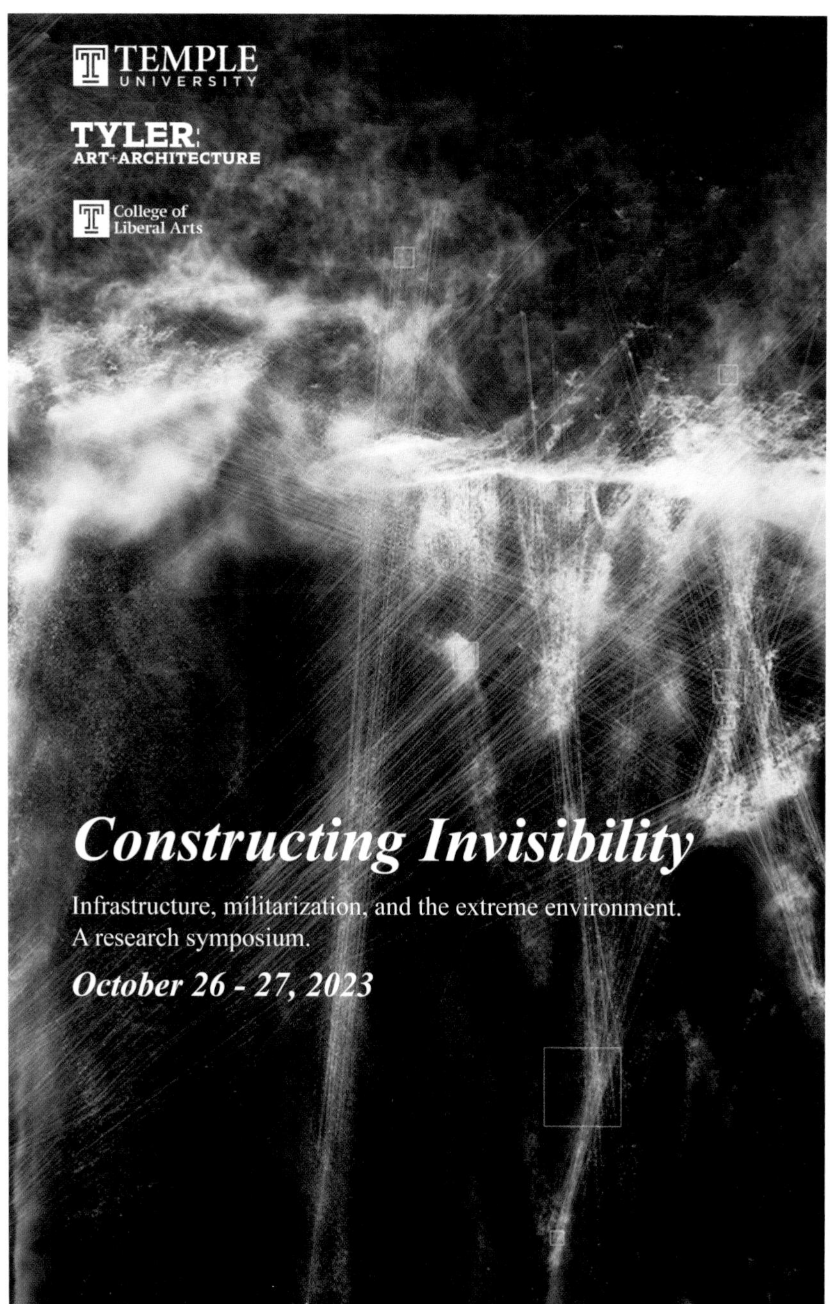

Fig. 1 "Constructing Invisibility," symposium poster, 2023.

Introduction

The World (In)Visible

Jeffrey S. Nesbit
Keaton Bruce

This volume is the first of a multi-year interdisciplinary research project for scholars, researchers, and designers to engage in the most pressing questions of our contemporary built environment. Supported by the Tyler School of Art and Architecture at Temple University, the series emerged as a platform for increasing contemporary discourse and scholarly research across the design fields in architecture, landscape, and urbanism, including diverse disciplines such as geography, media studies, and climate science more broadly.

Constructing Invisibility, the first volume in the series, began with a symposium co-hosted by the Architecture and Environmental Design department (AED) and the College of Liberal Arts at Temple University in Philadelphia on October 26–27, 2023, entitled "Constructing Invisibility: Infrastructure, Militarization, and the Extreme Environment." The symposium brought together scholars from across diverse disciplines in architecture, landscape architecture, urbanism, science and technology, military history, and political geography. Topics presented during the sessions garnered thoughtful conversations around themes including critical histories of infrastructural urbanization, planetary urbanism, military-industrial complex, Cold War geographies, nuclear landscapes, technical lands, and extreme environments. The essays collected here respond to the central theme of the symposium's many conversations—a discourse situated between ideas of (in)visibility, power, and the construction of space.

Modernity, Landscape, and the Worldview

From the scorched forest to the contested metropolis, from the remote desert to the deep Arctic, extreme scales of occupation imagined by the aggrandization of infrastructure, technology, and planetary urbanization extend state power quite literally to the edge of the world. These extreme scales of territorial occupation demarcate a new order of geographical boundaries and political networks rendered highly invisible through intentional methods of obfuscation and delineation.

The retreat from visible quests for state control reverses a linear development within modernity which increasingly interpreted the world as a vision of settler access to, and occupation of, territorializing lands. Modernity is the guise used to revolutionize the physical world.[1] From paintings to maps and airplanes to satellites, developing technology was used to visualize and ultimately enclose the world. To see the world once implied being seen by the world. But in a world fully monitored and fully enclosed, the outreached hand of state power now engages a surreptitious occupation of forgotten centers, frayed edges, and destroyed landscapes, the territorial extremes. Is it ironic, or more likely quite intentional, that in a world of total technological visibility, the question of invisible has become the unfettered territory of occupation?

For the earliest colonial states, castles and palaces constructed acres of measurable, and physical, occupation. Control was relegated to the human scale, the field of vision, the reach of the hand, the distance of the foot and the arrow. These tactics of seeing were methods of enclosure, of bounding the state within perceivable realities of presence. Alternatively, paintings and maps constructed infinitely imagined, conceptual worlds of occupation. Dutch landscape paintings of the seventeenth century, despite their celebrated naturalism, were a fantasy of the world, an imagination that rendered the actual world largely invisible. The landscape, or Dutch *landschap*, was not a reality but a representation of a specific idealized condition—a constructed view of land. This way of idealizing views of the world suggests that control has been exercised through constructed imaginaries, rather than on-site realities. Landscapes—constructed imaginaries that speak nothing of the brush, the pigment, or the painter—operate as stand-ins for land itself. From paintings to airplanes, from spaceships to satellites, technologies developed in militarized projects of infrastructural expansion have increasingly rendered the world an object to be seen. Through this act of total spatial representation, however, the spaces themselves become increasingly invisible.

In 1935, Le Corbusier suggested the new technological age, particularly the airplane, produced a new way of seeing; "seeing" the world and all its pre-machine civilization composed of a disorganized, economically driven order. Sight, from above, became "a new function added to our senses, a new standard of measurement, a new basis of sensation" that implicated the transformation of the built environment through an indication of the city as a malleable object.[2] Paul Virilio illustrates the latter view from the perspective of surveillance: "From the original watch-tower through the anchored balloon to the reconnaissance aircraft and remote-sensing satellites, one and the same function have been indefinitely repeated, the eye's function being the function of a weapon."[3] In this sense, the control over land, people, and economies transformed distance through the veil of so-called technological progress and pursuits of imperial visionary imaginaries. To put it quite simply, to see the world was to control the world.

But those perspectives changed quickly. On December 24, 1968, the image that came to be known as "Earthrise" engaged another transformation of the built environment based on a shift in perceptions of sight, and particularly of perceptions of self within the boundaries of sight. Taken aboard Apollo 8 as the capsule orbited the moon, the image resembles a swirling blue marble floating in a sea of darkness. It was not just the capturing of this image but the propagation of this image back to Earth which had a profound impact on human society. For the first time, individuals could picture the entirety of the globe and imagine themselves as single beings within a much larger but finite and enclosed earthen system, what Buckminster Fuller would term "Spaceship Earth."[4] Despite the profound impact on the individual's perception of self, of vulnerability in visibility, it is the state's perception of self that "Earthrise" impacted most.

Militarization and Visibility

The objects of seeing, from the painter and their easel to the satellite and its launchpad, have increasingly distanced themselves from the perception of the civilian population. The eye became an edifice, the canvas for projecting global access and measuring planetary coordinates. Throughout history, a linear development of technologies of access and documentation became objects of decreased visibility. If to see was to control, then to remain hidden was to retain self-control.

Building on the burgeoning discourse on technical lands—"those spaces defined and rendered invisible by their remote locations, delimited boundaries, secured accessibility, vigilant administration, and exceptional relation to the nonhuman world"—this issue examines the role, the power, and the implications of weaponizing a nondescript visual identity in a modern culture of hypervisibility.[5] As technology transformed the field of view of Virilio's weapon—the eye—so too did it transform the value of that which retreated from this seemingly unbounded vision.

Saskia Sassen speaks to this shift in the simplicity of traditional geographical narratives of seeing by emphasizing the complexities introduced in modern economic practices and geopolitical strategies. In "another geography of multiple seas on land, air, or water—seas that do not naturalize a single epic logic," modern empires occupy protected enclaves, free economic zones, and paper sovereignties "long enough to avoid taxes, engage inexpensive labor, or launder an identity."[6] Sassen notes that it is their very segregation from other worlds and nations that "helps them garner power, and shapes them into distended and dominating territories that are constantly expanding and excluding." Today's detached landscape is constructed not of rich pigments or dominant brushstrokes, but of infinite worlds with infinite seas. In this infinite, it is the invisible, the undetected, the unregulated, what Keller Easterling calls the "most ordinary forms of space," those governed by "invisible rules and relationships," that survive and ascend to the "major medium of political transformation."[7]

A world after "Earthrise" was a world seen in its entirety. Land and sea became instantly outdated constraints in the battlefield of territorial and imperial occupation. Adversaries shifted strategies to "invent nations that are no longer terrestrial, homelands in which no one could set foot; homelands that are no longer countries."[8] The physical, the visible, became a relic of the past, while the diffuse, the conceptual, the invisible, became the battlefield of, and for, the future. Antoine Bousquet writes in *Eye of War*, "Visual culture serves as both a lens and a battleground where the meanings of war are contested, constructed, and deconstructed."[9] War is not fought in physical space, but in the conceptual imagining of that space. In this transformation, like the landscape painting, reality is rendered invisible by conceived perceptions. The state of invisibility becomes not only a refuge, but a "condition with its own meaning and power."[10]

With similar concerns regarding the administrative management of territory, Stephen J. Collier and Andrew Lakoff explain how "distributed preparedness provided techniques for mapping national space as a field of potential targets, and grafted this map of vulnerabilities onto the structure of territorial administration in the United States. . . The rise of total war meant that the entire industrial capacity of a country was regarded as critical to its war effort, thus blurring the lines between civilian and military facilities and making civilian installations and populations into military targets."[11] As such, geopolitical boundaries and territories are both unstable, illegible, and continuously confronted at home and at a distance. In 1982, French film theorist Christian Metz coined the term "scopic regime" in his book *The Imaginary Signifier*: "What defines the specifically cinematic scopic regime is not so much the distance kept . . . as the absence of the object seen."[12]

The scopic regime, or visual culture, of modernity has been constructed and reconstructed by mass visibility. Martin Jay suggests that this modern culture can be best understood not as a "harmoniously integrated complex of visual theories and practices" but, rather as a "contested terrain." The impact of the built environment and technological progress has long been intertwined with the development of this contested visual culture. Ultimately, the desire to see necessitated distance, a distance between the object and its representation, from the seen, the scene, and the seer. The built environment has been transformed by the pursuit of sight, but it has equally, if not more dramatically, been shaped by the pursuit of invisibility. From remote technical lands to dense urban infrastructure, the modern world has been constructed by that which has intentionally retracted from sight. From Ascension to Mauna Kea to Diego Garcia, islands occupied by satellite regimes—quite literally—emphasize invisibility for the purpose of global vision. If the act of seeing is synonymous with the acquisition of control, then the creation of invisibility serves as a means of regulating access.

As the world increasingly confronts successive climate disasters, public cohesion deteriorates, communities become fragmented, resources grow scarce, and ecological systems face collapse. In this context, the state, along with its political messaging and constructed imaginaries—and invisibilities—emerges as one of the few enduring structures. How does the state dictate control in its creation of visible landscapes and spaces, people and problems? It is not the absence of the object but the intentional obfuscation of that object in the eye of publics, of enemies, of competitors which this issue most directly concerns. This is the intentionality of invisibility, whose retraction from the visual world has a lasting impact on the structuring of territory, nature, commons, boundaries, and identities.

Demystifying the Extreme Environment

Examining the impact of invisible infrastructures and delineated patterns of global urbanism becomes increasingly critical in a decreasingly visible world. Acknowledging and confronting systems of invisibility brings to light the people, places, and objects outside of common perception. The invisible is home to contemporary injustice. Keller Easterling defines the infrastructure space—the highways, pipelines, railways, ports, and sites of extraction—as "the secret weapon of the most powerful people in the world precisely because it orchestrates activities that can remain unstated but are nevertheless consequential."[13] The rules of contemporary urbanism are written not in laws or diplomacy, not in the territory of public conscious, but in "spatial, infrastructural technologies" rendered invisible by remoteness, ubiquity, and articulated propaganda.[14] People, labor, technologies, and operations "on the ground" in the extreme environment were implicated in the process of Cold War defense-related interests. How can we learn from these histories? What scales of control exert power over land, people, and territory? "Political belonging in the modern world has meant formal belonging to a spatially bounded state. . . Being political is always a matter of being, becoming, in place and through space."[15] Definitions of space are inseparable from regimes of control and ultimately have been relegated to militaries, corporate entities, and state occupations.

As part of *Architectural Design*'s issue titled "*Territory: Architecture beyond Environment*," Antoine Picon's concluding essay, "What Has Happened to Territory," seems to reference the seminal Koolhaas essay from 1994, implying that if the urban doesn't exist, then "territory" is now the object of confrontation.[16] As described by Picon, traditionally, perception of territory could be understood (made by institutions and corporations) by measurable distance from the "administrator" to the geographical area it comprised.

This distance has blurred, and the distinctions between natural and artificial have collapsed, including the distinction between territory and landscape. Furthermore, Neil Brenner and Stuart Elden describe the production of territory as a space constantly contested, transformed, and reconstructed across the wide range of spatial scales; therefore, the space that territory creates is not a fixed, nor visible, condition: it involves an "evolution of territory." As James Scott suggests in *Seeing like a State*, "Legibility implies a viewer whose place is central . . . [and] provides authorities with a schematic view of their society."[17] Scott continues, "A certain level of abstraction is necessary for certain forms of analysis and it is not at all surprising that the abstractions of state officials should have reflected the paramount fiscal interests of their employer," implying the state creates abstraction not for legibility of a participatory world, but rather for a world of control, one driven by economic interests. But also, for Brenner and Elden, Lefebvre's "illusion of transparency" renders the territory suspect.[18] Is the state's paradoxical ability to provide "transparency" incapable in and of itself, or does infrastructure becoming legible define the geometric, synthetic expression of power, imprinting the globe by human settlement? But outside of political geography, how does this correspond to the expansion of urbanization, its systemic processes of infrastructural access, and relationality with nature and technology?

In 2016, Brenner wrote "The Hinterland Urbanised?" in which he claims the design field saw the urban as a reflexively territorial orientation, rather than made of distinct conditions.[19] The "noncity" is no longer exterior to the urban; it has become a strategically essential terrain of capitalist urbanization and an operational landscape. Relations of power and the imaginaries of what nature is or should be complicate what David Harvey refers to as "accumulation by dispossession." But, for Picon, an inversion of nature and infrastructure has occurred, where now "urban infrastructure[s] that once were perceived as adverse to natural life now appear sometimes as wildlife preserves."[20] Stronger relationality between nature and infrastructural approach has emerged as a continuous fabric because "extremely large contemporary urban territories [and] natural elements can no longer be considered as artifacts."[21] Proposed by history of science professor Peter Galison, the "forbidden wilderness and nuclear wastelands" might not be as different as one might immediately imagine.[22] In this duality—opposite ends of the evolutionary spectrum—the contemporary world renders an intriguing argument for how we understand the role of infrastructure in the endless artificiality of nature. And therefore, the wasteland "leaves no place 'over there' that is untouched by human presence, but posits all places, all categories are interconnected: the domesticated and the wild, the urban and the rural, the local and the global," the visible and the invisible.[23]

For Jean-Louis Cohen, the "conflict of forms: territories, constructions and naval, aerial and land equipment" were all not only wartime facilities, infrastructures, and machines "designed," but they also come from cultural decisions specifically held across diverse concepts and interpretations in history.[24] Architecture, and human occupation more generally, expresses cultural practice, but is often ignored in conversations surrounding the military apparatus. According to American-British architect Anthony Vidler, "The shelter society is promulgated as a consumer necessity and a moral imperative."[25] Interestingly, cultural reflections regarding national defense turned into the emergence of fallout shelters embraced by Western economics. From Cold War fallout shelters to the quick reconstruction of war, architecture had become completely disillusioned. Modernists seem to have incorporated the "postwar reconstruction" as a parallel response with "consumerist monsters, development triumphs, and nostalgic dreams" in which the architect's utopian construction can be fully embraced and celebrated.[26] Paul Virilio refutes the dichotomy of "wartime/peacetime." The apparatus and "rupture point" between a dormant capable power and the immediacy of an operationally armed site complicates the argument.[27] British geographer Rachel Woodward investigates "military geographies," explaining that even during "nonconflict situations [military sites] exert control over space . . . which frequently render this control invisible" and that this kind of "control is both material and discursive."[28] She asserts that military landscape is as much about power as it is about revealing national identity and forms of imagination.

Architecture professor Alessandra Ponte described the impact of operationalized grounds, or what she referred to in "Desert Testing" as the blending of human artifact in the American landscape.[29] Illuminating the realm of "double enhancements" makes for a useful illustration when evaluating the infrastructure and process of urbanization. Similarly, Pierre Bélanger argues military infrastructure and political landscape are key to understanding the transitions from industry to urbanization. Not surprising, then, his earlier work on landscape and infrastructure lead to *Ecologies of Power*, focusing on the Army Corps of Engineers, and became a key study to understand how civil engineering as a discipline directly came out of military practices during a period of peace at the end of the nineteenth century.[30] As a military activity and from a distinctive political landscape perspective, for Bélanger, infrastructure is the state control in which "super urbanization opens new territories for occupation, renewal, and redistribution." Infrastructure, for Bélanger, is both physical technologies in space formed by processes of military operation and an "expression of power": just as the city can be seen as a history of militarization, so too can geospatial territoriality.

Constructing Invisibility continues the exchanges initiated during the first symposium and builds upon the diversity of knowledge shared. The late French philosopher Bruno Latour reminds us that "politics has always been oriented toward objects, stakes, situations, material entities, bodies, landscapes, places. What are called the values to be defended are always responses to the challenges of a territory that it must be possible to describe. This is in effect the decisive discovery of political ecology: it is an object-oriented politics. Change the territories and you will also change the attitudes."[31] This issue uses these economies, landscapes, and places, including the boundless corporations and destructive climate realities, to better see the world. Further, the collection of essays seeks to understand how the construction of such sight impacts civilian occupation in the remaining world. Illuminating stories and places has become the aim of this volume, as shedding light on distant territories has become confounded by extremity, complexity, disparity, and secrecy.

The first collection of essays in the volume explores nuclear narratives, place-based science, damaged environments, and technologies from the Cold War. The section begins with "Atom-Blasted Seeds" by Lindsey Freeman to introduce heritage stories from the Oak Ridge, Tennessee, context. Freeman's chapter describes how "atomic gardening" helped illuminate the American imagination and was formed through connections between nuclear technology and everyday culture. Mark Stanley's chapter, "Nuclear Blue: The Manhattan Project and Its Quieter Effects," unpacks the science behind nuclear technologies, focusing particularly on the Oak Ridge National Laboratory to make explicit the subliminal dangers and environmental devastation such practices have caused. Continuing along the lines of narrative and wartime technologies, "Mountain Time," by Eliyahu Keller, provocatively weaves questions of technology, war, mountains, and time and reminds us that the environment is perpetually entangled with the invisible presence of military-industrial information. Ryan Bishop's chapter, "Spectral Pursuits in Secret Gardens: Of Phonetics, Surveillance, and Cold War Lab-Prisons," shares a unique history of two seemingly diverse audio research labs, one hidden and the other glorified, to describe landscapes of imagination and labor-enabled telecommunication technologies and science. And to conclude this section, "Techno, Techné: Raves, Abstractions, and Militant Subjecthood," by

Philip Glahn, offers an intriguing provocation for how questions of hidden information, media, and culture are enmeshed with the rise of our "technocene"—a space situated between enacted technology and a worldview of colonial aesthetics.

The second series of chapters investigates the spatial politics, design agency, and militarization in conflicted and contested geographies from technical objects situated in distant landscapes. This section begins with Ghazal Jafari's "Silent Siege: In the Shadow Landscapes of Sanctions," which outlines the difficulty of tracing nation-state sanctions of humanitarian aid and environmental consequences in modern-day Iraq and Iran. What may initially seem like a peaceful program can have everlasting impact on the environment and society. Following questions of conflict and landscape, "Designing within Conflict (No one asked me to come, but here I am)," by Malkit Shoshan, presents novel design tools to both better understand and engage with conflicted places at a variety of scales and contexts, with particular interest to propose how design agency can be an advocate for change. May Khalife then demonstrates in "Core and Coastline: The State of Political Exception in Beirut" how urban conditions are formed through militarization and motivated by underlying political forces. The study of two urban areas in Beirut reveals how militarization since the early 2000s worked toward the protection of economic interests and financial profits at the expense of defense and security. Moving over the Pacific Ocean, Pedro Ignacio Alonso and Hugo Palmarola's chapter, "Soviet Telescopes in Latin America's Cold War," documents a technical object to unpack the relationship between the Soviet Union and Latin America during the Cold War and highlights the role of science and its geographic reach. And the final chapter in section two, "Border Blimp Bomb," by César A. Lopez and Jeffrey S. Nesbit, moves into North America to highlight how the construction of a celebrated bomb and surveillance blimp produces mythologized military practices in the American desert to control the border and national security.

The third assemblage of contributions examines seemingly common architectural artifacts entangled with national defense, military geographies, and urbanization. These chapters tend to describe the design, construction, and engineers behind shaping invisibility practices. The final section begins with Gretchen Heefner's chapter entitled "Engineering the Underworld." For Heefner, Cold War military engineers in Greenland during the 1950s and '60s led to furthering research and development in the frozen underground. And it is this extreme environment that allowed the military to feel authorized to expand their territorial reach. Continuing with histories of engineers shaping geographic space, "Atlantic Networks and Geometries: Visualizing Military New York (1783–1815)," by Victoria Sanger, studies the work of Joseph-François Mangin, a French-American military engineer who came from military practices and yet designed the early New York City grid networks. And in the final three chapters we slide between the territorial scale, or an urban grid, down to the architectural one. "Basements as Invisible Defense," by Dongwoo Yim, shares how the rise of defense interest on the Korean peninsula made its way into the common urban block, embedded underneath typical housing and public space in Seoul. Randy Crandon then follows with "Forgotten Fire Control Towers in Plain Sight" to consider the obsolete and decommissioned naval defense artifacts along the Northeastern United States coast as a cultural infrastructure for networking early national defense. To conclude the third section, Charles Waldheim writes about "Carter Manny and the Design Industrial Complex" to share how an architect's experience in the military informs a design practice, in background, which ultimately becomes a ubiquitous organizational model for operationalizing airports in plain sight around the world. And finally, the volume concludes with a series of smaller provocations by select graduate students. Such excerpts come directly from a research seminar entitled, "Technical Lands: Surveying Invisibility at the End of the World" held in the spring of 2024 at Temple University.

Each student positions an environmental concern up against a technical apparatus and economy.

Such histories and speculations show that territorial possession—rendered by wealthy nation-states—produces economic disparity and leaves behind ecological devastation now at the scale of planet. Confronting and dismantling contemporary regimes of dominance, authority, and suppression requires a critical interrogation of the invisible condition as a constructed reality. Our discussion of the unseen begins first with an understanding of the power of sight. A look back at the technologies of control implicated in documenting the world reveals the closely intertwined evolution of imperial occupation and technological progress. Today, designers, researchers, and scholars must responsibly engage these entangled networks and delineated systems far beyond boundaries of typical design practice to thoughtfully critique the past and consider counter-imaginations of the future.

-----

[1] Jason W. Moore, *Capitalism in the Web of Life: Ecology and the Accumulation of Capital* (Verso, 2015), 112.

[2] Le Corbusier, *Aircraft: The New Vision* (The Studio, 1935).

[3] Paul Virilio, *War and Cinema: The Logistics of Perception* (Verso, 1989).

[4] Buckminster Fuller, *Operating Manual for Spaceship Earth.* (Southern Illinois University Press, 1969).

[5] Virilio, *War and Cinema*, 1989.

[6] Saskia Sassen, *Expulsions: Brutality and Complexity in the Global Economy* (Belknap Press of Harvard University Press, 2014).

[7] Keller Easterling, *Enduring Innocence: Global Architecture and its Political Masquerades* (MIT Press, 2005), 70.

[8] Paul Virilio, *Speed and Politics*, trans. Mark Polizzotti (Semiotext, 1986; originally published 1977), 39.

[9] Antoine Bousquet, *The Eye of War: Military Perception from the Telescope to the Drone* (University of Minnesota Press, 2018).

[10] Akiko Bush, *How to Disappear: Notes on Invisibility in a Time of Transparency* (Penguin Press, 2019).

[11] Stephen J. Collier and Andrew Lakoff, "Distributed Preparedness: Space, Security, and Citizenship in the United States," *War, Citizenship, Territory*, ed. Deborah Cowen and Emily Gilbert (Routledge, 2018), 119-122..

[12] Christian Metz, *The Imaginary Signifier* (Indiana University Press, 1982).

[13] Keller Easterling, *ExtraStateCraft: The Power of Infrastructure Space* (Verso, 2014), p 15.

[14] Ibid.

[15] Cowen and Gilbert, "The Politics of War, Citizenship, Territory," *War, Citizenship, Territory*, (New York: Routledge, 2018), 25.

[16] Antoine Picon, "What Has Happened to Territory," *Architectural Design* 80, no. 3 (2010), 94-99.

[17] James Scott, *Seeing like a State: How Certain Schemes to Improve the Human Condition Have Failed* (Yale University Press, 1999).

[18] Neil Brenner and Stuart Elden, "Henri Lefebvre on State, Space, Territory," *International Political Sociology* 3 (2019): 353–377.

[19] Neil Brenner, "The Hinterland Urbanised?", *Architectural Design* 86 (2016): 118–127.

[20] Antoine Picon, "What Happened to Territory," in *Architectural Design*, 80, no. 3 (2010), 94-99.

[21] Ibid.

[22] Peter Galison, "Underground Future," *Ecological Urbanism*, eds. Mohsen Mostafavi and Gareth Doherty (Lars Müller Publishers, 2010), 304-305.

[23] Vittoria Di Palma, *Wasteland: A History* (Yale University Press, 2014).

[24] Jean Louis Cohen, *Architecture in Uniform: Designing and Building for the Second World War* (Yale University and Canadian Centre for Architecture, 2011).

[25] Anthony Vidler, "Air War and Architecture," *Ruins of Modernity*, ed. J. Hell and A. Schonle (Duke University Press, 2010), 29-40.

[26] Ibid.

[27] Paul Virilio, *Bunker Archaeology* (Princeton Architectural Press, 1994).

[28] Rachel Woodward, *Military Geographies* (Wiley, 2004).

[29] Alessandra Ponte, "Desert Testing," *Architecture and the Sciences: Exchanging Metaphors*, ed. A. Picon and A. Ponte (Princeton Architectural Press, 2003), 80-117.

[30] Pierre Bélanger, *Ecologies of Power: Counter-mapping the Logistical Landscapes and Military Geographies of the U.S. Department of Defense* (MIT Press, 2016).

[31] Bruno Latour, *Down to Earth: Politics in the New Climatic Regime* (Polity Press, 2018), 52.

0.4

0.6

0.7

0.8

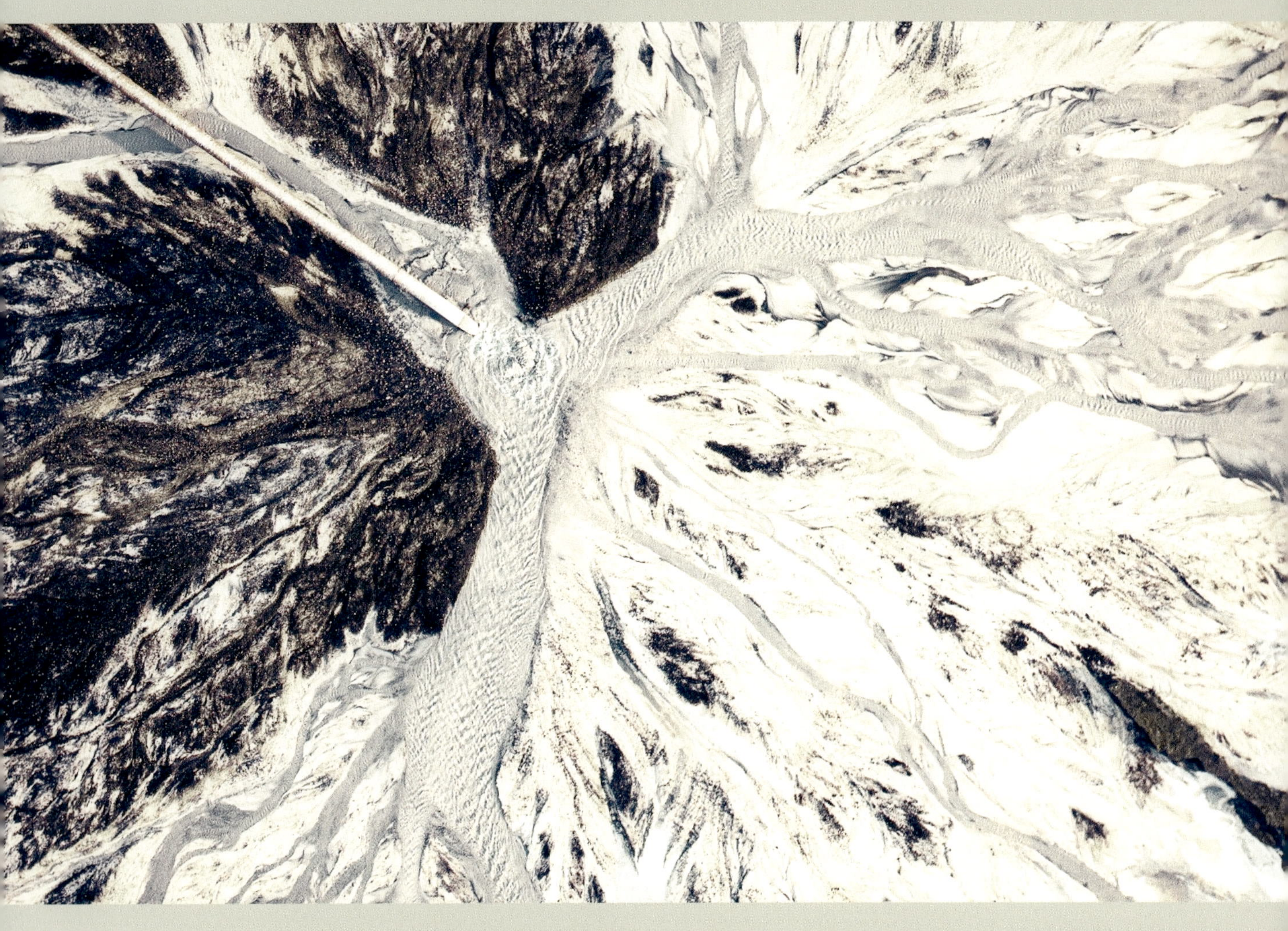

0.13

0.4 Industrial smokestacks rising above a sea of clouds in Kentucky, United States.

0.5 MERLIN Dish at the Mullard Radio Astronomy Observatory near Cambridge, United Kingdom.

0.6 *USS Yorktown* near Charleston, South Carolina, United States.

0.7 Shifting dunes in the Namib Desert, Namibia.

0.8 Combustion of decaying landfill waste from methane gas.

0.9 Coal ash pond sediment delta.

0.10 Communication tower at Mount Climie Track in Upper Hutt, New Zealand.

0.11 Chernobyl Radar Duga, part of the Cold War Soviet missile defense network.

0.12 Mountaintop radio towers above enshrouded by fog, Brazil.

0.13 Oil geyser flare, rural landscape.

Part 1

Environments and Technologies

Atom-Blasted Seeds

Lindsey A. Freeman

In most places in the United States today, heritage gardening with heirloom seeds can be seen as an effort to get back to practices of growing food more organically: a way to participate in the Slow Food movement, to resist factory farming, pesticides, artificial gene manipulation, and the industrialization of food writ large. It can also have a nostalgic bent, allowing gardeners to imagine growing plants as our great-grandparents did, giving us a way to eat the past. In this kind of thinking, Brandywine and Mr. Stripey tomatoes become time machines while Painted Serpent and Tendergreen Burpless cucumbers are transformed into archives. But what if you are from a place where a particular version of an atomic future was and is your heritage, where heirlooms are atomic and green thumbs connote not only skills with chlorophyll but also macabre jokes about radioactive glow? In this case, the most heritage way to garden in the place where I was born, Oak Ridge, Tennessee, might just be with irradiated seeds.

Oak Ridge was a former secret city of the Manhattan Project, built in the early 1940s for the sole purpose of creating fissionable materials for atomic bombs. After World War II, the small city in East Tennessee ceased to be a secret, but it was still actively contributing to the US nuclear arsenal. Today, the Oak Ridge National Laboratory is engaged in multiple areas of research, including isotope science, supercomputing, fission and fusion.[1] The Y-12 National Security Complex, which was initially used to enrich uranium for the Manhattan Project, continues to store and process materials associated with nuclear industries, including housing the world's largest supply of fissionable uranium in the hubristically named Uranium Center of Excellence. It is

Fig. 1 Atom Blasted Seeds, 1958. Photographed by Grey Villet.

perhaps no surprise then that Oak Ridge is the place where backyard experimentation with irradiated seeds began.

Atoms for Peace

The impetus for the atomic gardening movement can be found in President Dwight D. Eisenhower's 1953 "Atoms for Peace" speech, which was intended to educate the American public about the possibilities for nuclear technologies beyond bombs. At the top of the list were nuclear power plants, nuclear medicine, and atomic agriculture. "Atoms for Peace" was an attempt to manage Americans' fears by diverting attention away from the dangers of nuclear catastrophe and toward dreams of a radiant future fueled by fission and fusion. It was also an effort to justify the enormous costs of the atomic infrastructure.

Atomic agriculture grew from these utopian and practical sentiments. The driving idea behind irradiating seeds was that evolution could be sped up, with useful mutations occurring at a faster rate. The hope was that these lasting changes, which could be bred into future generations, would result in heartier and more productive plants that could put an end to food shortages, resist diseases and pests, and thrive in previously inhospitable places.[2] While large-scale operations were put into place to produce plants by highly scientific methods, such as the world's first Gamma Garden established at Brookhaven National Laboratory in 1949, here I'm more interested in how the amateur atomic gardening movement began alongside more controlled scientific pursuits through practitioners' atomic utopianism and ad-hoc

Fig. 2 Atom Blasted Seeds, 1958. Photographed by Grey Villet.

relationships to serious research institutes.[3]

Backyard atomic gardening began on Patchwood Farm, just outside of Oak Ridge, where Dr. Clarence J. Speas, an oral surgeon, was having a devil of a time with his hillside crops. Every time there was a hard rain, his fertilizers were washed away and his plants suffered. Speas mentioned the problem to his friend Dr. Marshall Brucer, who was known for his cancer research conducted at the Oak Ridge National Laboratory. They both arrived at the conclusion that atomic-induced mutant strains might solve the problem.[4] This is a very Oak Ridge way to think.

In 1957, the Atomic Energy Commission (AEC) sold Speas 10 curies of radioactive cobalt-60. Members of the AEC also helped to push a cement bunker-laboratory against the rolling hill that was causing Speas such trouble. This may sound like a top-secret project, but it wasn't. The AEC understood Speas's plan to sell his irradiated seeds to the public under the company name Oak Ridge Atom Industries.[5] Speas even demonstrated his process to visitors and schoolchildren on field trips, which was documented by the photographer Grey Villet of *Life* magazine.

Although there was a lot of cobalt by-product around, Speas noted in a paper titled "Advice on Atom-Energized Seeds" that "isotopes were practically impossible for the general public to obtain" because "of the usual government red tape which the average gardener cannot breakthrough in order to get his package of seeds irradiated for experimental purpose."[6] Speas was an oral surgeon and part-time farmer, but he also spent 20 years in isotope research in medicine and agriculture, working with the Oak Ridge Institute of Nuclear Studies."[7] Not just anyone gets handed radioactive isotopes from the government. Speas embodied the ethos of the atomic utopianism that was prevalent in Oak Ridge when he described the difficulty in obtaining radioactive isotopes for backyard experimentation as a matter of bureaucratic frustration.[8]

The goods that Oak Ridge Atom Industries sold were marketed as extraordinary, just the thing to push us closer to the good life, but the advertising was also schizophrenic—bombastic in suggesting possibility, while at the same time warning that even if you do everything as instructed nothing might happen. The back of the seed packets tried to ask and answer the concerns and hopes of potential atomic gardeners: "Will everyone find changes? We do not know. We have irradiated these seeds in an ATTEMPT to produce changes, and only by growing these seeds can you determine if you have a change. This is the challenge we offer you." And in the next paragraph: "What can you discover? No one knows—it may be the most exciting change ever found in this species. . . The change you find could be unique."[9]

Mutant Marigolds

Speas planted corn, marigolds, petunias, and tomatoes from irradiated seeds, as well as nonirradiated seeds for a control group. In a 1960 profile in *Flower and Garden*, it was reported that tomatoes from his atomic garden were twice the size, sausage-shaped, more delicious, and stayed fresh longer than normal tomatoes. His petunias were said to germinate early and were more bountiful and colorful than flowers grown from run-of-the-mill seeds. The most fantastic results were with the marigolds: many refused to grow normally, and when tied to stakes, they climbed up and around them and then continued to grow horizontally along the ground. They produced enormous blossoms, some trumpet shaped, some half yellow and half blue on the same blossom. These wild and massive marigolds also reportedly produced double the seeds of regular marigolds.[10]

Marigolds were popular with atomic gardeners because they were easy to grow and tended to yield more dramatic blooms than other flowers. Even though the results of atomic gardening were pretty tame overall, the copy in the advertising of atom-blasted seeds teased at a new future and created a charged atmosphere that had some backyard tinkerers nervous. In 1960, British horticulture expert Beverly Nichols attempted to alleviate some of these concerns by promising that "there is nothing dangerous about atomic gardening… Your marigolds will not blow up the herbaceous border."[11]

Atomic-enhanced marigolds had their biggest cultural moment in 1964 when they featured in a play by Paul Zindel with the wild title *The Effect of Gamma Rays on Man-in-the-Moon Marigolds*. The plot revolved around the relationships between a mother and her two daughters and one of the daughter's science fair projects, which utilized "seeds exposed to various degrees…of gamma rays from radiation sources in Oak Ridge."[12] The play went on to win the 1971

Fig. 3 A garden show featuring "super atomic energized seeds," 1961. Photo by Frank Scherschel for Life.

Pulitzer Prize for Drama and in 1972 was adapted as a film directed by Paul Newman and staring Joanne Woodward. Woodward won best actress at the 1973 Cannes Film Festival for the role of Beatrice, where on that glamorous shore, cinephiles took in the story of complicated relationships and irradiated seeds from Tennessee.

Atomic Peanuts

In 1959, just two years after Speas began irradiating seeds, Dr. Walton C. Gregory of North Carolina State College, head of the college's peanut improvement

Fig. 4 A garden show featuring "super atomic energized seeds," 1961. Photo by Frank Scherschel for *Life*.

program, "bombarded" 50 pounds of peanut seeds at the biological laboratories in Oak Ridge with 37 times the radiation necessary to kill a person.[13] Gregory, along with his research team, developed 11,000 mutations. Most of them were useless, but a small portion were found to be more wilt resistant.[14] The *Kansas City Times* reported that Gregory had given "mother nature a herculean boost" by being "one of the first to develop an improved strain of any living thing through atomic research in the United States."[15] Harland Manchester, writing in *Popular Mechanics*, quipped: "If anyone wants to grow a giant cocktail peanut, Dr. Gregory has it."[16]

Meanwhile, across the Atlantic, Muriel Howorth, an eccentric, wealthy British atomic enthusiast, established the Atomic Gardening Society after hearing about the experiments coming out of the United States. Howorth was a society mover and shaker, as well as an advocate of all things atomic. She had already established the Ladies Atomic Energy Club in 1948, and now she wanted to bring some of the excitement around atomic gardening to the UK. She contacted Dr. Gregory and arranged to have four pounds of his mutant peanuts mailed to her by post.[17] This began the connection between three of the earliest practitioners of atomic gardening: Speas, Gregory, and Howorth.

To show off the goobers produced from the irradiated seeds from North Carolina, Howorth organized a dinner including many of her "scientific friends" in the dining hall of the Royal Commonwealth Society in London. Guests remarked on the size of the peanuts—"big as almonds"—but overall Howorth was disappointed by the underwhelming responses.[18] Back at home, Howorth was wondering what to do with the rest her irradiated stock, when she had the idea to "plop an irradiated peanut in the sandy loam" of a pot she had handy. She took care to place the peanuts in a window to mimic the North Carolina climate.[19] She reported that the peanut grew "with uncanny speed" and, proud of the results, she named it after herself: the "Muriel Howorth peanut."[20] Then she called the press. On British TV, gardening expert Beverly Nicholas reported, "To me, it had all the romance of something from outer space. It is the first 'atomic' peanut. It… gives you a strange, almost alarming sense of thrusting power and lusty health. It holds a glittering promise in its green leaves, the promise of victory over famine." [21]

After her peanut experiments, Howorth wanted to expand her practice with the Atomic Gardening Society.[22] She wrote to Speas and they began an international trade partnership. Over several years, Howorth imported millions of irradiated seeds from

Oak Ridge Atom Industries, which she then dispersed to amateur gardeners across Europe. The society had hundreds of members and counted an impressive number of scientists on its advisory board and as patrons, including Albert Einstein. Howorth referred to the members of her society as "Atomic Mutation Experimenters." Individual gardeners in the society set out to seed their own plots across the UK and Europe, and there were a few larger endeavors as well. One of note was located in an old rabbit warren in Wannock Gardens, a "model village" composed of miniatures in East Sussex. There nine varieties of garden plants from irradiated seeds were planted alongside control group plants in what Howorth referred to as "the first purely lay atomic garden in the world." [23]

Howorth delighted in her relationship with Speas and Oak Ridge Atom Industries, except she did not care for his marketing term "atom-blasted seeds." In *Atomic Gardening*, she wrote: "Gardeners thought it disturbed the peaceful atmosphere of the garden: housewives felt it was reminiscent of the bomb: the school boys used it with a different meaning! But Dr. Speas had copyrighted the name, said it was 'catchy'; and wrote 'it did not frighten any of us over here!'" [24]

Atomic Utopianism

The mid-twentieth-century atomic gardening fad grew out of a genuine disposition of atomic utopianism, a trust in a controllable radioactive future that included a belief that once these experiments were moved from the backyard to large-scale farming operations,

Fig. 5 "Atoms for Peace" traveling exhibit in Oak Ridge, 1957, 57-1239 Department of Energy. Photo by Ed Westcott.

irradiated seeds could make "the deserts bloom" and render famines impossible thanks to mutated plants.[25] We can think of the atomic gardening craze of the late 1950s–1960s as a newer type of victory gardening, one that emerged in the same places where there had been a culture of tending victory gardens during World War I and World War II. Although in this iteration, the practice was less about immediate survival, and the feelings attached to it were more diffuse and future oriented. By hoping for useful mutations through atomic gardening, people were desiring to never be in the position of food desperation again. They also wanted nuclear technologies that were not dedicated solely to weapons of mass destruction. People wanted to believe that not only could nuclear technologies wipe us all out, but that they might also save the world. Dreams like this shaped the atomic zeitgeist. Like so many other atomic-based fantasies circulated during the first couple of decades of the Cold War, atomic gardening was appealing as a practice because it could glide up and down on that roller coaster of imaging the worst and thrilling to the possibilities of the future. While the atomic gardening movement, especially for amateur gardeners, did not live up to its promise for reasons both practical and political, it was not well-documented and so it is impossible to know what ghostly fragments of these experiments might exist in our backyards and gardens today. Next time you pass a garden, take a close look at the marigolds.

Acknowledgments

This essay grew out of a talk I gave at the Lavender Festival in Oak Ridge, Tennessee, in June 2019. I want to thank the organizer, Barbara Ferrell, for the invitation and all the Oak Ridgers who shared their anecdotes about atomic gardening with me over lavender lemonade.

-----

[1] For more on what the Oak Ridge National Laboratory does today: https://www.ornl.gov/.

[2] Using radiation to experiment with crops was not an entirely new practice; scientists first started doing this in the 1920s, when X-rays were new technology, but the results were far from spectacular, so it was largely abandoned in the United States. The practice picked up again with nuclear fission after World War II.

[3] While I have relied on primary sources as much as possible for this essay, I also want to note the scholars who sparked my interest in this topic, including Helen Anne Curry, especially her book *Evolution Made to Order* (University of Chicago Press, 2016), and nanoscientist and garden historian Paige Johnson's "Atomic Gardens: An Online History," https://www.atomicgardening.com/.

[4] Muriel Howorth, *Atomic Gardening for the Layman*, (King Bros and Potts, 1960), 19.

[5] Speas's company was the first incorporated company in Oak Ridge to be traded publicly.

[6] C. J. Speas, "Advice on Atom-Energized Seeds," Oak Ridge Atom Industries, Oak Ridge, Tennessee, February 2, 1960. Reprinted in Howorth, *Atomic Gardening*, 25–26.

[7] Howorth, *Atomic Gardening*, 39.

[8] I write extensively about the particular qualities of atomic utopianism in Oak Ridge, as well as a more general American atomic utopianism, in *Longing for the Bomb: Oak Ridge and Atomic Nostalgia* (University of North Carolina Press, 2015).

[9] Speas was the first atomic entrepreneur to market "gamma energized" seeds, but other companies soon followed. In *Onward and Upward in the Garden*, Katherine S. White mentions the Ransom Seed Company of Arcadia and San Gabriel, California, which offered "atom blasted seeds" to home gardeners and schoolchildren for science projects. In a seed catalog from 1960, the company implores caution, stating that seeds should be handled only by adults and high school students and that no one should put the seeds in their mouth. Katherine S. White, *Onward and Upward in the Garden* (North Point Press, 1997), 98 – 99.

[10] Robert. W. Miller, "These Seeds Have Been A-Bombed," *Flower and Garden*, (February 1960), .

[11] Quoted in the foreword to Howorth's *Atomic Gardening*.

[12] Paul Zindel, *The Effect of Gamma Rays on Man-in-the-Moon Marigolds*

(Harper Trophy, 2005), 97–98. A film adaptation of Zindel's work was directed by Paul Newman and released by 20th Century Fox in 1972.
[13] Walter C. Gregory, "First Atomic Peanut Is Product of U.S. Scientist," *Kansas City Times*, January 12, 1959, 1.
[14] The new, more resistant strain was called: NC4x, which stood for North Carolina 4th generation X-rayed. In this generation, the "X" was used for the first time to mean radiation-treated, whereas in previous iterations regular X-rays had been used. Howorth, *Atomic Gardening,* 11.
[15] Gregory, "First Atomic Peanut Is Product of U.S. Scientist," 1.
[16] Gregory practiced atomic gardening at home as well as at the office. The same Popular Mechanics profile mentions that "when Mrs. Gregory was nostalgic for the hibiscus of her Florida childhood, Dr. Gregory planted some but found that they didn't bloom until October, a few weeks before the frost killed them. By irradiating a few hundred plants, he produced a hibiscus that blooms in the late summer, thus moving the plant habitat a few hundred miles north." Harland Manchester, "The New Age of 'Atomic Crops,'" *Popular Mechanics*, (October 1958), 282.
[17] By her own account, the seeds were mailed from North Carolina on March 13, 1959. Howorth, *Atomic Gardening*, 13.
[18] Howorth, *Atomic Gadening*, 14.
[19] Howorth, *Atomic Gardening*, 14–15.
[20] Howorth, *Atomic Gardening*, 15.
[21] Quoted in Howorth, *Atomic Gardening*, 16.
[22] Howorth was passionate about all things atomic. In addition to establishing the Ladies Atomic Energy Club and the Atomic Gardening Society (and naming herself president), she composed and directed an atomic ballet called *Isotopia: An Exposition in Atomic Structure*, which debuted at the Waldorf Hotel in the center of London's theater district. The cast of characters in Isotopia included: knowledge, protons, electrons, neutrons, a rat, a cow, and a Geiger counter.
[23] Howorth, *Atomic Gadening*, 23.
[24] Howorth, *Atomic Gadening*, 22.
[25] John Hillaby, "Atom May Unlock Arctic for Farms: Scientists at Geneva Say Also Irradiated Seed Will Make the Deserts Bloom," *New York Times*, August 16, 1955, 6.

Nuclear Blue: The Manhattan Project and Its Quieter Effects

Mark Stanley

In 1934, after spending an hour waiting in a dark laboratory room for his eyes to adapt, Soviet scientist Pavel Cherenkov noticed a faint blue glow while irradiating uranium salts with gamma rays underwater.[1] Other glowing phenomena—like fluorescence and phosphorescence—were well studied by this time, but this effect from the heaviest known element, uranium, was something new, something more subtle. In much higher intensities, this blue glow, now known as Cherenkov radiation, can be seen at the bottom of any nuclear reactor pool today, including the High Flux Isotope Reactor at Oak Ridge National Laboratory. Like a sonic boom in the air, this light phenomenon appears when electrons, excited by ionizing radiation, move faster than the speed of light in that medium (in this case, water)—an almost impossible maneuver. If the reactor were not submerged in water, we would see no such glow, and the radiation it vivifies would remain invisible. Radiation is not a toxic green, but rather an intense and depthless blue—a nuclear blue—a sublime, numinous rendering of an extra-natural phenomenon. This nuclear blue is a marker of our encounters with the atom, of crossing quantum thresholds of the unknown. It is an explication of radiation—a vivid and unmistakable image of that which otherwise remains insidiously hidden.

The existential complexity of this blue is a signal to us of the deeper entanglements of "nuclearity," a term Gabrielle Hecht uses to describe the complicated (and contested) web of territories, (geo)politics, objects, bodies, and protocols through which we negotiate our relationships following our collective acquaintance with the concept of radiation:

> Nuclearity is a *technopolitical* phenomenon that emerges from political and cultural configurations of technical and scientific things.... Nuclearity is not so much an essential

> property *of* things, as it is a property *distributed among things*.[2]

There are no clear distinctions between nuclear things and non-nuclear things; rather, there are things negotiating each other within a nuclear paradigm. For Hecht, this has much to do with geopolitical questions of resource extraction and state power dynamics (topics to which we will return later). It also has to do with military-scientific developments and their extended ramifications in technical landscapes and environments. In explicating the atom, science, military, and environment became thoroughly enmeshed with one another and began to produce synthetic combinations between them (along with biotic, informational, and political things).

Nuclear blue is not just a metaphor for nuclearity—like the ambiguous green-glowing stick Homer Simpson tosses from his car window—it is a rare visual *expression* of broader techno-environmental associations that underlay it. It is the representative tip of a quantum iceberg, signaling to us an array of allied effects and conditions, ranging in scale, temporality, and visibility radioactive landscapes, science infrastructures, entangled radioecologies, and other hybrids between land, architecture, machine, animal, rock, and air.

Atomic bombs and their explosions were loud and overt; nuclear blue and its kin are among the quieter effects of the practice of unfurling atoms. These effects tend to bubble up in more secret places, out of the

Fig. 1 High Flux Isotope Reactor being refueled at Oak Ridge National Laboratory, 2015. Genevieve Martin / Oak Ridge National Laboratory.

nuclear weapons spotlight, where they enjoy their inherently fickle relationship with visibility. One special site through which to study these entanglements is the Oak Ridge Reservation, one of the earliest and most significant incubators of such complex hybrids. This essay charts some true tales from Oak Ridge, tracing how its landscapes, infrastructures, and ecologies have absorbed and reflected the uncertainties of the atom, quietly shaping the material and invisible worlds that surround it.

Explications and Accidents

First, it is useful to trace a historical thread through two other important explications of the atom, one before and one after Cherenkov. Only since 1895, when Wilhelm Röntgen discovered X-rays, has the invisible energy of ionizing radiation been a feature of our popular scientific imaginary. Seeing inside the body was a novel representational magic, but from the outset, there was also a profound unease about the specter of this invisibility and what could be made visible through it.[3] The ghostly skeletons of early X-ray images were an uncanny rendering of the existential anxiety that underlaid them. Upon seeing her own skeletal hand in the first-ever radiograph image, Röntgen's wife, Anna Bertha, exclaimed, "I have seen my death!"[4] While Röntgen is credited as the discoverer (explicator) of X-rays, it was Anna Bertha's instinctive and prescient reaction that forecast the profound existential ramifications ahead. Radiography was the first act of explication for radiation, and it dramatized the relationship between living beings and the invisible phenomena on which contemporary science had trained its attention.

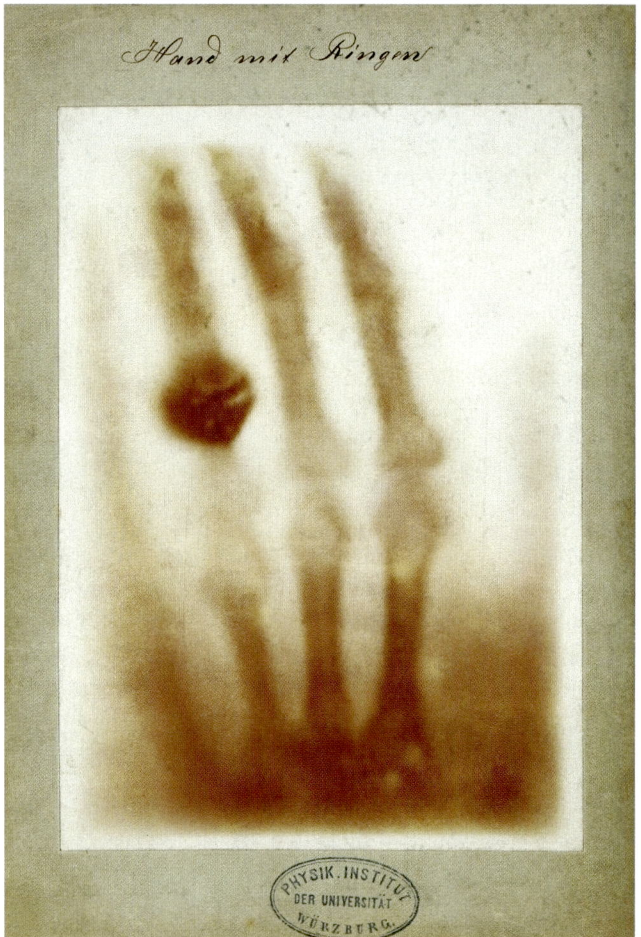

Fig. 2 The first radiograph image, by W.K. Röntgen, 1895. Wellcome Library / CC BY 4.0.

Over the next 50 years, physicists slowly demystified the inner workings of atoms and the energies that give them shape and order, including radioactive decay (the transmutation of one element into another), the first varieties of subatomic particles (electrons, protons, and neutrons), and most dramatically near the end of 1938, nuclear fission (the splitting of the uranium atom, converting tiny bits of matter into enormous energy).

But as acquaintance with the atom increased, so too did uncertainty. Dating back to Sir Issac Newton (1687), science was long accustomed to laws, certainties, and holistic models that described the nature of everything. The quantum mechanical model of the atom under development in the early twentieth century required a certain acceptance of uncertainty—not only because the tiny objects of study were directly unobservable, but also because it was *in their nature* to be incomplete and indeterminate. For example, in quantum theory, bizarrely, one may know only the location or the momentum of a particle, never both—to measure one is to affect the other. This physical anxiety was—and remains—difficult to understand and to describe. The concepts, terminologies, and metaphors were many: Heisenberg's *Uncertainty Principle*, Bohr's "indeterminacy," and Schrödinger's famous (and tragic) cat.[5] The atom enjoyed an ambiguous pendulum between inhibition and explication: it hid things away, then flashed them into immediate reveal and around again.

The discovery of fission rapidly accelerated this process, both in pace and scale. The abstract idea of a bomb preceded all these discoveries, but with every new atomic divulgence (and each passing day of worldwide war) its reality became more and more inevitable.[6] Human hubris took over to scale up and concentrate laboratory experiments toward war products. From 1939 onward, governments and militaries explicitly sought the power to annihilate each other through nuclear fission.[7] The most fervent (and consequential) operation was in the United States—code-named the Manhattan Project—through which a distinct scalar shift was enacted, from discovery to manufacture, from laboratory to factory, from tabletop to landscape.

While certainly not the final episode, a particularly dramatic and poignant explication of radiation came on August 6, 1945, with the anthropogenic invention of "atomic bomb radiation sickness." The thermal and mechanical energies of the bomb were extreme, abominable, and, of course, unprecedented; the "radioactive energies and [their] injurious effects" lingered insidiously in the bodies of those still alive.[8] A mysterious and incurable illness began to manifest in the days that followed the bombing of Hiroshima, slowly killing as many people as had the initial blast.[9] This time, the phenomenon of ionizing radiation was rendered not in eerie glows or ghostly images, but in the flesh, bone, and blood of hundreds of thousands of *hibakusha* (literally "bomb affected person").[10] Nuclear historian Richard Rhodes writes that, "No large population had ever experienced so extensive and deadly an assault of ionizing radiation before."[11] Upon crossing the threshold of military deployment against a city full of people, the atom flipped into its most explicit (and grotesque) mode.

These explications—to which dozens more could be added—might even be more productively considered as *accidents*. Paul Virilio argues that the invention of any technology is the simultaneous invention of its twinned accident: to invent the airplane is to invent the crash, to invent nuclear energy is to invent the meltdown and vice versa, the accident is itself a kind of explication, "The accident is the appearance of a quality of something that was hidden by another of its qualities."[12]

Under Virilio's logic of accidents, the explication of the atom (and, in its most extreme concentration, the technology of the bomb) coproduced its twinned accident(s). Not only did the blinding flash and all-consuming fireball atomize 140,000 people and obliterate the urban core of Hiroshima, but it also set in motion the ever-more insidious (and much longer-lived) *accident* of ionizing radiation. By extension, ionizing radiation coproduces the spatial and territorial accidents we might call *radioscapes*: target cities, test sites, exclusion zones, blast radii, no-go areas, restricted access, disposal facilities, isolation plants, and so on.[13] This network of sister sites conjoins into a generalized and interconnected territory (as a special subgenre of technical lands) marked by the invisible and practically infinite signature of radioactivity. And by further extension, the invention of radioscapes yields further techno-social, ecological, and geopolitical effects, organized as a series of cascading accidents.[14] Rippling with their associated uncertainties, each event coproduced the conditions for the emergence of the next, the scale of the atom continually recalibrating the scale of the globe.

The Scalar Conundrum of the Atom

One of the earliest radioscapes was the Oak Ridge Reservation (ORR). In 1942, the United States Department of War seized 54,000 acres of rural land in eastern Tennessee on which to establish the Manhattan Project—the full-fledged military-industrial effort to bring atomic bombs to fruition.[15] A presidential proclamation would be issued, under the Second War Powers Act of 1942, designating it as a military reserve and evicting the 400 families sparsely inhabiting the territory. This type of land acquisition was familiar to the Army Corps—the War Department acquired over 45 million acres in the United States during World War II, often compulsorily—but in most ways, the Manhattan Project was foreign to the normal logics of Army Corps business.[16] The goal was clear, "to provide our armed forces with weapon that would end the war and to do it before our enemies could use it against us," but every step to achieve such a goal remained hugely ambiguous.[17] As General Leslie Groves recounts (perhaps too dramatically) in his memoirs:

> Never in history has anyone embarking on an important undertaking had so little certainty about how to proceed as we had then. . .Not until later would it be recognized that chances would have to be taken that in more normal times would be considered reckless in the extreme. Not until later would it become accepted practice to proceed vigorously on major phases of the work despite large gaps in basic knowledge.[18]

In haste to be the first nation with the bomb, massive construction projects began well before the science was proven. The rarity of natural uranium was surpassed by the near non-existence of its fissile variety, U-235 (less than 1% of natural ore). One of the chief concerns of the project was to extract this more volatile substance and

Fig. 3 The K-25 Gaseous Diffusion Plant and its surrounding complexes entangled with the Clinch River, ridges, valleys, and forests. Photo by Ed Westcott, 1945. United State Department of Energy.

Fig. 4 The K-25 Gaseous Diffusion Plant under construction. Photo by Ed Westcott, April 1944. United State Department of Energy.

refine it to about 94% concentration—weapons grade. A new fissionable element, plutonium, too could be "bred" from uranium inside nuclear reactors, requiring altogether different processes. Thousands of tons of raw material would need to be broken down and sifted at an atomic level to yield a small, spherical bomb core about the size of a cantaloupe.[19] The upscaling of laboratory experiments to industrial manufacturing processes required audacious, and often enormous, architecture-landscape-machine hybrids. These were the first cases of *science infrastructure*, an accident of military-industrial invention at the ORR.

For example, the K-25 Gaseous Diffusion Plant was a half-mile-long, four story building housing a series of 2,892 pressure vessels ("diffusion stages"), five million barrier tubes, and "miles and miles of pipes and pumps" through which a gaseous concoction of uranium was filtered to achieve isotope separation.[20] At 5.2 million square feet of floor space, it was arguably the largest building in the world at that time.[21] A sprawling network of roads, rail, water, steam, and electrical lines extended the circulatory systems of the process well outside this footprint, to the degree that features of the landscape (river, ridge, forest) are wrapped and blended with the development of the complex, both formally and functionally. Another facility, the Y-12 Electromagnetic Separation Plant, was a series of giant mass spectrometers, using extreme magnetic fields to differentiate between the minuscule atomic weight differences between the two varieties of uranium (238 and 235). Whereas K-25 was one colossal process, Y-12 was organized as a series of 17 very large machines, each slowly processing slightly enriched product from K-25 to make *highly enriched uranium*, ready for shipment to Los Alamos.[22] Richard Rhodes writes, "... the Y-12 complex counted 268 permanent buildings large and small—the [electromagnetic separation] structures... a distilled water plant, sewage treatment plants, pump houses... a generator building, eight electric substations, 19 water-cooling towers—for an output measured in the best of times in grams per day."[23]

Science infrastructure is a product of this ironic scalar conundrum. Exfoliating the interiors of atoms too small to see (even with microscopy) required the construction of vast mechanized landscapes. The same logic extended to the organizational principles of the larger Manhattan District—a vastly distributed network of highly compartmentalized research and production facilities across the entire nation. In 1939, when fears of a German bomb arose after the discovery of fission, Niels Bohr thought the prospect was unlikely because the uranium refinement processes would require "turning the country into a gigantic factory." When he visited the United States after his escape from occupied Denmark in 1943, he remarked to Manhattan Project scientists, "you have done just that."[24] The blooming of science infrastructure at the ORR, while huge, is only a part of the more incomprehensible act of mobilizing a distributed war machine around the uncertainties of the atom. Further still, after the explosion of the bomb (and the many nuclear echoes that followed it), the unaccountable distribution of ionizing radiation produced a growing global network of radioscapes, including the ORR.

Fig.5 A few of The Alamogordo Cows, shipped from New Mexico to live the rest of the lives in Oak Ridge, Tennessee as objects of radiological study. Photo by Ed Westcott, 1946. The American Museum of Science and Energy.

Such a territorial promiscuity is also a reflection of the project's disposition toward information. Despite its enormous size and expense, the project was kept fastidiously secret and it precipitated the invention of new concepts and practices of government secrecy. It was kept secret from the enemy, the American public, Congress (lest they defund the effort because of its huge expense and uncertain outcomes), even the vast majority of the hundreds of thousands of people it employed, and especially from those it incinerated and poisoned from above.[25] The sprawling complexes were hidden not just by their location in the Appalachian foothills, but also through deliberate governmental and military efforts to obscure their true purpose. The siting of Oak Ridge was partly about geography and resources, but it was also about creating a self-contained, controlled environment where the intense secrecy of the project could be maintained. The ORR remained an isolated zone of militarized control even after the veil of absolute secrecy was lifted from the project, and as a side effect, its environmental exclusivity began to foster extended entanglements between living systems and radiological processes on the reservation.

Radioecology

While the accident of acute radiation syndrome was invented in Hiroshima, the accident of "fallout" was conceived in the New Mexico desert. Early on July 16, 1945, the first nuclear flash blinded the desert and the first mushroom cloud rose into the atmosphere. As much as "250 tons of sand were vaporized and sucked up into . . . the ball of fire," and with it, 360 types of radioactive fission products, some of which decayed in seconds or minutes, while others will wait decades or millennia.[26] About two hours later, the atomized particulates in the cloud began to fall back to earth, with the heaviest radiation falling over areas northeast of the test site. Uncertainties about testing made predictions and contingencies difficult. Up until the

Fig. 6 Radioecologists inoculating trees with cesium-137 in the Cesium Forest, circa 1962. Oak Ridge National Laboratory.

Fig. 7 Quick-trap device for capturing insects to irradiate them with cesium-137, circa 1967. United States Department of Energy.

moment of detonation, no one knew if the bomb would work, how big the blast might be, how much radioactive fallout would be produced, where it might go, or how dangerous it might be. The army chose a test site in New Mexico that, for them, was conceptually empty—a conventional bombing range they leased years before. The 97 families settled there were removed, but the plant, animal, and otherwise nonhuman inhabitants were not considered.[27] The lands adjacent to the army lease, however, were not so empty of inhabitants, whether human or nonhuman.[28]

Radioactive "snow" fell on people, animals, plants, farms, buildings—everything.[29] In a dark meteorological survey, military reconnaissance planes tracked the cloud as it merged with others of natural origin and made its way across the country, over the Midwest and Northeast, eventually circling the entire planet, applying the first blanket of radioactive fission products to the earth and inaugurating post-Trinity ecologies.[30]

While the human tragedies of atomic bombs multiply and abound, there are also deep chords of entanglement between nonhumans and radiological matter. Animals, as usual, encounter the most extreme varieties of cruelty. Ranch lands surrounded the

Trinity site, where herds of cattle grazed. As fallout settled on them, it caused hair loss, gave them sores and lesions, and turned their fur white in splotches. As described by Ferenc Morton Szasz, "it looked as though they had been scalded by something."[31] In the months following the war, when ranchers complained about the cows' lowered market value, the army purchased 60 to 70 of the most heavily affected cattle and shipped them to Oak Ridge Reservation.[32] The Alamogordo Cows became the first objects of study—irradiated mascots—at what became the UT-AEC Agricultural Research Laboratory, where intentional (and sometimes grotesque) radiation experiments were carried out on wide varieties of animals and plants to study the genetic and biological effects. Cows, donkeys, pigs, chickens, mice, cotton, corn, and many others were dosed with radiation.[33] Ostensibly, the studies accumulated data and intelligence about food safety and agricultural systems in the wake of a nuclear attack. The underlying pursuit was to map and understand the relationships between biological and radiological matter, leading eventually to the establishment of the discipline of radioecology, pioneered at the ORR in the 1950s.

Stanley Auerbach, an expert in soil-dwelling animals, was hired as the first ecologist at Oak Ridge National Laboratory. The first studies carried out under his direction were at White Oak Lake, a tributary to the Clinch River and a small, dammed drainage basin that accumulated low-level radioactive wastes from the Manhattan Project operations. It was a dry lakebed at the time Auerbach arrived, and various soil-dwelling animals made their homes in it. The ecologist mapped the lakebed according to radioactivity levels and studied incidence of cataracts and other ailments among the critters there. While it was the first meaningful radioecological study, the data was vague and inconclusive. Scientists needed ways to better trace and understand the movement of radioactivity through ecosystems. In 1962, Auerbach's team invented the Cesium Forest: a group of 30 trees inoculated with cesium-137, one of the most biologically dangerous fission products, but one whose lifespan and unique signature would make it easy to trace. Taking samples and measurements over the course of several seasons, they traced the cesium through root and branch systems, leaf litter, soil, and eventually insects, soil animals, and birds. In the quietude of the reservation, Auerbach was for the first time using radioactive tracers to render out the nascent concept of "ecosystems."[34]

Given what we know today about the endless and entangled nature of ecosystems, perhaps these experiments seem irresponsible, but radioecology has left us epistemological tools to understand and cope with the accidents of refining uranium and manufacturing plutonium. The couplings and entanglements between biology and technology are more navigable today at least in part because of advancements in radioecology—radiolabeling of acids led to the image of DNA sequences, for example.

Today, thanks to its military security and limited human occupation over the last 80 years, the ORR enjoys substantial biodiversity.[35] Plant and animal populations thrive in ways they cannot under "normal" human development patterns. Deer (and cars) multiplied to the degree that incidence of animal-vehicle traffic collisions on the reservation became problematic.[36] In 1993, Oak Ridge National Laboratory (ORNL) instituted a series of annual hunts to cull the population—or "harvest specimens" in the language of the event. Given the radioecological profile of the reservation (and that deer are relatively well-connected in the food web), each harvested animal undergoes scans for radioactivity in their bones and flesh before being released off the grounds for consumption. Most years at least a few deer are "retained" because they remain too radiologically *hot*.[37] Some quiet encounter in the woods imbued them with high alpha, beta, or gamma levels, some cesium in their flesh or strontium in their bones. This suggests to us that some unknown number of irradiated deer roam the reservation right now—allegorical Godzilla figures, the charismatic megafauna of radioecology on the ORR—their free-radical-laced bloodstreams disturbing DNA sequences around them as they brush against other agents. The stacking and repetition of automatic accidents are too difficult to trace.

Irradiated deer are an explication of the tight couplings between biology and technology borne out of the ORR from its earliest days, but the entanglements continue to ripple out into the future. At ORNL today, studies in synthetic biology, plant systems, bio-computing, nano-technology, gene-editing, computational chemistry, and medical isotope production probe the future. Undoubtedly, these probes produce as many human risks as they do benefits, but the vectors of entanglement only deepen and accelerate over time.

Radiogeology

Most of the uranium processed in the Manhattan Project was mined years prior in what its colonizers then called the Belgian Congo—the richest source ever found, deposited there in the Earth's crust as it cooled into solid rock billions of years ago.[38] The violence of Belgian colonial domination in the Congo Basin is notorious, where it conflated natural resources—rubber, copper, gold, diamonds—and human labor into a singularly cruel extraction regime. Millions of Congolese people died or were killed or maimed under this regime, laboring to extract resources from the earth; and their suffering is (literally) embodied in the ore, in what Kathryn Yusoff describes as "the shadow geology of disposable lives."[39] While, at the time, uranium was only a byproduct of mining for other precious metals, it was an inhuman geology from the start.[40] Yusoff theorizes an "inframaterialism" between biology and geology through the lens of inhumanity: "The language of materiality and its division between life and nonlife, and its alignment with the concepts of the human and inhuman, facilitated the divisions between subjects as humans and subjects priced as flesh (or inhuman matter)."[41] Under slavery and colonial extraction regimes, subjects are voided, and bodies are equated with matter. The deployment of uranium in weapons unfolded another tragic chapter of geologic inhumanity, especially as the volatile metals were later wielded on the other side of the globe against Japanese citizens and on indigenous Pacific Islanders and other "downwinders" in the form of fallout. Under radioactive ionization, bodies are atomized and disassembled along with everything else.

Over time, this geologic matter can be traced through vectors of concentration and dispersion—across continents and through bloodstreams. Uranium ore was extracted from the earth and sent to the ORR, where it was refined in giant machines, crafted into dense bomb cores, then redistributed into the "nuclear umbrella" of deterrence—a worldwide network of bombers, missiles, submarines, and other delivery vehicles. Some of this metal was atomized into the air, the sea, and even into our bodies, distributing itself so finely that it is imperceptible. The uranium and plutonium that remains unexploded continues its anxious passage between concentration and dispersion.

On the ORR today, the Highly Enriched Uranium Materials Facility (HEUMF) at the Y-12 National Security Complex is the nation's central repository for this mutant geology. Nuclear fuel from weapons in "the stockpile" is returned to Y-12 from all over the world, where it is arranged and stored in as dense a configuration as possible—like an extra-spacious nuclear reactor, kept sufficiently out of the range of criticality. 12,000 such cans, in addition to 12,000 barrels of "special nuclear materials," occupy serial stacks, dormant and quiet. Thanks to the sensitive and rarified nature of the materials it houses, the building is made to withstand catastrophic floods, 7.7-magnitude seismic events, 200 mph tornadic winds, and an "impact in excess of a general aviation aircraft."[42] Beyond its national security functions, the building, which shares characteristics of a temple, prison, a bunker, and even a castle, serves also as an archive of inhuman geology.

The Anthropocene is marked not only with fission products in the soil strata, but also with extensive families of other inhuman geologies that preceded and succeeded the explosions themselves: bone marrow of uranium miners, tooth enamel of downwinders,"black deposits" etched into buildings by Hiroshima shadows, Trinitite from New Mexico and Nevada, exhumed animals from Chernobyl, shellfish from Fukushima, beach sands from Hiroshima (still containing tiny granules of vaporized and melted buildings and people), "sludge" from Hanford, coral dusts from Bikini Atoll, seafloor sediment containing carbon-14 from the Mariana Trench.[43 44 45 46 47 48]

Fission products have shed an epistemological light on the many entangled geochemistries humans participate in. Thanks to atmospheric nuclear tests, I have strontium-90 and carbon-14 in my bones and teeth, but I also almost certainly carry PFOA in my blood and nanoplastics in my organs.[49 50 51 52] This is the *inhumanity* of this geology—both its utter indifference to the trivial goings of self-obsessed humans and its capacity to facilitate the most abstract forms of violence we have yet considered. These forms of "cellular Hiroshima," quietly violent as they are, perhaps also help us to re-navigate the fraught techno-environmental relationships brought on by co-living with the decay products of the Anthropocene.[53]

-----

[1] Michael F. L'Annunziata, *Radioactivity: Introduction and History* (Elsevier, 2007), 440.

[2] Gabrielle Hecht, *Being Nuclear: Africans and the Global Uranium Trade* (MIT Press, 2012), 14.

[3] For reflections on implications of X-rays on our technosocial and aesthetic imaginaries, see Beatriz Colomina, *X-Ray Architecture* (Lars Müller Publishers, 2019).

[4] Kelsey Kennedy, "The Existential Horror Created by the First X-Ray Images," Atlas Obscura, October 9, 2017, https://www.atlasobscura.com/articles/roentgen-xrays-discovery-radiographs.

[5] Karen Barad theorizes entanglement in both a quantum and a relational sense, especially through the lens of quantum physics. Karen Barad, *Meeting the Universe Halfway* (Duke University Press, 2007).

[6] Richard Rhodes describes H.G. Wells' *The World Set Free* (1914), in which Wells writes about the idea of super bombs with atomic power, Richard Rhodes, *The Making of the Atomic Bomb* (Simon & Schuster, 1986), 24.

[7] I.I Rabi described in 1986: "What we did was great. What we did was inevitable; what we did was fortunate for the United States and for the world—as of that period." I. I. Rabi Papers, "How Well We Meant," 1986.

[8] National Research Council, "Report on the Medical Studies of the Effects of the Atomic Bomb," *Atomic Bomb Casualty Commission General Report*, 1947, 68–75.

[9] Estimates vary for deaths and casualties inflicted by the atomic bombs in Hiroshima and Nagasaki. The most rigorous historical accounts suggest that 140,000 died in Hiroshima by the end of 1945, with 70,000 of those on August 6. For more, see Alex Wellerstein, "Counting the Dead at Hiroshima and Nagasaki," *Bulletin of the Atomic Scientists*, August 4, 2020, https://thebulletin.org/2020/08/counting-the-dead-at-hiroshima-and-nagasaki/. Richard Rhodes writes that 5-year deaths reached 200,000, see Rhodes, *The Making of the Atomic Bomb*, 734.

[10] Official numbers of *hibakusha* (survivors of exposure to radiation) are also difficult to account for, but both cities contained hundreds of thousands of residents, and the number of Hiroshima bombing victims recognized at the 79th anniversary ceremony at Hiroshima Peace Memorial Park was 344,306, see Hideki Soejima and Akari Uozumi, "Woman Behind Names Listed on A-bomb Cenotaph Dies of Cancer," *The Asahi Shimbun*, August 8, 2023, https://www.asahi.com/ajw/articles/15391834.

[11] Rhodes, *The Making of the Atomic Bomb*, 731.

[12] Paul Virilio, *The Original Accident*, trans. Julie Rose (Polity Press, 2007), 5-10.

[13] Wellerstein, *Bulletin of the Atomic Scientists, https://thebulletin.org/2020/08/counting-the-dead-at-hiroshima-and-nagasaki/.*

[14] Peter Galison describes "radioactive territories" and "radioactive lands" in his descriptions of the qualities and behaviors of technical lands, Peter Galison, "What Are Technical Lands?" *Technical Lands: A Critical Primer*, ed. Jeffrey S. Nesbit and Charles Waldheim (Jovis, 2022), 19–28.

[15] Leslie M. Groves, *Now It Can Be Told: The Story of the Manhattan Project* (Harper & Row, 1962), 26. See also, *Manhattan District History, Book I - General, Volume 10 - Land Acquisition*, prepared by the War Department for the Atomic Energy Commission, 1947.

[16] Alvin T. M. Lee, "Land Acquisition Program of the War and Navy Departments, World War II," *Journal of Farm Economics* 29, no. 4, Part 1 (Nov. 1947): 889–909.

[17] Groves, *Now It Can Be Told*, 11.

[18] Ibid., 72.

[19] Rhodes uses various spherical objects to describe plutonium cores' sizes under implosion—an orange, an eyeball, etc., see Rhodes, *The Making of the Atomic Bomb*, 670. The use of cantaloupe here is based on the author's own calculation of the Little Boy U-235 core, made up of 64kg of material at a density of 19 g/cc.

[20] Rhodes, *The Making of the Atomic Bomb*, 495–500. See also, Manhattan District History: Book II, Gaseous Diffusion (K-25) Project, Volume 3: Design (italicized) (War Department, Corps of Engineers, 1947), pp.7.7.

[21] The "largest" qualifier is a contentious claim, but it is often used in the lore of K-25. The Pentagon building, for example, was completed a year earlier and housed more total square footage. This sometimes leads to qualifiers for K-25 like "largest factory under one roof", etc. It was among the largest buildings in existence, even until its demolition in the early twenty-first century. See, *Manhattan District History: Book II, Gaseous Diffusion K-25 Project, Volume 4: Construction*," (War Department, Corps of Engineers, 1947), pp.3.29.

[22] Groves, *Now It Can Be Told*, 98.

[23] Rhodes, *The Making of the Atomic Bomb*, 490.

[24] Ibid., 500.

[25] See Alex Wellerstein, *Restricted Data: The History of Nuclear Secrecy in the United States* (University of Chicago Press, 2021).

[26] Ferenc Morton Szasz, *The Day the Sun Rose Twice: The Story of the Trinity Site Nuclear Explosion, July 16, 1945* (University of New Mexico Press, 1984), 121.

[27] Ibid., 115-129.

[28] For a thorough account of the Trinity Test and its impacts, see Nora Wendl, "Trinity Fallout," Places Journal, June 2024, https://placesjournal.org/article/trinity-fallout-nuclear-downwinders-manhattan-project-new-mexico/.

[29] See "Remembering the First Victims of the Atomic Bomb," *Nuclear Threat Initiative*, July 25, 2023, https://www.nti.org/atomic-pulse/downwind-of-trinity-remembering-the-first-victims-of-the-atomic-bomb/.

[30] Szasz, *The Day the Sun Rose Twice*, 116.

[31] Ibid., 133.

[32] For a comprehensive account of the Alamogordo herd, their roles as test subjects, and the misleading rhetoric used by the Atomic Energy Commission (AEC) to assure the American public that radiation was less dangerous, see Annamaria Haden, "Atomic Cows: The Alamogordo Herd at Oak Ridge, Tennessee, 1945–1965" (Master's thesis, University of Tennessee, 2023), https://trace.tennessee.edu/utk_gradthes/10108.

[33] University of Tennessee Agricultural Experiment Station, "UT-AEC Agricultural Research Laboratory" (1966). History of the Institute of Agriculture: Publications, https://trace.tennessee.edu/utk_aghistory/7.

[34] Patrick C. Kangas, *A History of Radioecology* (Taylor & Francis Group, 2023), 86–104.

[35] Martha S. Salk and Patricia D. Parr, *Biodiversity of the Oak Ridge Reservation*, Oak Ridge National Laboratory, September 2000/updated September 2006.

[36] Lisa I. Muller et al., "Spatial and Temporal Relationships between Deer Harvest and Deer–Vehicle Collisions at Oak Ridge Reservation, Tennessee," *Wildlife Society Bulletin* 38, no. 4 (2014): 812–820.

[37] Oak Ridge National Laboratory, "Oak Ridge Reservation Deer Hunts," accessed October 13, 2024, https://oakridgereservationhunts.ornl.gov/deer-hunts/.

[38] Groves, *Now It Can Be Told*, 33–37.

[39] See David Van Reybrouck, *Congo: The Epic History of a People*, trans. Sam Garrett (Ecco, 2014).

[40] Kathryn Yusoff, *A Billion Black Anthropocenes or None* (University of Minnesota Press, 2018), 24.

[41] Ibid., 9.

[42] "Highly Enriched Uranium Materials Facility | Y-12 National Security Complex," n.d., https://www.y12.doe.gov/about/transforming-y-12/highly-enriched-uranium-materials-facility.

[43] Hecht, *Being Nuclear*, 40-43.

[44] UNC Gillings School of Global Public Health, "Cold War Cache of 100,000 Baby Teeth Provides Unique Opportunity to Understand Long-Term Radiation Effects," *UNC Gillings School of Global Public Health,* September 14, 2021, https://sph.unc.edu/sph-news/cold-war-cache-of-100000-baby-teeth-provides-unique-opportunity-to-understand-long-term-radiation-effects/.

[45] *Silent Witness: Human Shadow Etched in Stone.* (n.d.). 中国新聞ヒロシマ平和メディアセンター. https://www.hiroshimapeacemedia.jp/?p=120719

[46] E. Francis and J. M. Inuma, "Japanese Ministers Eat Fukushima Sashimi to Show Water Release Is Safe," *Washington Post*, August 31, 2023, https://www.washingtonpost.com/world/2023/08/31/japan-fukushima-water-release-fish/

[47] Mario M. A. Wannier et al., "Fallout Melt Debris and Aerodynamically Shaped Glasses in Beach Sands of Hiroshima Bay, Japan," *Anthropocene* 25 (2019).

[48] Adam Levy, "Bomb Carbon Has Been Found in Deep-Ocean Creatures," *Scientific American*, August 28, 2023, https://www.scientificamerican.com/article/bomb-carbon-has-been-found-in-deep-ocean-creatures/.

[49] Yusoff, *A Billion Black Anthropocenes*, 44.

[50] R.Fisher, "The Atomic 'Bomb Spike' in Your Body," *BBC*, August 9, 2023, https://www.bbc.com/future/article/20230808-atomic-bomb-spike-carbon-radioactive-body-anthropocene

[51] Nathaniel Rich, "The Lawyer Who Became Dupont's Worst Nightmare," *New York Times Magazine*, January 6, 2016, https://www.nytimes.com/2016/01/10/magazine/the-lawyer-who-became-duponts-worst-nightmare.html.

[52] S. Osaka, "With Microplastics, Scientists Are in a Race against Time," *Washington Post*, March 13, 2024, https://www.washingtonpost.com/climate-environment/2024/03/11/microplastics-health-impacts-unknown/

[53] Virilio, *The Original Accident*, 11.

Mountain Time

Eliyahu Keller

The December 2019 issue of the *MIT Technology Review* was edited with a particular theme in mind. Titled "The War and Peace Issue," it was published only a few months before the world was sent into the disarray and calamity of Covid-19. Seeking to explore the contemporary use of technology in the context of war, the journal posited a simple, albeit somewhat rhetorical, question: "Can technology can be a force for good even in something as bad as war?"[1]

The question, in and of itself, was not novel. More than seven decades earlier, British author George Orwell reflected somewhat similarly on the nature of technology and war, while adding the question of culture and government to the mix. In a short essay titled "You and the Atom Bomb" and published in the British democratic socialist magazine *Tribune*, Orwell responded to the invention of nuclear weapons by formulating a connection between the instruments of war, economic domination, and systems of government:

It is commonplace that the history of civilization is largely the history of weapons. In particular, the connection between the discovery of gunpowder and the overthrow of feudalism by the bourgeoisie has been pointed out over and over again. And though I have no doubt exceptions can be brought forward, I think the following rule would be found generally true: ages in which the dominant weapon is expensive or difficult to make will tend to be ages of despotism, whereas when the dominant weapon is cheap and simple, the common people have a chance. Thus, for example, tanks, battleships, and bombing planes are inherently tyrannical weapons, while rifles, muskets, long-bows, and hand-grenades are inherently democratic weapons. A complex weapon makes the strong stronger, while a simple weapon—so long as there is no answer to it—gives claws to the weak."[2]

In the essay's last lines Orwell coined the term "Cold War." Focusing on the atom bomb's technological complexity, he suggested that the costliness of its production would prevent it from becoming a commonplace weapon and prophesized that its invention could "end large-scale wars" but at the "cost of prolonging a 'peace that is no peace.'"[3] However prescient and precise, this projection is of less importance than Orwell's observation connecting civilizational progress, war, and the technologies by which these opposite—nay, entangled—manifestations of humanity are sought. Indeed, whether in its modern or ancient forms, war is, has been, and always will be technological, and it is in this sense that its tools are inseparable from culture, pushing forward the violent storm of progress, as Walter Benjamin famously observed.[4]

The cover of "The War and Peace Issue" is, in this regard, quite remarkable. The headline directed readers to the journal's main story, the burgeoning relationship between the web services giant Amazon and the U.S. Department of Defense. The cover art featured an image referencing the poster for *Full Metal Jacket*, Stanley Kubrick's noted Vietnam War film of 1987. Floating in the middle of a white background and under the title THE EVERYTHING ~~STORE~~ WAR, it presented a GI helmet covered with military camouflage cloth. On its front side, the words BORN TO KILL, which appeared in the original poster, have been replaced with a more current and somewhat cynical BORN TO SELL. The iconic peace symbol was exchanged, in turn, for a different sign of pacification—Amazon's iconic smiling arrow—while the bullets lining the helmet's rear were swapped with their contemporary counterpart: a row of slightly

Fig. 1 Illustration for the *MIT Technology Review* "The War and Peace Issue" by Tim O'Brien. © Tim O'Brien.

less intimidating yet equally penetrating USB sticks. The message was almost vulgar in its simplicity: in today's trenches and fighting fields, information equals ammunition. The opposite implication, however, is slightly more terrifying: it is the world of information—that is, to say, anywhere and everywhere—that is the new battleground.

The *Review*'s issue is telling in more ways than one. The journal, as its name suggests, is owned by MIT; an institution that is arguably the most consolidated manifestation of the military-(tech)-industrial complex. Importantly, the *Review*'s editors acknowledge this seeming conflict of interests and stand firm that it does not influence their journalistic integrity and work.[5] Nevertheless, the journal itself is, in some respect, reflective of the kind of cultural and political entanglements that are inherent to this terrain. These are made most visible through instances like that of Amazon, exposing the contemporary intertwinement of military infrastructure with communication technologies, and the physical and material landscapes which make these networks virtually invisible.

The *Review*'s cover story focused on the newly established Joint Enterprise Defense Infrastructure (aptly titled JEDI) and Amazon's somewhat questionable relation to it.[6] The foundations for this story—ones that connect the U.S. military and the nation's industry—were laid decades earlier, during the years of the Manhattan Project and continued with the dozens of projects developed throughout the decades of the Cold War and beyond.[7] This history found its contemporary culmination in the centralized JEDI project—canceled, as some reports suggested, because of then President Trump's animosity toward Jeff Bezos—and its replacement, a distributed acquisition vehicle with a much less suggestive acronym, the Joint Warfighting Cloud Capability or JWCC.[8] Through it, the Department of Defense could directly purchase

Fig. 2 The War Room with the Big Board from Stanley Kubrick's 1964 film, *Dr. Strangelove*. Public Domain

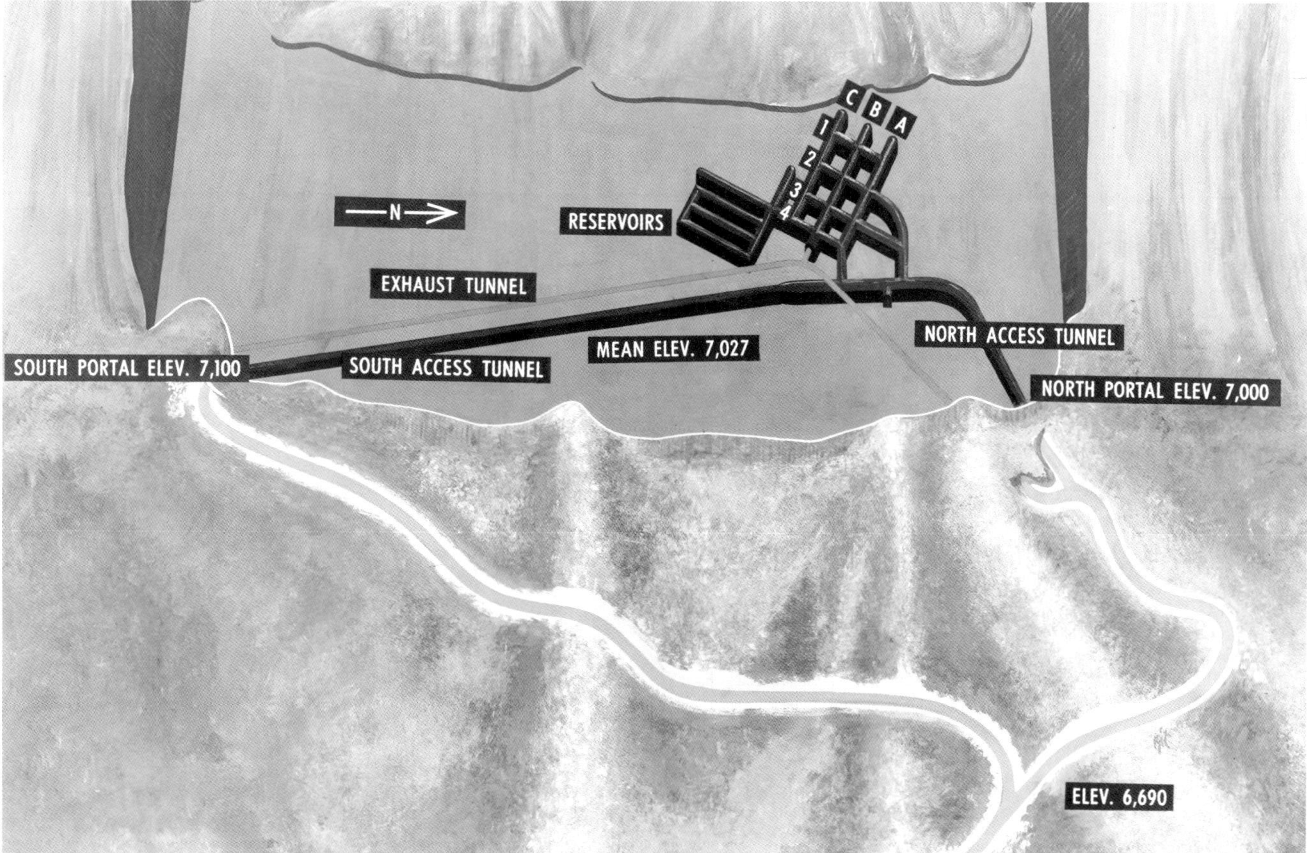

Fig. 3 Cheyenne Mountain cutaway diagram, date unknown. USAF photo, Public Domain.

cloud services from four different technological goliaths, Microsoft, Google, Oracle, and the already mentioned Amazon. Thus, the material path set by companies such as DuPont and Union Carbide during the material production of the nuclear bomb, or by more contemporary industrial giants such as Lockheed Martin, Raytheon, or General Electric—all of which have been providing the military with hardware—was now to be complemented by the abdication of the military's intelligence to a privately owned and seemingly intangible cloud.

War Room

Six decades earlier and almost 20 years before his poignant Vietnam critique was promoted by the noted poster, Kubrick created what is widely considered to be one of the most emblematic Cold War films. In part a reaction to the Cuban Missile Crisis, Kubrick's 1964 *Dr. Strangelove* mocked the prospect of mutually assured destruction (again, with an apt acronym, MAD) and portrayed the politicians, generals, and experts trusted with the power to annihilate humanity as nothing more than a group of irresponsible backyard boys.

The ultimate decision to end the world, however, was relegated to the "doomsday machine": an emotionless computer designed by a mad scientist (himself inspired by an array of actual figures), operating purely in response to data points and information and equipped with the ability to launch an irreversible nuclear attack.[9]

Setting aside the ways in which Kubrick's satire demonstrated the seeming irrationality that underpinned the strategy of deterrence, what is pertinent about *Dr. Strangelove* in this particular context is the setting of the film: an underground war room, designed by British production designer Ken Adam, of James Bond glory. With its dark and atmospheric lighting, its egalitarian round decision-making table, and its enormous and ominous screens communicating the location of missiles, bombers, and nukes in real time, Kubrick's war room both embodied pervasive Cold War imaginaries and conditioned those for years to come. Indeed, the Cold War underground was a paradoxical space hosting, on one hand, the instruments that could bring about humanity's destruction and, on the other, the place of refuge, the only space in which a nuclear apocalypse—unleashed from the very same location—could be survived.

In the film, a short montage discloses the war room's location to be somewhere around or underneath the Pentagon. Though Adam noted in a late interview that he was not inspired by any real military spaces in the world outside the set, its design demonstrates how this particular cultural imaginary was rooted in the reality of countless Cold War–era command centers, hidden and buried beneath the earth.[10] The most familiar of these is the Combat Operations Center (COC) in Cheyenne Mountain, known in part for its own cinematic fame in the years and decades to come.[11] The former home of the North American Aerospace Defense Command (NORAD), it is located in central Colorado, on a site chosen for its strategic geographical remoteness and geological qualities, and where it still serves as an alternate site for NORAD and as the Cheyenne Mountain Space Force Station.[12]

However coincidentally, the COC was built from 1961 to 1965, a period paralleling, in part, *Dr. Strangelove*'s production and release. Not unlike Kubrick's war room, it too became symbolic in terms of how one imagines Cold War environments, and specifically the spaces of decision making. As author and curator Layne Karafantis noted, NORAD's combination of advanced computer and communication technologies and their placement within a "hardened" environment that could withstand a nuclear attack "spoke to Cold War national security needs" and fostered the creation of a "command and control environment that was qualitatively distinct from its predecessors."[13]

At the outset, Cheyenne Mountain comprised approximately 154,000 square feet of space, most of which the Utah Construction and Mining Company excavated during the first year of construction.[14] The majority of this space was dedicated to housing

Fig. 4 NORAD entrance to Cheyenne Mountain, 1968. USAF Photo, Public Domain.

chambers, exhaust and access tunnels, as well as fuel and water reservoirs. Importantly, the COC was designed, conceived in a manner that would allow it to function autonomously in the event of an emergency.[15] With its vast amounts of supplies, equipment, and sprawling spaces, Cheyenne Mountain could continue operations for approximately 30 days after the world outside descended into chaos.

The COC was not the only underground fortress built by the U.S. government during the Cold War. Rather, it was part of a network of bunkers located underneath or within mountains, serving as the physical infrastructure for the government's Continuity of Operations plan. In addition to Cheyenne Mountain, these included the Raven Rock Mountain Complex and the Mount Weather Emergency Complex, both built in the 1950s. Also known as Site R, Raven Rock was located on the southern border of Pennsylvania and within the northern portion of the Blue Ridge Mountains. Its official function was to serve as an emergency communication and command center, or a kind of alternate Pentagon. Mount Weather, on the other hand, was located about 70 miles southwest of Washington, DC. Its role within a projected apocalyptic scenario was to be the evacuation location for senior government officials and military personnel.[16]

Within the depths of Cheyenne Mountain, chiseled more than 1,400 feet into the rock, lay a new advanced command and control system dubbed "the Western world's most important military data processing installation."[17] Designed by the MITRE Corporation, an offshoot of MIT's Lincoln Laboratory, it brought together data from various sources, including "the Ballistic Missile Early Warning System (BMEWS), the DEW line and coastal radar networks, picket planes and ships, and other information sources and field commands," and consolidated those on a series of screens for the NORAD commander to observe.[18]

The system responsible for coordinating the arriving data was called the Semi-Automatic Ground Environment, or SAGE—a most appropriate acronym, once again, for a technology designed to predict the future. Indeed, a big portion of the Cold War was fought (and, for that matter, the equally dreaded war that was never fought but only imagined) and relied on communication technologies and networks of information, whether internal or external. Within the depths of the mountain, it was not only security that was provided to the inhabitants but the possibility of omniscience, the knowledge of everything that was taking place outside, and the ability to observe either the future or the demise of the entire world.

We Are as Mountains

With the security offered by the underground environment and the omniscience given to those settled within it by the ever-flowing stream of data, the image of the mountain bunker offered a mythical, if not religious, power. As historian of religion Mircea Eliade noted, both imaginary and real mountains have served as liminal locations between sacred and profane spaces throughout human history and across diverse and global cultures.[19] Whether Olympus, Sinai, Juktas, Fuji, or Six Grandfathers Mountain—to name only a few mythical, sacred, and symbolic peaks—mountains have long been considered and worshiped as focal points of an *axis mundi*, as spaces from which divine authority speaks and communicates with the terrestrial world, or as places that lead to the "summit of the universe."[20] Within the history of architecture mountains too have played a prominent role. In Hindu traditions, for instance, temples are modeled after the holy peak of Mount Meru, representing a cosmological order through their form, while holding a sacred hidden space within their depths.[21] In many other instances, as Michael Jakob noted, artificial mountains were constructed as "meaningful cultural signals," asking to symbolize the various universal concerns of humanity.[22]

Though Cheyenne Mountain itself is not considered a sacred site, it certainly extends the cultural and mythical symbolism associated with and implied by the history and images of the mountains.[23] Connecting knowledge, visions, security, and hiddenness, it produced an invisible presence of military-industrial informational deity, carving a space out of solid rock to give place to an all-knowing and all-seeing system; a technological divinity designed to consume information in order to anticipate and counter the destruction of the world. And, if all preventive measures were to fail, then, at the very least, it would serve as a refuge to survive the nuclear flood.

The ever-growing and entangled network of industrial corporations, academic institutions, and military research teams formed the framework for much of the research into communication and information technologies. Surprisingly, however, this complex had a somewhat unanticipated echo and an entanglement within a growing countercultural movement in the United States during the very same years. As author Fred Turner demonstrated, the postwar history of military-industrial research culture and that of counterculture are deeply intertwined.[24] In Turner's view, it was "the same military-industrial research world that brought forth nuclear weapons—and computers," which concurrently fostered and relied on a "free-wheeling, interdisciplinary, and highly entrepreneurial style of work."[25] This individualist spirit, he suggested, resonated with tens of thousands of young Americans who were seeking an alternative lifestyle and setting up communes across the United States. The most noted and well-known representative of this somewhat unexpected cultural exchange—and the protagonist of Turner's study—was author and serial entrepreneur Stewart Brand.

Brand's brand, pun intended, is both unique and elusive. As journalist Malcolm Harris noted in a recent scathing review of Brand's biography—he labeled Brand a "huckster"—it was mostly salesmanship, posturing, and an ability to be at the right place, at the right time to connect with the right people that had made him into a figure of historical magnitude.[26] Whatever may be the truth about his actual role in shaping counterculture or the computer industry, Brand at the very least made sure to place himself at the center of a whirlpool that came to characterize technological and cultural production in the Cold War United States. Out of that current came the entangled world we know today: a globalized and interconnected reality in which the spheres of military, academic, and civilian research are inseparable from one another and from the daily life of many citizens of the world.

Brand first achieved fame with the creation of the *Whole Earth Catalog*, a counterculture magazine he coproduced sporadically between 1968 and 1972. Influenced both by his education in biology at Stanford and by his short military training, the catalog was labeled as an "evaluation and an access device."[27] It included an array of texts as well as information about countless DIY products, from tents to lamps to mills or knife sets, which could be used by anyone. Its first paragraph began: "We *are* as gods and might as well get used to it." What followed was a critique of the power held by "government, big business, formal education, church" and of the wealth and glory accumulated by them; the development of a "realm of intimate, personal power" would, by contrast, allow individuals to form and shape their own education and environment, with the catalog being a first step in that direction.[28]

Following the publication of the catalog, Brand became a "network entrepreneur," moving from one intellectual milieu to another and using the connections made to promote various projects and ideas. In the first years, these connections were made primarily between the worlds of art, design, counterculture, and scientific research: one such project was the 1985 Whole Earth "Lectronic Link," or WELL for short, labeled as the world's first virtual community. In parallel, and by the turn of the century, Brand's cultivated network would be cast much wider and materialize in 1987 in a consulting firm he established with several partners called Global Business Network (GBN).[29] Founded in Berkeley in 1987, it provided services to various Silicon Valley corporations and software companies, branches of the U.S. and

Fig.5 Prototype model of the Clock of the Long Now, photo by Rolfe Horn.

other governments, as well as oil companies.[30] Given this evolution, the critique that Brand first expressed in the *Whole Earth Catalog* might seem quite ironic in hindsight. And yet, these connections, some perhaps more direct than others, present the formulation of that opening line—that is, the godlike power that humanity as a whole or individual humans could and should assume—that gains a different meaning than before.

Time, Denaturalized

It should come as no surprise that Brand approached Jeff Bezos, who has been pushing to solidify the long-term relationship between cloud computing corporations and the military, and asked him to fund his latest endeavor, christened with an awe-inspiring title: the Clock of the Long Now. The clock was the flagship project of the eponymous Long Now Foundation, a San Francisco–based nonprofit presided over by Brand. It was cofounded by him and several of his longtime collaborators, including the clock's inventor, engineer Danny Hills, the founder of the Thinking Machines Corporation and formerly of Disney R&D, and the musician Brian Eno, who notably gave the foundation its name. Its purpose is "to promote long time thinking," to encourage "imagination at the timescale of civilization—the next and last 10,000 years," and to "preserve possibilities for the future" by being "good ancestors."[31]

Serving as the foundation's crown jewel, the Clock of the Long Now is the epitome of these so-called best intentions. Its idea is as simple as it is megalomaniac: to construct a clock buried deep within a mountain that would keep time for the next 10,000 years, synchronizing itself in relation to the sun's position as well as Earth's rotation. Most important, Brand noted, if "sufficiently impressive and well engineered, [it] would embody deep time for people."[32] Constructed with "long-lasting materials, including titanium, ceramics, quartz, sapphire, and 316 stainless-steel" components, the clock is meant to be wound by its visitors or to be powered by "energy captured by changes in the temperature between day and night."[33] While its final version will be placed within Mount Washington, in a secluded, dry, and remote area of northwest Nevada, its prototype, about 200 feet tall, is currently being constructed in the Sierra Diablo in western Texas, on a piece of land owned by Bezos, and with funds donated by him.

In response to its request to be considered a nonprofit, the Internal Revenue Services asked the Long Now Foundation to provide a detailed description of the experience offered by the clock. The former executive director of the foundation, industrial designer Alexander Rose, responded with a striking text, supposedly written by someone in the year 11,567. Among the features of Clock of the Long Now would be a "flight of shallow steps, each step carved from a layer of rock representing approximately 10,000 years" and which would make one feel "belittled by the greatness of geologic time"; or a "hemispherical mirror lighting up the whole room" and actuating a "synchronization mechanism which automatically adjusts the time of the clock to local noon."[34] The clock's enormity and design, Rose continued, would be so thoughtful that it would strike visitors upon arrival, injecting them with the thought of himself and his fellow members—"the people of this ancient time"—who all "had the foresight to think this far into their future and create this place."[35] Finally, visitors would arrive at a library that Rose, with typical hubris, equated to "the truly ancient library of Alexandria." In it, they would find not only data in "increasingly better and denser methods of storage" but also the first one thousand books chosen by the clock's founders and makers, which though obsolescent "helped to teach people the value of knowledge over long periods of time."[36]

For Brand and his collaborators, the clock is meant to act as a culturally transformative device: the temporal equivalent, Brand noted, of the photographs taken of Earth by astronauts, thus conditioning our temporal perspective in the same way that those photos supposedly influenced our environmental thinking.[37] The choice to place the clock within a mountain is, in this regard, intriguing. The comprehensive view afforded by Apollo's eye is reversed and replaced by a peering not into the planet's form, but into its flesh, its geological strata indicating and indexing its formation over millions over years, a process too slow to be noticed by the chronologically insensitive human sight.

Brand's desire to construct this audacious temporal temple within a mountain is rooted not only in the mythical symbolism associated with mountains—of which he was likely aware—but also in his own formation by Cold War culture and history.[38] As Brand himself acknowledged, his adolescent years were shadowed by fears both of nuclear holocaust and of the loss of his personal will to a homogenizing Soviet machine.[39] These anxieties, Turner noted, resulted not only in a deep need to keep one's individuality, but in the belief that cultural and artistic expression could play a significant role in saving the species from its own

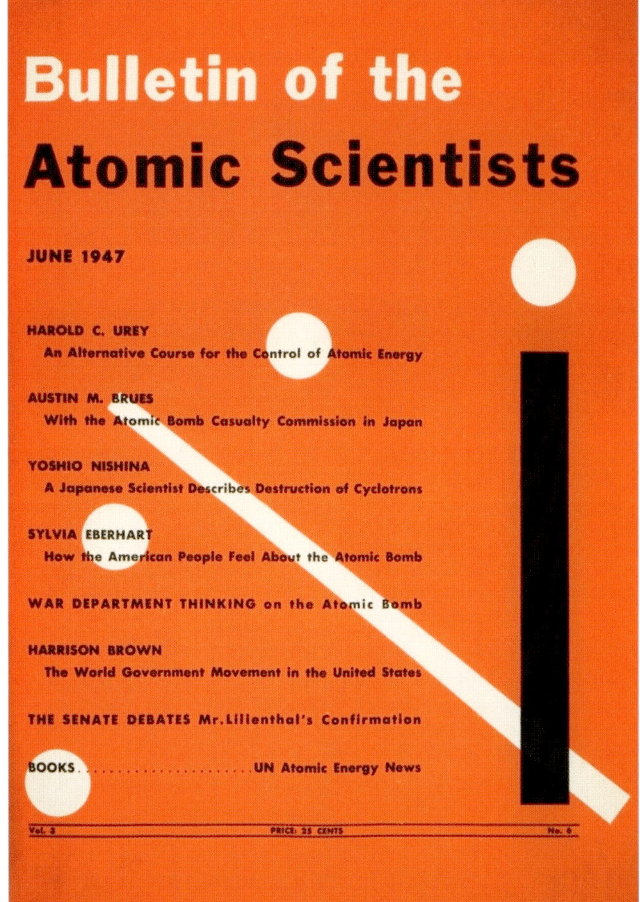
Bulletin of the
Atomic Scientists
JUNE 1947
HAROLD C. UREY
An Alternative Course for the Control of Atomic Energy
AUSTIN M. BRUES
With the Atomic Bomb Casualty Commission in Japan
YOSHIO NISHINA
A Japanese Scientist Describes Destruction of Cyclotrons
SYLVIA EBERHART
How the American People Feel About the Atomic Bomb
WAR DEPARTMENT THINKING on the Atomic Bomb
HARRISON BROWN
The World Government Movement in the United States
THE SENATE DEBATES Mr. Lillenthal's Confirmation
BOOKS .... UN Atomic Energy News

Fig. 6 The June 1947 issue of the *Bulletin of Atomic Scientists*, featuring the first image of the Doomsday Clock. Courtesy and with the permission of the Bulletin of Atomic Scientists.

destruction and helping humanity to both confront and avoid nuclear war.[40] The Clock of the Long Now, then, is the last manifestation in a long list of cultural and artistic artifacts meant to placate, at least in part, Brand's apocalyptic fears.

What we end up with, however, is not an artifact embodying some new understanding of humanity's temporality or an acknowledgment of the minuscule scale of human history in relation to geological, let alone cosmological, timescale. Rather, the Clock of the Long Now seems to be a representation not of a renewed relationship with a different scale of time but of the persistence of the old scales: of how difficult it is for humans—in this case, very particular, voracious, and extractive humans—to reformulate humanity's relationship with the environment, with the planet, with time itself. Indeed, the clock does not offer an imaginative leap into the next 10,000 years, but a mélange of past forms stripped of any real sense of wonder or transcendence. Not unlike the idols of old, which masked the economic reality of temples, what the Clock of the Long Now hides behind its mechanism is a planetary network of materials and infrastructure that supports an aging, omniscient, and omnipresent military-industrial data deity that offers no real grace. A strange hybrid of a holy mountain, an ancient temple, a nuclear bunker, an earthwork, and a server farm, it emerges as a space not so much of future sacredness, but a kind of secularized *axis mundi*, obscuring and disguising the nexus between our world's terrestrial and finite material existence and the supposed immaterial infinity and airiness of data clouds.

Postscript

The experience of time, according to Einstein's relativity theory, diverges depending on one's location in relation to gravity's pull. In general, at higher altitudes, where gravitational forces are comparatively weaker, time progresses marginally faster than at lower elevations, where gravitational forces are stronger. For an individual standing atop a mountain, time will move faster than for someone situated within the mountain's depth. This disparity, though imperceptible to the human mind, stands true when tested with the most precise measurements. What it might mean, in somewhat pragmatic terms, is that for those standing inside a mountain there is, comparatively of course, more time.

The military infrastructures hollowing the forlorn deities that we once revered as mountains and now apprehend as geological formations have, quite literally, more time. The information held within them, supplied and supported by corporate giants, allows one to anticipate—that is, to peer into the future—perhaps not with certainty, but certainly with growing accuracy and probability. In this sense, the mountain is neither a deity nor a geological formation. Rather, it is a material consolidation of geopolitical and military interests, constructed not from rock but out of notions of security, defense, and secrecy. Whether the Clock of the Long Now will tick for the next 10,000 years or whether humanity will survive to witness its ticking is, in some respects, of no importance at all. What is at stake, in fact, is what the clock is hiding within a mountain, located somewhere, if not sometime, else.

One of the first artifacts of the atomic age was the Doomsday Clock. Established by the *Bulletin of the Atomic Scientists*, it was first published on the cover in June 1947, marking humanity's distance from self-annihilation at seven minutes to midnight. What that number actually meant is, in all fairness, quite vague. Originally, it was set by Eugene Rabinowitch, the *Bulletin*'s editor, who consulted various experts and policymakers and, perhaps as a reference to its apocalyptic connotation, set it on seven minutes to midnight, indicating humanity's temporal distance from the world's nuclear doom. Since Rabinowitch's death in 1973, the responsibility for the dials' setting has been taken up the *Bulletin*'s Science and Security Board, a group of 18 experts with "diverse backgrounds ranging from policy and diplomacy to military history and nuclear science."[41] Over the decades, the clock has ticked back and forth, moving slowly but confidently toward oblivion. Adding anthropogenic climate change and the war in Ukraine, among other things, to their calculations, the *Bulletin of the Atomic Scientists* decided, in 2023, to place the hands of the dial as close to the end of the world as it has ever been: only 90 seconds before doom.

There could not be two artifacts as similar in their supposed function, yet as different in essence, as the Doomsday Clock and the Clock of the Long Now. While the graphic clock is printed on a piece of paper or flickers as pixels on a computer screen, the Clock of the Long Now is a heavy, and heavily material, entity. Both clocks express a kind of hope for humanity, yet they do so in fundamentally diverging ways. While the Doomsday Clock freezes an everlasting and ever-shortening moment before the end of time, it does so to visualize something as abstract as time and propel humanity into action by making the end of the world unbearably near. The Clock of the Long Now, however, takes time differently. Its slow ticking does not suggest that we have all the time in world to wait for action, but it does speak to a kind of bourgeois mentality that soothes itself through the creation of symbolic and out-of-scale artifacts, among other things.

As it stands now, carved into one mountain and awaiting the excavation of the next, the clock offers the same perspective that has been offered by modernity for centuries, that sees humanity as external, if not superior, to the planet, or as the crowning achievement of a forlorn god. If Brand and his companions were to adhere to their task truly, they might realize that a clock that measures time for scales that are beyond human perception already exists—*it is the mountain*—and that it would require some time to shed the kind of civilizational goggles that make us see it as a place to put something of our own within it rather than experience ourselves and our temporality differently. Perhaps 10,000 years.

-----

[1] "The War and Peace Issue," *MIT Technology Review* (2019), https://www.technologyreview.com/magazines/the-war-and-peace-issue/.

[2] George Orwell, "You and the Atomic Bomb," *Tribune*, October 19, 1945.

[3] Orwell, "You and the Atomic Bomb."

[4] I refer to Benjamin's noted reading of Paul Klee's painting *Angelus Novus*, in his "Theses on the Philosophy of History," and his assertion that the angel in the painting represents the dynamics of history and its catastrophic progression. "This storm irresistibly propels him into the future to which his back is turned, while the pile of debris before him grows skyward. This storm is what we call progress." Walter Benjamin, "Theses on the Philosophy of History," *Illuminations* (Schocken Books, 1969), 257–258.

[5] The *MIT Technology Review* states that it is a "not-for-profit media company, wholly owned by MIT but editorially independent from it." Moreover, it notes that the Review benefits "from the Institute's many resources, including easy access to its prominent faculty and researchers. At the same time, our coverage of technology is independent of MIT. We do not favor people or technologies simply because they are associated with the Institute. We are not part of MIT's communications functions; it is not our job to promote its activities." "Editorial Guidelines," *MIT Technology Review*, https://www.technologyreview.com/editorial-guidelines/.

[6] The Joint Enterprise Defense Infrastructure, of 2019, was a ten-billion-dollar cloud computing contract initiated by the Department of Defense and canceled after legal controversies that followed its awarding to Microsoft.

[7] See, for instance, Stuart W. Leslie, *The Cold War and American Science: The Military-Industrial-Academic Complex at MIT and Stanford*, rev. ed. (Columbia University Press, 1994).

[8] David Shepardson, "U.S. Judge Declines to Dismiss Amazon Allegations Trump Interfered in JEDI Contract," *Reuters*, April 28, 2021, sec. Technology, https://www.reuters.com/technology/us-judge-declines-dismiss-amazon-allegations-trump-interfered-jedi-contract-2021-04-28/.

[9] The character of Dr. Strangelove is said to have been inspired by various Cold War intellectuals, strategists, and scientists, including the RAND Institute strategist Herman Kahn; the so-called father of the hydrogen bomb, Edward Teller; and German American rocket scientist Wernher von Braun. See Paul Boyer, "Dr. Strangelove" in Mark Carnes, ed., *Past Imperfect: History according to the Movies* (New York: H. Holt, 1995), 267.

[10] Ken Adam, quoted in Fionnuala Halligan, *Filmcraft: Production Design* (Focal Press, 2012), 14.

[11] Cheyenne Mountain and NORAD have been referenced in countless films as a secret location for U.S. military operations, and often in apocalyptic or disaster contexts. See, for instance, *War Games* (1983), *Independence Day* (1996), or *Interstellar* (2014).

[12] David W. Shircliffe, *NORAD's Underground Combat Operations Center, 1956–66 - Historical Reference Paper no. 12* (Declassified; North American Air Defense Command, January 1966), 10–14.

[13] Layne Karafantis, "NORAD's Combat Operations Center: A Distinctively Cold War Environment," *Information & Culture: A Journal of History 52,* no. 2 (2017): 139.
[14] Shircliffe, *NORAD*, 21
[15] Shircliffe, *NORAD*, 23
[16] For a detailed account of the US Continuity of Operations plan, see Garrett M. Graff, *Raven Rock: The Story of the U.S. Government's Secret Plan to Save Itself—While the Rest of U.S. Die* (Simon & Schuster, 2017).
[17] Karafantis, "NORAD's Combat Operations Center," 146.
[18] Karafantis, "NORAD's Combat Operations Center," 147.
[19] Mircea Eliade, *The Sacred and the Profane: The Nature of Religion*, trans. Willard R. Trask (Harcourt Brace Jovanovich, 1987), 36-47.
[20] Eliade, *The Sacred and the Profane*, 40-41.
[21] Francis D. K. Ching, Mark M. Jarzombek, and Vikramaditya Prakash, *A Global History of Architecture*, 3rd edition (Wiley, 2017), 254-255, 320, 615.
[22] It is worth noting Michael Jakob's inquiries into artificial mountains. For many cultures have designed artificial mountains "as meaningful cultural signals" in order to express and symbolize matters of great concern for civilization: death and immortality, work and leisure, time and space." See: Michael Jakob, "On Mountains: Scalable and Unscalable" in Stan Allen and Marc McQuade, eds., *Landform Building: Architecture's New Terrain* (Lars Müller Publishers ; Princeton University School of Architecture, 2011), 136-164.
[23] Cheyenne Mountain is named after the Cheyenne people, comprising two native tribes. Unlike Pikes Peak, located several miles to the west, which is considered a sacred site to the Cheyenne and various other Indigenous peoples (it is called Sun Mountain by the Ute people), the particular mountain itself has not been considered as such. Nevertheless, it was used by the Cheyenne people and other Indigenous tribes as a rendezvous and as a site well suited for hunting, gathering trees for tepee construction, and hiding from enemies.
[24] Fred Turner, *From Counterculture to Cyberculture: Stewart Brand, the Whole Earth Network, and the Rise of Digital Utopianism* (University of Chicago Press, 2008).
[25] Turner, *Counterculture*, 4.
[26] Malcolm Harris, "Stewart Brand's Dubious Futurism," *The Nation*, June 13, 2022, https://www.thenation.com/article/society/stewart-brand-whole-earth/.
[27] Stewart Brand, ed., *Whole Earth Catalog*, Fall 1968 (self-published), 3.
[28] Brand, ed., *Whole Earth Catalog*, 3 (emphasis in original).
[29] Fred Turner borrows the term from Ronald Burt to describe Brand. Turner, *Counterculture*, 5.
[30] Turner, *Counterculture*, 5.
[31] "The Long Now Foundation," Long Now, https://longnow.org/.
[32] "About: The Long Now," https://longnow.org/about/.
[33] "The Clock of the Long Now," https://longnow.org/clock/.
[34] Rose, quoted in Stewart Brand, *The Clock of the Long Now: Time and Responsibility*, rev. ed. (Basic Books, 2000), 46–48.
[35] Ibid.
[36] Ibid.
[37] Brand, quoted by Brian Eno in an essay titled "The Big Here and Long Now," accessed June 23, 2024, https://longnow.org/essays/big-here-long-now/.
[38] Brand quotes Mircea Eliade's book *The Myth of Eternal Return.* It would not be far-fetched to speculate that Brand was familiar with Eliade's other texts, and that his choice of site for the clock was influenced in part by the mythical history and symbolism of mountains. Brand, *Time and Responsibility*, 43.
[39] Brand, quoted in Turner, *Counterculture*, 41.
[40] Turner, *Counterculture*, 43.
[41] "What Is the Doomsday Clock?" University of Chicago News, https://news.uchicago.edu/explainer/what-is-the-doomsday-clock. For a current list of the board's members, see "Science and Security Board," *Bulletin of the Atomic Scientists* (blog), https://thebulletin.org/about-us/science-and-security-board/.

Spectral Pursuits in Secret Gardens

Of Phonetics, Surveillance, and Cold War Lab-Prisons

Ryan Bishop

Constructed between 1959 and 1966, Bell Laboratories-Holmdel marks a deliberate shift toward a modernist design befitting the modern research housed within. The property is characteristic of the mid-century move toward suburban landscaped campuses for corporate headquarters and research sites. Listed in the National Register on June 26, 2017, the Bell Laboratories-Holmdel, New Jersey, is significant for the architectural design work of Eero Saarinen and Associates and the corporate campus landscape design by Hideo Sasaki of Sasaki, Walker and Associates. From 1959 to 2007, the building functioned as a research and development facility for Bell Laboratories and its successor, Alcatel-Lucent. The facility gained significance as a key research and development facility for Bell Laboratories, which spearheaded scientific significant breakthroughs. Over the course of the twentieth century, and in its various organizational incarnations, the company was responsible for innovative work related to radio astronomy, the transistor, lasers, and physics.[1]

—National Parks, *Bell Laboratories - Holmdele*

Day was breaking. A thick, rich hoar-frost feathered the posts of the fences, the score of intertwined strands, the thousand stars of the barbed wire, the sloping roof of the watch-tower and the tall grass in the wilderness outside the compound…Turning their backs to the room, they looked out of the window and the lights in the compound, the watch-tower faintly outlined in the darkness, more lights near the distant greenhouses, and the column of shimmering fire over Moscow.[2]

—Alexander Solzhenitsyn, *The First Circle*

Two Sites and (at least) One Shared Goal

Invisibly blended into suburban landscapes lie two Cold War research labs for audio technological development with military remits: overt in their size and covert in their function, hiding in plain sight like Poe's purloined letter, they operated for decades.[3] The gardens in this chapter's title are not gardens in the traditional sense and the spectral pursuits were not those of the supernatural or metaphysical varieties. Rather, the "gardens" were carefully curated grounds for two very different but related sites—one a corporation in the United States, Bell Labs, and the other a *sharashka*, or Soviet secret research and development lab, stocked with hand-picked prisoners (Mavrino). Each entity pursued state-directed secret research in telecommunications during the Cold War. The spectral pursuits were the aural spectra that still shape the telecommunications world and its future-directed potential in ways that were not supernatural, though they can have that effect. The "tele-" or "at-a-distance" nature of the technologies involved can seem supernatural, allowing the metaphysical overcoming of corporeal time-space constraints and allowing, for example, the dead to speak to the living through audio recordings.[4] And it is through spectral research, including audio analysis-synthesis technologies, that time overcomes space: over there becomes right now, as Paul Virilio pithily put it, thus altering our sense of metaphysics.[5]

Warped *döpplegangers*, or bad doubles of each other, Murray Hill and Mavrino are semi shadow sites occluded through the lens of competing materialist ideologies during the Manichean struggles over global futures fraught with eschatological consequences. Murray Hill, New Jersey, and Mavrino, Moscow, wrapped their cutting-edge, speculative technological research in swaths of flora and foliage. The grounds of Murray Hill exemplified the budding corporate campus landscape design, while Mavrino occupied the appropriated gardens and grounds of a seminary near the city limits. Alexander Solzhenitsyn's novel *The First Circle* provides the primary source for any understanding of Mavrino, a thinly fictionalized version of the *sharashka* in which he was imprisoned, and the research he undertook there. The novel devotes several passages to various inmate-researchers deep in meditations inspired by the cultivated beauty of the compound, moments of pause and near-freedom sparked by nature's glory, as found in the "century-old lime trees." Such sensorial pleasures had been long withheld from them in grueling prison or gulag conditions. The invisible secrets of nature, revealed by synesthetic technologies that rendered spectra legible starting at the end of the nineteenth century, deepen the awe and wonder with which the "specialists" immersed themselves in Wordsworthian reveries. The ancient manse, we are told, required retrofitting for its new purpose, a process facilitated by the German occupation during World War II. Stalin, in turn, continued the building-lab palimpsest with seized German and American gear and manuals. With newly installed radiators, temporary floors, makeshift labs, and idyllic grounds, the researchers took solace in unfettered access to the latest foreign insights into the audiovisual applications of the Fourier series and unrationed portions of sliced black bread. Murray Hill, by contrast, offered its researchers more carefully coiffed environs in which to take gentle strolls, and the new compound inspired less bucolic admiration and nostalgia than the makeshift barn-centered configuration found on the same site decades earlier, and instead gestured to the brave new world of US global superpower status in politics, economics, and technoscience innovation, a future being generated on that very spot.

Capturing moments in a dynamic process such as speech into small storable units, the process can be held and rearranged in repeatable units for transmission. This method of manipulating and controlling dynamic systems provided multiple advantageous applications for the Cold War strategy known as C3I (communication, command, control, and information). These strategic goals provided the primary rationale for the construction of compounds and the employment of researchers to work in these dynamic gardens. Capturing elusively fast spectral dynamics into manageable forms for transmission, dissemination, clarification, and obfuscation led to the establishment of cybernetics and information theory as essential building blocks for the post-WWII world. What emerged from these gardens and various spectrally driven research constitutes our spectrum-rich telecommunications contemporary existence, technologies as invisible to and through our use as the spectra they leverage.

Those who labored at Murray Hill undoubtedly thought of it as a work camp, a corporate prison that promised blue-sky thinking and research within the proprietorial parameters of profit and/or governmental agendas. Mavrino, on the other hand, was an actual *sharashka*, an R and D lab of a specifically penal variety stocked with academicians and researchers carefully culled from more punitive prison camps/gulags. If Bell Labs hyperbolically smacked of indentured servitude with the promise of cutting-edge technological playgrounds, future-changing innovations, and potential Nobel prizes, Mavrino offered freedom from incarceration, a clean state record, and enough money to restart a brutally paused life after WWII service . . . if workers were successful in fulfilling their assigned research goals (if not, it was a return to the gulag). Solzhenitsyn explains that "the prison took its name from the nearby village, which had long since been swallowed by Greater Moscow."[6] As a converted seminary, the grounds came replete with contemplative but mostly unkempt orchards and gardens and an onion-domed tower. The compound conversion chimes with the Dantean allusion of the title while also indicating the suspended state in which the prisoners labored there. They could bask in the beauties of nature and allures of Moscow but only as points on an unreachable horizon. Along with their fellow prisoners, their companions in limbo are the works of Homer, Socrates, Aristotle, Vedic philosophers, and others encountered by Dante in the first circle of hell, populated by unbaptized pagan souls condemned by ignorance or their place within the cruel historical timing of Christianity's presence on earth. When Mavrino first opened, the prisoners felt its "pastoral simplicity" when they were allowed to "wander the compound as they pleased . . . lie in the long wet grass . . . [and] gaze at the stars at night."[7] In those early days, their assignment remained vague, though deliveries of equipment for "telephone, ultra high frequency radio communications and acoustics" gave them a clue: a top-secret plan to develop a vocoder clone for cryptographic communication and another project to identify voices in telephone calls and "discover what makes every human voice unique." Each of these tasks involved audio analysis and synthesis. To accomplish these tasks of camouflaged speech and aural fingerprinting, linguists and mathematicians followed the equipment to the site. The effort necessitated intensive pursuit of the current promising research on Russian phonetics, such as that pursued in the US by the Moscow-born linguist Roman Jakobson. The project came straight from Stalin, who also wrote at length on Russian linguistics and phonetics.[8]

Bell's development of Murray Hill began in the 1930s and grew at a prodigious rate, soon outstripping its New York City facilities and satellite counterparts.[9] The New Jersey suburbs could furnish a campus with enough space to house all the lab work in one central site in a semirural setting. The campus was envisioned more as university campus than factory, with the essential difference of consolidating all activity in "a model of sleek and flexible utility" with an agenda to modernize both the lab's look and function.[10] Drawing on principles from spatial determinism, Building I opened in 1942 with an open-plan interior designed to have everyone get in one another's way and force discussion and a free flow of interaction between often-siloed areas of expertise. The virtues of the pastoral ambience and the architecturally open floor plan were highlighted in a 1944 *Life* magazine spread touting the "Modern Laboratory" with the tagline "A workroom for any experiment can be set up in 48 hours."[11] The apparent freedom and lack of managerial oversight extolled in the magazine article was belied by the realities:

> Everyday responsibilities of the government-sponsored scientific researcher were as likely to involve, in addition to research itself, managing contracts, projects, and staff, and committee and government agency work. The bureaucratic demands of the new order, increasingly set either on campus itself or in faux university environments like Murray Hill, produced a kind of R&D version of William H. Whyte's organization man.[12]
>
> —John Beck and Ryan Bishop, *Technocrats of the Imagination*

In this way, Bell Labs drew vague resonance with the work conditions at Mavrino. Termed the "House of Magic" by Jon Gertner, the labs at Murray Hill offered an abundance of opportunity, intellectual stimulation, and world-changing inventions but did so under the auspices of an invisible but firm corporate molding. Such a situation chafed many pure research scientists, several of whom eventually decamped to help facilitate the emergence of what would become Silicon Valley in California's Bay Area.

Murray Hill and Mavrino shared more than shared acoustic research, intensive expertise and leafy grounds. Each was a shadow of its respective national agendas and aspirations, as well as of each other. And each shared the same source of seemingly strategic advantage: the phoneme.

To Control Floating Phonemes in Secret Gardens

> He who rules the signals rules the nation.
>
> —Bernhard Siegert, "Mineral Sound and Missing Fundamental"

These two not-so-invisible research sites explored the invisible dynamic systems of sound spectra, especially that of speech. Not only did this research further the commercial fields of telecommunications and the burgeoning interest in "information" as a research object, but it was also directly channeled into covert applications for the state. Such applications included, but was by no means limited to, cryptography, the vocoder, voice prints (pursued as the aural analog to the tactile fingerprint), and other automated voice-recognition systems (ultimately leading to such current applications as Alexa). To say that Bell held a far more public profile than Mavrino, which essentially had none, is a massive understatement. As Gertner notes, Bell held a grip on electronic inventions second to none in the US and helped secure the US's lead in that role for most of the twentieth century. Bell research also resulted in collaborations with top-secret acoustic research labs in German, Italy, France, Brazil, and Argentina, while the Mavrino research remained within Soviet borders, including its intranationally colonized states.

These seemingly innocuous sites are steeped in the histories of spectral research, as indicated in the National Parks description of the Bell Labs complex in New Jersey. With both figuring in the history of quotidian infrastructural hardware, software, and theory, these labs perpetuated technologies of today such as telephony, voice compression, synthesis and generation, fiber optics, information theory, electronic music, and ambient aural environments. They also embraced the research fields of solid-state telecommunications, real-time teletechnologies, remote sensing, geoacoustic and hydroacoustic surveillance technologies, and (most relevant here) linguistics. Springing from "the idea factory" of the semiprivate labs of a commercial corporation, the discursive and material production was trumpeted widely during the "American Century."[13] And yet the related and simultaneous research undertaken in the former Soviet Union at the start of the Cold War remained largely unknown, except by intelligence agencies, until the publication of Solzhenitsyn's first novel.

The scientific results from each site differed vastly, but they shared at least one common goal, to gain control of dynamic phenomena found in aural and visual spectra for the benefit of geopolitical advantage. The general method to capture, store, and control temporal phenomena proved exceptionally powerful and productive from the second half of the twentieth century onward. Given the scope and speed of this research, long separated from its original development and rationale, we can turn to perhaps the smallest unit of telecommunications in each suburban complex: the modest phoneme. A phoneme is the smallest meaningful unit of sound in speech and language, and its import for the reconstitution of linguistics as a strategic research field during WWII and beyond helped turn it into a foundational social science during the historical Cold War without that status necessarily surviving the fall of the Berlin Wall.[14] Despite being numbingly prosaic, the US Cold War funding for this work is nonetheless fascinating for its eccentric institutional linkages that so shaped this specific historical moment and its multifaceted resonances in the present. The postwar funding went to and stemmed from Bell Labs/ATT, the US Department of Defense, the Rockefeller Foundation, the Macy Foundation, and major research universities, including MIT, Princeton, and Harvard, in pursuit of the shared promise held in phonetics and structural linguistics as well as all the other dual use applications, from telephony to cryptography.

The peripatetic structural linguist and literary theorist Roman Jakobson embodies various incarnations of these trajectories. His multiple areas of linguistic research and its manifest reach into areas aesthetic, cultural, scientific, national, and geopolitical. Jakobson provides a fulcrum between postrevolutionary linguistic developments and literary studies in the new Soviet Union, developments of literary formalism, poetics, and semiotics in Prague and later post-World War II structuralist linguistics and phonetics in the United States. He provided a common thread linking the Moscow Linguistic Circle, the Prague Linguistic Circle, and the Linguistics Circle of New York when the field was shifting from the capacious humanities and arts directions found in the work of Edward Sapir to the more instrumentalist and deterministic goals espoused by Leonard Bloomfield. Jakobson immersed himself in poetics and literary theory throughout these decades, and his travels drifted ever close to "scientific" and quantifiable formal traits of language in the 1940s without losing the grand gestures of "national identity" resident in some strands of early-twentieth-century literary study. The post-World War II world afforded a landscape in which such concerns as "the Soviet mind" and Soviet nation-building out of a Russian feudal past resonated in US policy and geopolitical plans. In the United States, Jakobson drifted along the shifting tides of government funding to support ideas gleaned from Ferdinand de Saussure as well as those found in Claude Lévi-Strauss's writings on structuralist analyses of language and/as culture but tinged with a specific Cold War justification.

The Moscow Linguistic Circle, on the other hand, emerged on the eve of the Russian Revolution and pursued similar revolutionary ideals and agendas found in the post-feudal moment of future-directed arts with an eye toward an anarchic remaking of Soviet Russia. Simirnov and Pchelkina called the decades between 1910 and the 1930s in Rusisa/Soviet Union a series of "cataclysms" wrought from sloughing off foreign values and "official culture" to build a uniquely Russian culture from scratch through the "development of various technologies in numerous areas of the arts and sciences." This was the crucible in which Jakobson forged many of his nascent ideas about the implicitly generative capacities of language, even in its most minimal elements, to create a culture, a nation, a mind, and a worldview (in this way drawing close to the Sapir's take on language). It also became part of the intellectual backdrop of the Mavrino prisoners. Mavrino emerges in Solzhenitsyn's novel (and actual internment) as the co-opted and corrupted inheritance of this idealistic cultural past. The synergistic coupling of arts and technology for the perfection of a classless society, as evolutionarily charted by thinkers such as Solomon Nikritin, who developed a universal typology of the human voice and anticipated cybernetics a decade before Norbert Wiener and Arturo Rosenblueth, transmogrified into a prison camp dedicated to control and surveillance of the population at large. Just as the acoustics labs of the 1950s in the US and Europe explored electronic music alongside cybernetics and information theory in the same labs that helped generate these theories, in the 1920s Lev Teremen (aka Leon Theremin) worked in electroacoustics and machine music sites and created the Theremin, only to end up serving an eight-year sentence in a *sharashka* in the 1940s alongside intellectuals such as Solzhenitsyn.[15] The specters of revolutionary ideals accompany the Mavrino prisoners' musings while engaged in the instrumentalist applications of linguistic spectra to serve the paranoid whims of Stalin's state apparatus.

In the US, science advisor to the presidents during World War II, Vannevar Bush, convinced President Truman to continue the "blue-sky research" at the heart of the government's collaborations with corporations and universities operative in the war effort in order to further the nation's postwar global advantage in science and technology.[16] The investment in the postwar interdisciplinary domain of Area Studies meant investment in phonetics could naturally follow.[17] Russian-American linguist and literary theorist Roman Jakobson's lead in phonetics research and his earlier work in historical phonology helped unlock entire language and linguistic systems. From the phoneme, then, one could discover the hidden origins of ethno-nationalist thought and cognitive patterns, rather like an updated version of *geist* in German Romanticism. The focus on phonemes developed when working with the Prague Linguistic Circle; he argued that phonemes, as the smallest unit of binaristic difference in a language system, connect well with structuralism and could be conveniently plugged into the emergent digital computational practices. Jakobson referred to phonemes as part of the search for "invariants" in language, with "invariant" understood as a math term designating constant units to which all languages were reducible.[18] Jakobson and Morris Halle influenced not only linguistics but also information theory by positing phonemes as "bits" of information and differentiation (following Shannon). The electronics labs in the US and Europe pursued phonemes as bits of information suitable for machinic analysis and replication. Information theorist Colin Cherry, in collaboration with Halle and Jakobson, developed a group of Russian phonemes into binary bits suitable for computer processes by following Shannon and Weaver's lead to find the *minima* of information-bearing material to convey for storage, manipulation, and communication. As the smallest unit to carry a signal in the noise that is language, with every other element deemed "redundant," phonemes constitute the difference in sound that makes a difference and determine the signal strength.

In the context of this research and its direct or indirect connections to C3I, it is worth remembering that Jakobson held an editorial role at the journal *Information and Control*. His Rockefeller Foundation–funded project on Russian phonemic distinctions and typological arrangement, "Language, Logic, and Symbolism," deployed the same logics operative in Weaver and Shannon's work on communication and information. In fact, it was thanks to Weaver's role as head of the Rockefeller Foundation's Division of Natural Sciences and Agriculture that Jakobson received the funding to pursue this project.[19] The acoustic structure of a language's phonemes, according to this thesis, not only provides the basic structuralist distinctions of a given language but also, as noted, determines the language's entire structure and clues to the noetic world of its speakers.[20]

The research at Murray Hill and Mavrino contributes to the control component of C3I political agendas. Thus it is of little surprise that the linguist whose epigraphs appear atop Cherry, Halle, and Jakobson's 1953 article "Toward the Logical Description of Languages in their Phonemic Aspect" is Leonard Bloomfield.[21] The final line of his hugely influential tome Language states: "It is only a prospect, but not hopelessly remote, that the study of language may help us toward the understanding and control of human events." Such prospects were certainly in the Cold War air and borne aloft by the analytic power of phonemes. One of the epigraphs Cherry et al. take from Bloomfield reads: "Distinctive features occur in lumps or bundles, each one of which we call a phoneme. The speaker has been trained to make sound-producing movements in such a way that the phoneme-features will be present in the soundwaves, and he has been trained to respond only to these features and to ignore the rest of the gross acoustic mass that reaches his ears.[22]" This passage suggests the digital, calculative logics at play in the direction that the human sciences were taking under the influence of Shannon and others. Phonemes, in such a model, become the digital unit that yields calculation and prediction in a probabilistic world, thus providing language opportunities as a tool for control, a long-standing goal in cybernetic correction.[23]

The storable and computational attributes of phonemes in human speech and language provided numerous and varied interactions between speech synthesis research underway in telephony at Bell Labs, MIT, and IBM, but not, of course, Mavrino. The study of phonetics at these research sites was occasionally directed to disability research but primarily pertained to military and commercial applications in the post-World War II era while also co-developing theoretical research, as previously noted, into structuralism. The prisoners at Mavrino with the mandate to build a cryptographic vocoder for Stalin used phonemes in the same way that Jakobson had with his Rockefeller-funded Russian language project. As a character in *The First Circle*, Stalin shows an interest in voice analysis-synthesis beyond cryptography, speech spectrograms, and surveillance (external and internal to the state). Solzhenitsyn devotes Chapter 19 of the novel to the Great Leader's thoughts on linguistics, many of which echo those of the Moscow Linguistics Circle in their updated Cold War form found in Jakobson's research (with Halle, Cherry and others). These similarities attributed to Stalin's thought, and indeed in his publications on the matter, relate linguistic elements to mathematics and, more importantly, reveal national character through sound, phonemes, and grammar, all of which are bereft of class burdens. The liberatory and revolutionary work undertaken by the Moscow Linguistics Circle had become in Stalin's hands the very stuff of intranational state surveillance and the terror campaigns realized in the gulags and *sharashkas*.

At Mavrino, they conducted research into speech analysis-synthesis and vocoder development in what the researchers termed "the Clipped Speech Laboratory." In addition to borrowing the term, they also borrowed the design by copying the machine from US technical manuals and magazines. This site was essentially a digital speech lab not unlike that in Bell Labs in their remit. Here, they engaged in "clipping, damping, amplitude compression, electronic differentiation and integration of human speech" by breaking it down "into small groups of electrical impulses" that were reconstructed to perfectly mimic speech and speaker alike.[24]

In his book on computer speech, compression, and synthesis, Manfred Schroeder references Solzhenitsyn's novel when stating that speech can be "infinitely clipped" or sliced into storable units (e.g., phonemes) while maintaining their intelligibility. Schroeder explains that both an undistorted speech signal and a clipped speech signal maintain regular temporality and dynamics. In spite of sounding very distorted, "clipped speech" nonetheless remains intelligible and spectrographically legible. The discernment of signal from noise at play with clipped speech research leads directly to Shannon's theoretical work on information. The title of one of his classic essays indicates the unavoidable condition under which communication occurs: "Communication in the Presence of Noise."[25] Admitting that all real channels unavoidably generate noise, the incapacity can be turned to advantages of all kinds, including cryptographic ones (as both the US and Soviet governments understood) "because," as Friedrich Kittler explains, "messages can be generated as selections or filterings of noise."

These insights reach back to the late 1920s at Bell Labs, when Homer Dudley was given the key problem for long-distance communication: how to use existing telegraph lines to carry a voice signal. This necessitated the compression of broadband speech signals, which can exceed 3,000 Hz, to operate on telegraph cables with far narrower bandwidth capacities. Dudley's solution was the vocoder, the foundational apparatus for sound analysis-synthesis, a version of which exists in every smart phone and computer with audio capacity. In terms of infrastructure, the long telecommunications quest to cram as much input down a wire as possible eventually gave digital technologies the advantage over their analogue counterparts. Optical pulses and optical fiber wires followed, seemingly sealing the deal for the near future.

Distant Sites and Sounds: A Conclusion

> Therein, as far as I by listening knew
> There was no lamentation save of sighs
> Whence throbbed the air eternal
> through and through.
>
> —Dante, Canto IV, *The Inferno*

> Nerzhin went into the booth thinking how shabby its sackcloth covering looked (thanks to the external shortage of proper materials) and locked the soundproof door.
>
> —Alexander Solzhenitsyn, *The First Circle*

Our telecoms present and near future emerged from these suburban landscapes of imagination and labor. In 2024 Bell Labs, now Nokia Bell Labs, announced it would be moving its research lab from the campus/country club grounds of Murray Hill to a new complex within a tech hub underway in New Brunswick, New Jersey. Home to 10 Nobel Prize winners and tens of thousands of patents, the site will no longer have a Bell Labs presence by 2028. Nokia's public relations tends to leverage its Bell Labs past in terms of heritage, lineage, genealogy, and avant-garde experimentation, and continues that pattern by conjuring the spirit of Claude Shannon and other (Bell and non-Bell) drivers of the American Century.[26] The prison that served as the model for Mavrino, and which indeed housed Solzhenitsyn for a time, Butyrka, announced in 2018 plans to close its operations. Once standing in a semirural suburb, the imposing structure now is swallowed by central Moscow and bears little resemblance to the bucolic seminary grounds described in the novel. Even if the grounds held material enchantment for the specialists and provided inspiration from well-turned or aged gardens, the pursuits at both sites sought ways to render the immaterial ephemerality of spectra into manipulatable forms for materialist ideological pursuits, espionage, communication, and information for control. In these gardens was hatched our collective contemporary aural existence, the history and provenance of which vanish into the ether like the spectra, or the lamentations of the barely visible souls heard by Dante and Virgil in the first circle.

-----

[1] National Parks website: Bell Labs complex, https://www.nps.gov/places/bell-laboratories-holmdel.htm.

[2] Alexander Solzhenitsyn, *The First Circle*, trans. Michael Guybon (Collins Fontana, 1968).

[3] I am indebted to ongoing conversations with many colleagues whose insights inform elements of this chapter, including John Beck, Bobby Pietrusko, Jussi Parikka, Sasha Anikina, Tania Roy, Sunil Manghani, Victor Burgin, Louise Siddon, and Peter Middleton. I owe a special thanks to my colleagues Vinicius Andrade Pereira and Erick Felinto at the State University of Rio de Janeiro; I was able to work through some of these of ideas with them and a stellar group of graduate students. Some of the issues pursued in this chapter appear in a different but related set of arguments in a forthcoming book coedited with John Beck, *Cold War Imaginaries: Technology, Temporality, Culture* (Edinburgh University Press, 2025).

[4] For an evocative and influential take on the role of media technologies and supernatural phenomena, see Jeffery Sconce, *Haunted Media: Electronic Presence from Telegraphy to Television* (Duke University Press, 2000).

[5] See Paul Virilio, *Speed and Politics: An Essay on Dromology*, trans. Mark Polizzotti (Semiotext(e), 1986).

[6] Solzhenitsyn, *The First Circle,* 32.

[7] Solzhenitsyn, *The First Circle,* 33.

[8] The fictional veneer here is thin as Stalin's 1950 articles and "letters to the author" exchanges in *Pravda* on these topics indicate. These articles were titled "Marxism and Problems of Linguistics" and "Marxism in Linguistics". Solzhenitsyn's characterization of "the Boss" moves metonymically from his paranoid and vindictive concern with language found in the applied focus of the prison lab to his historico-political musings found in these articles as well as the novel. The passages attributed to Stalin are really just slightly modified versions of material found in these pieces. Stalin as linguistics expert, and indeed final word on any and all topics related to it, emerges regularly in the novel, including a section in which his Pravda pronouncements blunts other theoretical explorations of language origins aligned with Engles' writings on labor and the hand and the theories generated by Nikolai Marr. The "Greatest Linguist of all Time", Solzhenitsyn writes, "had raised the blade of the ideological guillotine over Marr's head" (362).

[9] Jon Gertner, *The Idea Factory and the Great Age of American Innovation* (Penguin, 2012), 75-77.

[10] Gertner, 77.

[11] John Beck and Ryan Bishop, *Technocrats of the Imagination: Art, Technology and the Military-Industrial Avant-garde* (Duke University Press, 2020), 79-80.

[12] Beck and Bishop, *Technocrats of the Imagination*, 79.

[13] This is the title of Gerner's book.

[14] See John R. Pierce, *An Introduction to Information Theory: Symbols, Signals and Noise*, 2nd rev. ed. (Dover Press, 1980). Jennifer Iverson, *Electronic Inspirations: Technologies of the Cold War Musical Avant-garde* (Oxford University Press, 2019); Bernard Dionysius Geoghegan, *Code: From Information Theory to French Theory* (Duke University Press, 2023); Mara Mills, "Media and Prosthesis: The Vocoder, the Artificial Larynx, and the History of Signal Processing," *Qui Parle* 21, no. 1 (2012): 107–149.

[15] Andrey Simirnov and Liubov Pchelkina, *Russian Pioneers of Sound Art* i(La Casa Encendida, 2011), 3. Catalog of the exhibition "Red Calvary: Creation and Power in Soviet Russia Between 1917 and 1945."

[16] Bush's book *Science—The Endless Frontier* made this case to the executive branch before it became part of the public domain a little later, in 1945. This proved to be the road map for what Eisenhower some years later decried as the military-industrial complex, conveniently ignoring the role of universities in this mutually profitable triangle of R and D. Thus emerged the Global R and D university that is the current model embraced and mimicked throughout the world. The supposedly benign role of the university sector in military R and D and covert action led to much abuse in the Cold War (see Noam Chomsky et al., *The Cold War & the University* (New Press, 1997), the Korean War, and of course the Vietnam War (see John Beck and Ryan Bishop, *Technocrats of the Imagination* (Duke University Press, 2020).

[17] See Gayatri Spivak's excellent *Death of a Discipline* for an analysis of the emergence of Area Studies and its influence on humanities and social sciences research, including languages.

[18] Roman Jakobson and Morris Halle, *Fundamentals of Language* (Mouton, 1956), 19.

[19] The Rockefeller Annual Report 1950, available through the Foundation, describes Jakobson's work as collaborating with scholars in "acoustics, psychology, logic and criticism" as well as linguistics. Even though the focus was Russian phonetics, the report indicates its remit will include "morphology, syntax, lexicology and pragmatics" as phonemes scale up to inform larger language elements, attributes, and functions. Warren Weaver ran this part of the Rockefeller funding program, which also funded in the same round Norbert Wiener (on biofeedback and cybernetics), Linus Pauling (alpha helix), and Dorothy Hodgkin (X-ray crystallography). To recap, some of the funding sources for Jakobson and others working in phonetics at the time includes ATT/Bell Labs, US Department of Defense, the Macy Foundation, major research universities (such as Harvard, MIT, and Princeton), as well as the Rockefeller Foundation. This coalition embodies Vannevar Bush's vision for the post-WWII R and D in order to keep the US in its newly acquired global power status.

[20] All of this chimes with the discussions among incarcerated researchers in Solzhenitsyn's novel's, drawing on Jakobson's theoretical developments with both the Moscow Linguistic Circle and the Prague Linguistic Circle.

[21] Leonard Bloomfield, *Language* (George Allen and Unwin, 1923/1957); Colin Cherry, Morris Halle, and Roman Jakobson, "Toward the Logical Description of Languages in their Phonemic Aspect," *Linguistic Society of America 29*, no.1 1953): 34–46.

[22] Cherry, Halle, and Jakobson, *The Fundamentals of Language*, 34.

[23] The goal of control plays a central role in the general US Cold War policy knows as C3I, including communication and information. The establishment of the journal *Information and Control* in 1957, with

Jakobson on the editorial board and an article by Shannon on coding for noisy channels in the inaugural issue, helped further this nexus of language, communication, information and control, with all roads leading back to the usual funding and research bodies.

[24] Solzhenitsyn, *The First Circle*, 69.

[25] Claude Shannon, "Certain Results in Coding Theory for Noisy Channels," *Information and Control* 1(1957): 6–25.

[26] Beck and Bishop, *Technocrats of the Imagination*, 175-177.

Techno, Techné

Raves, Abstractions, and Militant Subjecthood[1]

Philip Glahn

Logics of Abstraction

The history of modernity is also always a history of territory and of the technologies that render spaces as territories. These technologies include the tools that work and shape the land, its plows and canals, fences and settlements, as well as devices of transportation and transmission that make geographical thinking and logic of land possible to begin with, as it positions the modern subject as increasingly autonomous and mobile, shrinking distances and increasing a material and psychological-ideological mastery over the world. Further contributing to these what Shannon Mattern has called "indexical landscapes," are aesthetic technologies that not only make visible what is to be seen in different places at various moments but also create imaginaries that shape a given territory according to the perspectives brought to it, thus rendering them both "'intelligent' and intelligible."[2] Land surveys and photographs, topographical plans and property lines, satellite imaging and traffic patterns, landscape and plein-air painting and public sculptures all map, demarcate, and chart, thus allowing us to make sensible and knowable our environments. Though the techniques of this aestheticization have traditionally operated under and relied on an ostensibly scientific and artistic disinterestedness, territorial assessments are not only partial but actively formative. Mapping and indexing both *extract* and *abstract* and in that sense hold power and exercise control.

As Mabel O. Wilson has argued, the interconnected development of artistic and technological innovation, as forcefully presented in nineteenth-century world's fairs, expositions, and exhibitions, "put the metropolitan and cosmopolitan world on view"—a world and a view reliant on the construction of subjecthood situated via the selective reification and ordering, quantification *and* qualification of (other) people, things, and sites.[3]

Colonial and neocolonial territorialization has created a horizontal image of a world that is in fact administered vertically. A spatial imaginary of nation-states, horizons, and frontiers is overlaid and governed by various material and immaterial infrastructures and networks, be they informational, financial, or ideological.[4] Power is exerted not only by managing the flows through these networks but by determining the quality of the relationalities between the different layers: how particular ecological resources are valued and represented, economically as well as culturally, for example, and how that in turn affects which resources are harvested and exploited or replenished and protected. *What* is made visible or sensible and *how* greatly determines its place and level of agency and mobility within the infrastructure that is our contemporary *technocene*. People are just as much subject to these mediations and dependencies as any other element. Embodiment within the planetary spatial order is determined by how one is made to appear. Sovereignty means having the ability to determine the construction of a self through the degree and quality of its enmeshment. The state exercises its sovereignty by abstracting its subjects as citizens, while the military abstracts people as combatants, the market as consumers. None of these abstractions are necessarily exclusive, but they are strategic in their selective designation and *de*-figuration of otherwise complex bodies and their ways-of-being.

The question is, What kind of alternate forms of individual and social subjecthood are possible within this structure? What kind of sovereignty can embodied subjects exercise? What mediations of self provide a degree of relative agency? What is a model of resistance that does not revert to a more "authentic" and romantic version of subjecthood rooted either in a fantasy of a space outside any entanglements of control or in the affirmative catharsis of a corporeal immediacy—or in a more "complete" and "genuine" visibility of self or self-sense-ability asserted not as part but in spite of the subject's constant mediation and selective presence? Rather, what is a resistance based in the potential for what Sebastian Egenhofer has called abstraction as "*re*-figuration," as the construction of new relationalities between the various layers and platforms that are and make people, things, and spaces?[5]

The Stack and Minerva

The spatial order and logic of the *technocene* might be best grasped by what Benjamin Bratton has theorized as "the Stack." The Stack is an attempt to come to terms with the fact that "the new normal twists distant sites into one another":

> Discontiguous megastructures cohere from molecular, urban, and atmospheric scales into de facto jurisdictions. Ecological flows become a public body of intensive sensing, quantification, and governance. Cloud platforms take on the traditional role of states, as states evolve into cloud platforms. Cities link into vast and tangling urban networks as they multiply borders into enclaves inside of enclaves, nesting gated communities inside of gated communities. Interfaces present vibrant augmentations of reality, now sorted as address, interface, and user.[6]

The Stack consists of several interwoven and interdependent platforms; it is material and immaterial, both hardware and software, an "accidental megastructure," a new logic of "vertically thickened political geography." It is, as Bratton explains, "a machine that serves as a schema, as much as it is a schema of machines."[7]

As a totalizing theory, the Stack is strategic. It "make[s] the composition of new governmentalities and new sovereignties both more legible and more effective," offering insights into the constantly changing and thus arguably change-able constructedness of a shared contemporeality.[8] Within this structure, embodiment is the degree of enmeshment, of being embedded in the geography. There is a relative distinction between the virtual and the material, the digital and the analog, but there is no separation, no outside. The continuity between the Stack's interrelated platforms offers new ways of being as forms of identity and action can be forged in the manipulation of images and imaginaries as long as one is aware of the machine's techno-logic and its tendency to obscure the apparatus's inner workings. As Legacy Russell has observed, "*AFK* [away from keyboard] and *IRL* [in real life] are Westernized myths, dualities that support the notion that what happens online does not have the capacity to impact and affect real change. Arab Spring, Occupy Wall Street, and the recent London riots are all prominent illustrations of the continuous loop between that which takes place on and off screen."[9] What is hailed here as the potential to organize and mobilize new social actors as part of a vertically integrated body politic finds its technocratic correlate in the oppressive and exploitative mediations of advanced consumer and surveillance technologies.

Cognition and knowledge, and thus embodiment and mobility within and through the Stack, are subject to what Matteo Pasquinelli has called capitalism's "mega-machine of governance," relying as much on the logics of traditional nation-state power as on the new high-tech economies of Amazon, Apple, etc.[10] What all of these mechanisms have in common is that they collect and produce data in order to generate and "predict" ideas and desires, habits and behavior. The distinction between governance and economy remains vague at best, and at worst collapses in the assertion of sovereignty over the Stack's platforms, modeling very specific pathways and movements of subjects and their formations within material and immaterial territories. The evolution of the military-industrial complex into intelligence industries continuously doubles the subject as consumer and combatant, weaponizing the technical apparatus to extract and abstract a limited set of data to in turn provide restrictive possibilities of movement, differing only within their variations, leaving little room for technological emancipation and change. The Department of Defense's Minerva Project employs a system of "algorithmic governance" most commonly associated with search engines, social media, and generative consumption. Launched in 2008, it is designed "to model the dynamics, risks and tipping points for large-scale civil unrest across the world."[11] In collaboration with university research programs and under supervision of US intelligence services, the project aims to develop software that both observes and predicts social mobilization and "contagions." The project scans digital traces like Twitter and other new media communications during occasions like the Arab Spring, the 2011 Russian Duma elections, or the 2013 Gezi Park protests in Istanbul. Posts and conversations are examined "to identify individuals mobilized in a social contagion and when they become mobilized."[12]

Nora Khan has discussed a similar iteration of machine-driven sensing-and-ordering with regard to Project Green Light Detroit.[13] The project is an initiative of the Detroit Police Department, designed to prevent crime and make business owners *feel* safer. Cameras watch over specific areas in particular neighborhoods, generating feeds to a real-time crime center where the footage is monitored by a specially trained and computationally assisted officer at the moment a crime happens *or is about to happen*. The Motorola Solutions–developed software used here and in several other Green Light projects throughout the country ostensibly makes policing and response more efficient, more connected, more integrated. Furthermore, it employs "AI-based analytics," which "transform[s] video surveillance from reactive monitoring to *automated proactive alerts when a person, object or vehicle of interest is detected.* Intelligence analysts using Commandcentral Aware will be automatically alerted when *unusual activities* are detected."[14] What is the logic, Khan asks, that governs the sequence of "seeing-naming-knowing" in these instances? "What does 'aberrant' or 'threatening' look like, on this block in Detroit, and how is it named, and how is it understood?"[15] What qualifies as "unusual" and "of interest" in a society where the normal, the normative, the default is inscribed by race, gender, and class, yet "seen" and sensed by a disembodied eye and "read" by a machine that flattens difference into deviation rather than complexity, heterogeneity, and transformation?

The space of the street and bodies moving in it is mapped onto and into the Stack just as the Stack is mapped onto the body, creating visibilities and invisibilities according to selective criteria on what the sensors are made sensible to pick up on. The old techno-adage "data > information > knowledge > wisdom" exercises and reveals the always-ever partiality of mediation, the instrumentalization of technology's "god eye," the ostensibly disembodied and disinterested view from above. The complexity and specificity of human experience falls outside of the equation, raising an increasingly urgent question, What is the quality of the relationality between experience, knowledge, information, and data as the apparatus's view is not only partial but an *abstracting as de-figuration*, an embodiment of selfhood in the Stack that produces particular subjects and subjectivities? Detroit, like many other cities in the US and the world, has been the historical site of such abstraction, a global territory of the extraction of labor and the reductive embeddedness of working bodies—especially the poor and Black ones—within the interlinked platforms of the global megastructure as pure labor power and property value and as potentially deviant bodies to be policed. As Nadim Samman has argued, technology materializes as the double of abstraction: "Against the promise of unlimited extension and remote control, the inability to extract oneself [*one self?*] from certain platforms, surveillance systems, and other infrastructures becomes a waking nightmare."[16] Within this "vertically thickened political geography," this "sensory order" of control, this "spaceship infrastructure" of weaponization that organizes and optimizes being(s) and experience, how are we to image and imagine, to model and enact modes and spaces of resistance?[17]

Ranting and Raving

While today techno is a global phenomenon, the music's place of origin is Detroit. As DeForrest Brown Jr. and others have chronicled, techno emerged in the early 1980s as a Black form of sonic labor working its way through the ruins of the failed social and economic promises of technological progress: "Formulated out of an intuitive response to the urban degradation plaguing Detroit and other cities around the United States in the late twentieth century, techno is evidence of post–Civil Rights Movement Black youth adapting to the industrialized Northern States, using the technology available."[18] Techno is an act of refusal to partake in the myths and materializations—whether generically utopian or dystopian—of a linear futurity, one that reduces bodies and spaces to objects and sites of reification and exploitation. The music is an appropriation of the machines and sensories of technological modernism, a reorientation of movement geared toward a diffusion of the categorical boundaries that define the spatial imaginary of the Stack: "Techno attests to a collective engineering of stereophonic intelligence."[19]

Techno is the music of the rave. Technically, techno is "repetitive, four-to-the-floor beats, from about 120 to 140 per minute. Few vocals, if any. Few sounds that bear any relation to a recognizable musical instrument."[20] Historically, techno is complex, contradictory, and tied to "the African American musical continuum," Black and queer in its exuberant futurist evasion of preconceived designations of who and how to be.[21] "The party is the riot, and vice versa."[22] The rave is a collective manifestation of techno, and although it has grown to take all kinds of shape—from regularly scheduled events in commercial metropolitan megaclubs to word-of-mouth one-off underground happenings—as a refusal and abstracting refiguration, the rave relies on a dynamic of ephemerality and assertion, of transparency and obfuscation. To some, the rave is a site and performance of loss, or rather, of getting lost: going off the map and out of sight and losing sight of everyday paths and demands and confirmations of conformity. Raves are durational (rather than directional) and pleasure-oriented, occupying spaces that have yet to be remonetized by landlords and developers. The dancing provides a surplus energy that is harnessed by nobody other than the ravers themselves. To Hannah Baer, the rave space is potentially the site for a "liberatory protagonism," "centering everybody at the party . . . humanizing people across structural divides like race and class but also age."[23] To McKenzie Wark, the rave is constructivist and situationist, an "art of copresence."[24] The rave offers an alternate dynamic of dis/embodiment, one that is dissociating and alienating but in a way that is different from more technocratic mediations of selves: it offers a "ressociation," a new mix with those around oneself, the music, technology, the time, the space—"sequenced together": "What can still be shared between humans and machines, between humans and humans?"[25]

Where does the rave point within the Stack, as part of a dynamic of time and organized experiential direction? Maybe the rave need not be, cannot be, emancipatory labor in a traditionally productive sense as long as productivity and progress remain forces of violence—forces that aggressively embed the subject in the vertical order in a way that extracts and exploits, surveils and surveys to make the march of history plow its way ahead in a preordained fashion, the subject a mere mechanism serving the capital machine. Wark describes the rave as "a collaborative practice that makes it possible to endure this life."[26] Where history seems to hold nothing but an assertive continuum of territorial and extractive violence, the rave offers a "machinic, sonic time that can be endured. An endurational time . . . for a period in which durational time is no longer available to us. A trans time, with no future, which makes it a present of the present."[27] In this iteration, the aforementioned ressociation begets an assertive immediacy in the face of fettered mediations. To Brown Jr., techno and the rave are a defiant amplification of the Stack's ostensibly omnipotent power to appropriate all liberatory impulses. Techno has its roots in the 1960s riots and the assembly lines of American capitalism; it is not escapist but confrontational, an uprising and a monstrosity:

> All I ever wanted to do was give you all a map to go and tear this shit down. . . . It's about opening up a black hole in front of people and just showing them what's in there, because that's all I got is just a big black hole, an expressionless, genderless, faceless black hole of pain, joy. . . . To just profess this dark truth of what America is and we'll never ever, ever be able to transcend.[28]

On the other hand, what if the rave is more than the event, but is a technological *model* that *defies* presence and immediacy in favor of a different kind of abstraction? What if, as part of the spaceship infrastructure or *as* a spaceship infrastructure, the rave constructs a vertical orientation that defies the sovereignty of entities such as "America"? To insist on the Blackness and queerness of the rave is *not* to point to a place of origin where origin is an abstraction defined through a techno-logic of extraction and essentialization. Rather than being a thing, an objectification, it is a process of continuous refiguration. In the recent work of artist William Toney, the rave is a new Stacking, the modeling of an enmeshment-to-come. (Fig. 1) Using a constellation of images and projections, sounds and objects, the artist creates less an experience than a plan of occupying a space temporarily, of making territory, supplying tools

Fig. 1 William Toney, *Untitled* (2024); courtesy of the artist.

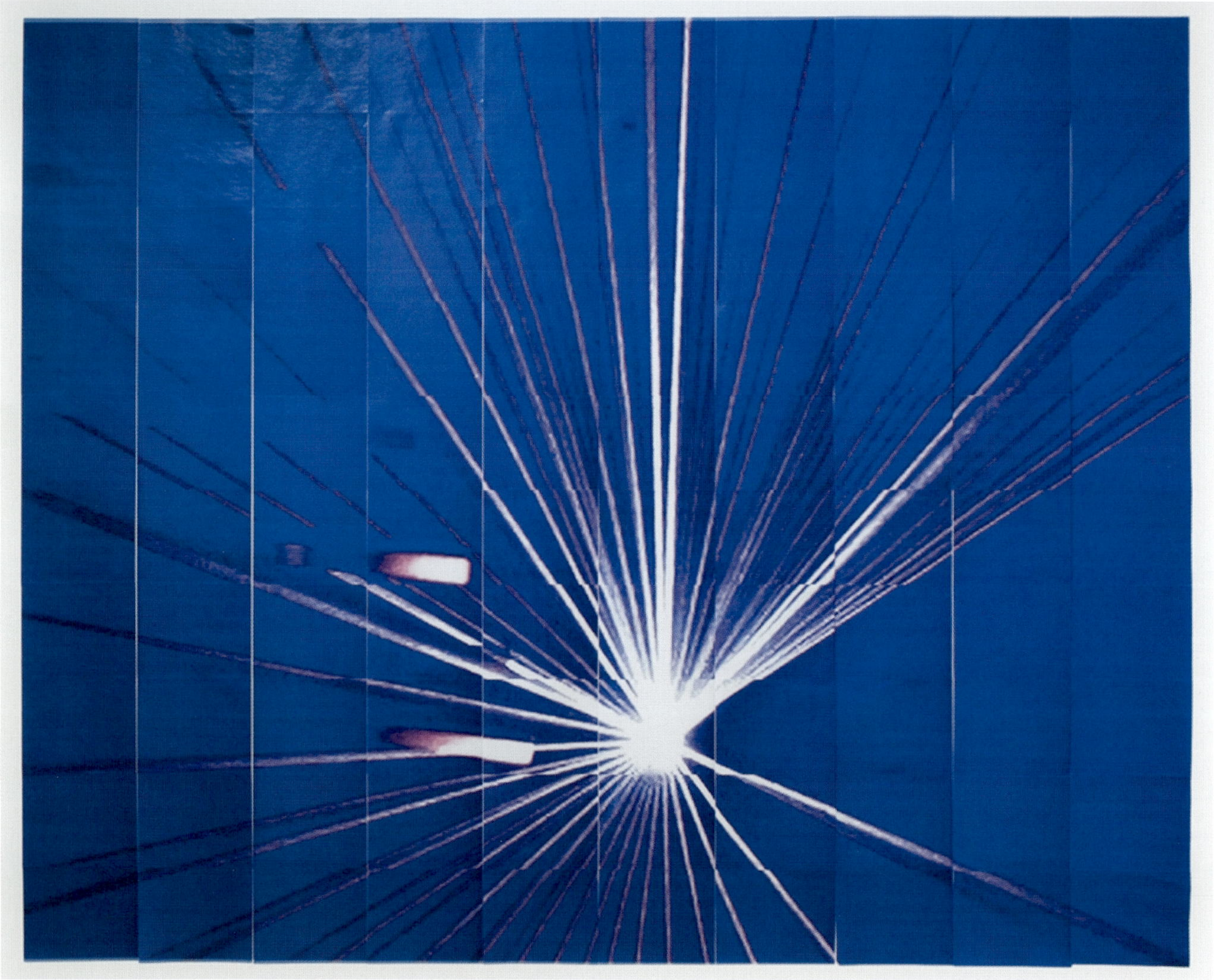

Fig. 2 William Toney, *Untitled* (2024). Photograph by Neighboring States; courtesy of the artist.

Fig. 3 William Toney, *Untitled* (2024); courtesy of the artist.

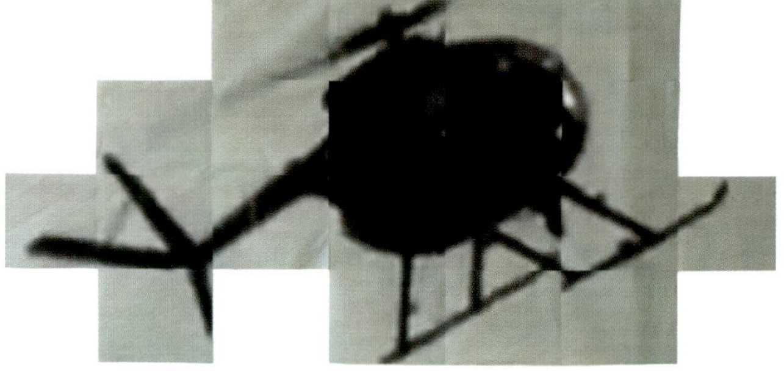

Fig. 4 William Toney, *Helicopter.1* (2024); courtesy of the artist.

Fig.5 William Toney, *Untitled* (2024); courtesy of the artist.

of both analysis and production, of navigation and transformation. Pictures of unpopulated club spaces contain vibrant colors and the flash of a strobe light; a wall-size version is assembled from multiple smaller plates arranged in a grid evoking a sensory map to something "just-beginning-to-stir."[29] (Fig. 2) All of the pieces evoke mobility, are portable, to be broken down and moved at a moment's notice only to pop up somewhere else, at some other time. Images and material support are interdependent protagonists—in some instances, the base of the display doubles as the work's crate. (Fig. 3) The pixelated image, assembled of a helicopter (Fig. 4) is a reminder of the policing of bodies and identities, placing the rave territory within a structure of power and violence; against this iconoclastic abstraction and technocratic optimization the artist offers a dynamic of anticipation: "Blackness, queerness, and marginalized people's technological mediations modify conventions. Repetition, sampling, looping, and countless approaches to undoing and reworking are methods of abstraction. These types of space, time, and sonic collage give participants a chance to 'be' in a way that is fugitive."[30] The rave is not escapist but a process of modification, the fugitivity of Blackness and queerness a refiguration of embodiment that refuses to be reduced to existing images and materializations essential to the power structure of the current vertical order. It is a Blackness that, according to Stefano Harney and Fred Moten, "cuts the regulative, governant force of (the) understanding."[31] Toney rejects the containment of any bodies within imaginary and manifest confines of defiguring abstraction, of efficiency and integration, but proposes the rave as a laboratory and technology of experimentation and innovation. The looping projection of two dancing figures moves to and against the sequenced soundtrack of a helicopter, the ocean, and a "bass test." The bodies evade easy description and recognition, testing the viewer's compliance with and complicity in deducing knowledge from the sensory data provided and the governing logic mapping it. On the third loop, the figures pixelated image beyond the boundaries of corporeality, never quite dissolving in space but enact and propose a new concept of personhood. (Fig. 5) It is in this sense that "nightlife as form" constitutes, according to Madison Moore, a "space of performance, where we go to experiment with identity. . . One of the most crucial sites for the production of selves . . . it is an always already ideal site for acts of transgression, possibility, and innovation."[32] Here, the rave is *not* the assertion of selfhood through cohesive, experiential presentness—whether individual or collective—in light of the self's iconoclastic abstraction in the Stack. It is not a "safe" territory or a world off the map. The body of the "meatspace" is no more real than the ostensibly disembodied, liberated online persona: they are a different Stacking of being, different embodiments of an always-already mediated self. To engage in the rave as modeled by Toney is to inhabit what Bratton calls "a long-duration project of abstraction: of distance, alienation, depersonalization, scaffolding, quantification as qualitative judgment, and mediation in all its guises. These are not what distracts each of us from the intensity of being alive but what focuses our patient attention on its strangeness."[33] This engagement is one example of what Ernst Bloch describes as "materially comprehended hope," of knowing and being willing to experience the world in its constructedness and the "militant optimism" of acting within and upon this constructedness in order to transform it.[34]

As process and project of duration, the rave as model is the future as undecided material, "which can however be decided through work and concretely mediated action," not as the realization of abstract ideals, "but rather the repressed elements of the new."[35] The rave makes visible a re-figured self—one that through and as technology within the sensory infrastructure refuses to be abstracted into an easily measured, positioned, and surveilled product of calculated reduction. It is a self reconstructed through an ongoing process of possible mediations and tangible enmeshments. The raving body (both individual and collective) is more than mirrored in its layered complexity of relationalities, but a fugitive presence within the Stack. The sovereignty of the militant subject is made of its insolent and itinerant connections and disconnections, its partial and shifting relationality within a topographic-senso-graphic space. This results not in a denial of or escape from the technocene, but in a temporal (and temporary) re-ordering of its spatial logic. The images and sounds, structures and projections, movements and bodies have pasts and presents without being limited by or to them: "I'll never disown who I am, who we are, but I don't want to be confined by it."[36] The militant subject is asserted in its connections and disconnections, the ones that are given and the ones that are possible. They have a direction toward the future that is not linear or progressive, a temporality that charts what in its intertwined and moving complexity is latent, is deviant and dissident, what neither fits nor is fixed. As a model, the rave is a configuration of embodied territorial possibilities, of a subjecthood unclosed.

-----

[1] The thinking around this topic has evolved out of my ongoing collaboration with Cary Levine and in conversations with William Toney, Daniel Cappello, and Gianna Santucci.

[2] Shannon Mattern, "Scents of Spatial Order: Sensing Technical Lands," in *Technical Lands: A Critical Primer,* ed. Jeffrey S. Nesbit and Charles Waldheim (Jovis, 2022), 39.

[3] Mabel O. Wilson, "The Cartography of W.E.B. Du Bois's Color Line," in *W.E.B. Du Bois's Data Portraits: Visualizing America*, ed. Whitney Battle-Baptiste and Britt Rusert (Princeton Architectural Press, 2018), 39.

[4] See, for example, Saskia Sassen, "Reading the City in a Global Digital Age," in *Urban Screens Reader*, ed. Scott McQuire et al. (Amsterdam: Institute of Network Cultures, 2009), 29–44; Arjun Appadurai, *Modernity at Large: Cultural Dimensions of Globalizations* (University of Minnesota Press, 1996); Benjamin Bratton, *The Stack: On Software and Sovereignty* (MIT Press, 2015).

[5] Sebastian Egenhofer, "Figures of Defiguration: Four Theses on Abstraction," *Texte zur Kunst* 69 (March 2008): 139–145.

[6] Benjamin Bratton, "The New Normal," *Strelka Mag* (2017), https://strelkamag.com/en/article/the-new-normal-essay-bratton.

[7] Bratton, "The Black Stack," *e-flux Journal* 53 (March 2014), https://www.e-flux.com/journal/53/59883/the-black-stack/.

[8] Bratton, "The Black Stack."

[9] Legacy Russell, "Elsewhere, After the Flood: Glitch Feminism and the Genesis of Glitch Body Politic," *Rhizome* (3/12/2013), https://rhizome.org/editorial/2013/mar/12/glitch-body-politic/.

[10] "The mega-machine of cognitive capitalism is easily described by the assemblage and stratification of the global infrastructure of computing, such as, for instance, search engines and social media (Google, Facebook), logistics networks and the 'internet of things' (Amazon, Walmart), intelligence agencies assets (see NSA's Utah datacenter and PRISM program) and climate research institutions too." Matteo Pasquinelli, "The Eye of the Algorithm: Cognitive Anthropocene and the Making of the World Brain," *Fall Semester* (2014), https://www.librarystack.org/eye-of-the-algorithm-cognitive-anthropocene-and-the-making-of-the-world-brain-the/.

[11] Nafeez Ahmed, "Pentagon Preparing for Civil Mass Breakdown," *The Guardian*, June 12, 2014, https://www.theguardian.com/environment/earth-insight/2014/jun/12/pentagon-mass-civil-breakdown.

[12] Ibid.

[13] Nora N. Kahn, *Seeing, Naming, Knowing* (The Brooklyn Rail / Crossed Purposes Foundation / Visual Arts Foundation / School of Visual Arts, 2019); https://www.librarystack.org/seeing-naming-knowing/.

[14] "Motorola Unifies Command Centre Software with Avigilon ACC," *Security World Market.com* (09/08/2018), https://www.securityworldmarket.com/na/Newsarchive/motorola-unifies-command-centre-software-with-avigilon-acc1. Emphasis added. For a more detailed discussion regarding "smart cities" and the uneven "optimization" of urban life through selective sensory technologies see Shannon Mattern, "A City Is Not a Computer," *Places Journal* (February 2017), https://placesjournal.org/article/a-city-is-not-a-computer/ and *Deep Mapping the Media City* (University of Minnesota Press, 2015).

[15] Kahn, *Seeing, Naming, Knowing*, 4–5.

[16] Nadim Samman, *Poetics of Encryption: Art and the Technocene* (Berlin: Hatje Cantz, 2023), 14–15. Emphasis added.

[17] Ibid., 31.

[18] DeForrest Brown Jr., *Assembling a Black Counter Culture* (Primary Information, 2022), 5. See also Dan Sicko, *Techno Rebels: The Renegades of Electronic Funk* (Wayne State University Press, 2010); madison moore and McKenzie Wark, eds., *Black Rave, e-flux Journal* 132 (December 2022).

[19] Brown Jr., *Assembling a Black Counter Culture*, 6.

[20] McKenzie Wark, *Raving* (Duke University Press, 2023), 5.

[21] Brown Jr., *Assembling a Black Counter Culture*, 6. For an in-depth discussion concerning the constellations of Blackness, queerness, techno, and rave, see the contributions to moore and Wark, *Black Rave*.

[22] David Riley, DeForrest Brown Jr., madison moore, and Alexander Ghedi Weheliye, "Black Vibrations: Techno as Queer Insurrectionist Sonics," *Journal of Visual Culture* 22, no. 1 (2023): 26.

[23] Hannah Baer, "Dance Until the World Ends," *Artforum* (December 2021): 175.

[24] Wark, *Raving*, 9.

[25] Ibid., 21, 31.

[26] Ibid., 66.

[27] Ibid.

[28] Riley et al., "Black Vibrations," 40, 38.

[29] Brian Massumi, quoted in madison moore, "Nightlife as Form," *Theater* 46, no. 1 (2016): 49.
[30] William Toney, flyer, 2024.
[31] Stefano Harney and Fred Moten, *The Undercommons: Fugitive Planning & Black Study* (Minor Compositions, 2013), 50.
[32] moore, "Nightlife as Form," 51, 55.
[33] Benjamin Bratton, "Not Right Now," *Tank* 10, no. 19 (Spring 2024): 126.
[34] Ernst Bloch, *The Principle of Hope* (MIT Press, 1986), 200.
[35] Ibid., 199.
[36] Wark, *Raving*, 17.

Part 2

Politics and Geographies

Silent Siege

In the Shadow Landscapes of Sanctions

Ghazal Jafari

The borderline in the mountainous Kurdistan region has no physical existence beyond scattered checkpoints. Known as "point zero," it's an imagined red line delineated on maps in 1911. Today, in this rugged and impenetrable terrain, the trace of old passages, nomadic migration routes, and depressions carved by ancient streams connect the tightly packed Kurdish villages on both sides of the border in the two neighboring nation-states of Iran and Iraq. The Kurdistan region encompasses one-third of the 906-mile western border of Iran and houses the headwaters of a vast riverine region that stretches between the high altitudes of the Zagros Mountain Range in the north and the Persian Gulf in the south. The riverine region has undergone major geospatial transformations under the influence of U.S. international development programs from 1954 until the 1979 Iranian Revolution.

These programs, driven by U.S. foreign policy that emphasized technical assistance and cooperation, aimed to extend and reinforce American geopolitical influence and economic presence during peacetime, particularly across the "Third World," where movements for national emancipation were hostile towards Western imperialism. Iran, at the time, was regarded as a client state of the United States and its largest military ally in the region. As part of its military aid, the United States assisted in launching a national nuclear energy program in 1957 for the Pahlavi Dynasty (1925–1979) under President Eisenhower's "Atoms for Peace" initiative, among other projects.

Along the borderline, thousands of Kurdish koolbars ("couriers" or smugglers) make a round trip of 27.5 miles on foot from Iran to Iraq and back every day. According to locals, smuggling across the border is nothing new.

If anything, these trade routes are much older than the borderline, which has made the flow of goods and people a matter of state permission. But the traffic and scale of cargo have swelled exponentially as a direct result of the U.S. embargo and unilateral sanctions, particularly after the Trump administration imposed a "Maximum Pressure" policy and placed new sanctions on Iran in 2018. The human chain along informal border crossings marks a fragment in the shadow landscapes of black market networks necessary for circumventing economic sanctions. More than vectors of flow, these networks imply sociospatial transformation and emergence of new uneven geographies with lasting impact.

Economic sanctions are often represented as peaceful and diplomatic alternatives to war, an international apparatus for promoting world peace or confronting terrorism, armed violence, and political oppression within targeted nation-state boundaries. Sanctions often go unnoticed since their destruction cannot be captured in photographs or live broadcasts. "While their consequences for human life and suffering may be equally ruinous, the quotidian rhythm of sanctions' necropolitical impacts lacks the drama of war and seldom provokes mass demonstrations."[1] While the banality and the unquestioned benevolent intent of sanctions permeate contemporary geopolitical debates, they have become one of the most popular policies of the so-called peacetime, precisely due to the invisibility of their consequences. This invisibility is constructed on the one hand by the neutralized language used to describe sanctions in the sphere of law and diplomacy, and on the other hand, by the elusiveness of their environmental and humanitarian effects. Confronting sanctions' constructed invisibility by mapping their shadow landscapes—the geographic, biopolitical, and necropolitical imprints—begins to reveal an otherwise overlooked system of oppression and systemic dispossession of marginalized populations around the world amid contemporary financial capitalism and its extractive geographies.

Covert Interventionism

The normalization of contemporary economic sanctions as "humanitarian, peaceful policy," according to human rights and international law professor, Vasuki Nesiah, is framed by constructed dichotomies between "the domain of war and the domain of peace, between military relations and economic relations," understood as opposing transactional spheres, exchanging goods and weapons, promise of life and threat of death.[2]

Modern sanctions were formally defined in the Article of Peace by the League of Nations at the end of World War I. They were designed, according to the US president of the time, Woodrow Wilson, as an "economic weapon" holding excitement of being "something more tremendous than war." According to Wilson, sanction "brings a nation to its senses just as suffocation removes from the individual all inclinations to fight… It is a terrible remedy. It does not cost a life outside of the nation boycotted, but it brings a pressure upon that nation which, in my judgment, no modern nation could resist."[3] The modern definition of sanctions represented a pivotal point in geopolitics ever since. As one of the most important outcomes of world war policies, sanctions emerged as a so-called peacetime weapon, recognized as measures so extreme that the initial aim of their design was not to implement them: "To interwar internationalists, economic sanctions were a form of deterrence, prefiguring nuclear strategy during the Cold War."[4]

Despite the initial intention, not only sanctions have been used pervasively ever since, but with no need for a declaration of war, they conveniently fell into "a normalized domain of foreign relations."[5] Because they are promoted as a "tactic of peaceful relations" often under the auspices of humanitarian purposes, they are not subject to International Humanitarian Law (IHL) that should be met in times of war.[6] The unquestioned legitimacy of sanctions makes them a "form of untargeted collective punishment and notoriously disproportionate even within its own terms."[7]

Despite their stated purpose, sanctions have long been used as a weapon against the colonized subjects or nations that resist imperialist submissions, knowingly or unknowingly creating necropolitical zones by proliferating deprivation, famine, disease, and mass expulsion—as seen in the Bengal famine (1943), Iraq (1990-2003), and Venezuela (2017-current).[8] As an example, the case of the full-on embargo on Iraq is well documented. Sanctions made infrastructural reconstruction after the Gulf War impossible, wreaked havoc on civilians, and brought all social services to halt, as if conditioning the ground for military occupation by weakening the enemy so to speak.[9]

This dehumanization of target nations is an underpinning of a deeply racialized geographies of sanctions. A closer look at the timeline of international sanctions and the list of most sanctioned countries in the past century further debunks their neutrality. It is the wealthiest countries that almost exclusively enforce sanctions against the most vulnerable.[10] The majority of sanctions in the past few decades have been enforced by the US, the European Union, and the United Nations, and as sanctions historian, Joy Gordon, notes, against countries in Latin America, Africa, and the Middle East, many of them among the most economically deprived nations.[11]

Iran has a dark recollection of sanctions, dating back even before the 1979 revolution. The first haunting memory is related to the Persia's Great Famine (1917–1919), caused by the concurrent illegal occupation of the country by European armies, the hoarding of grains by the British military, and an embargo imposed by the British government, among other actions. These factors led to the deaths of 2 to 10 million people—up to 50% of the entire population.[12]

Another case is the oil embargo imposed by the British government in response to the nationalization of oil industry in 1951 under Prime Minister Mohammad Mosaddegh. This bold move sought to end the exploitation of Iran's resources by the British and marked an unexpected assertion of political autonomy. Although it became evident that the country could survive under British embargo, the attempt to nationalize oil was ultimately thwarted by the Anglo-American coup known as Operation Ajax in 1953.[13] This operation was the first of its kind carried out by the newly established CIA.

While sanctions have been historically framed as a humanitarian tool of peacetime diplomacy, historical facts tell a different story. At least, we should be suspicious of whether sanctions have been tied to the continuous Anglo-American imperialism in the post–World War II era. Sanctions perhaps might be better understood as another weapon in the arsenal of "hybrid warfare" that relies on a combination of low-intensity military conflict, recruiting native guerrilla fighters, and the support of compliant state governments.[14] This approach was explicitly outlined in language of policy by President John F. Kennedy in his "U.S. Overseas Internal Defense Policy" (1962).[15] Central to Kennedy's statements, and to the ideological foundation of hybrid warfare, was a commitment to covert interventionism—enabling nation-building and dismantling without exposing the United States to accusations of colonialism.

Financial Imperialism

Enforcing unilateral sanctions relies entirely on the structure of international banking system and uneven power dynamics in the global financial market. Today the United States holds an exceptional role in the global financial system. It has the largest economy, financial market, stocks of foreign assets, and liabilities.[16] The U.S. dollar is the main currency of international exchange, accounting for about 59 percent of all global transactions.[17] This "dollar supremacy" is considered an essential component of the US "financial hegemony" in the global trade market even when trade does not involve the United States or American corporations: "To deal in dollars, financial institutions must often borrow, however temporarily, from US counterparts and comply with the rules of the US government. That makes the Treasury Department, which regulates the U.S. financial system, the gatekeeper to the world's banking operations."[18] With emergence of electronic banking and political justification for close monitoring of national and international transactions after the 9/11 terrorist attacks, The US Treasury Department found itself in a superior place of control never dreamed of.[19]

In addition, despite the global reach of electronic banking, international transactions are often regulated by central standardized systems—such as the Brussels-based Society of Worldwide Interbank Financial Telecommunications (SWIFT) which processes transactions for many countries. These systems become inaccessible to sanctioned countries, in effect isolating them from global transactions by standard means. In addition to the centralization of information and control over standard systems, the centrality of the US dollar in international trade has become a means for the United States to force third-party financial institutions, businesses, and manufacturers to comply with the United States foreign policies, on the pretext of evading sanctions. "For any international bank that conducts dollar transactions, the risk of being suspended from the US banking system is existential; it is known as the "death penalty." No such bank can risk running afoul of the US Treasury Department, however burdensome, unreasonable, or illegal the US policies may be."[20]

Simultaneously, due to the vague language of sanction policies, many financial institutions prefer "over-compliance" and opt out of any relations with banks in the sanctioned countries, even if they are not listed in the sanctions' target institutions or when the transaction is done for civilian purpose. This means that under the benevolent surface of "smart sanctions" and exemptions in humanitarian cases, the chilling effect of sanctions is still blanketing the whole nation.[21] If a country is listed as a supporter of terrorism even humanitarian aid groups, NGOs, and individuals have trouble finding banking support for sending aid supplies or running their errands.[22] Foreign banks refuse to provide services for those residing in geographies listed as sanctioned or "high risk" by the Financial Action Task Force (FATF), even if they are not located in sanctioned territories.[23] Effectively, what is called "unintended consequence," or "casualty" in the deceitful language describing impact of sanctions, respectively represents the design outcome—the result of policies, institutional structures, and protocols—and dehumanized target populations. Against this uneven terrain of financial power, sanctions have become an apparatus of pressure for compliance with the United States' superior position in a fragile monopolar economic sphere.

The Making of the Enemy

After the 1979 Iranian Revolution (partly fueled by anti-colonial sentiments of the younger generations against years of American interference in every sector of the government and society), the US foreign policy changed from one invested in cooperation to one waging asymmetric proxy warfare. The country has been subject to four waves of sanctions ever since.

In the 1990s, the invention of the so-called "smart sanctions" claimed to target specific industries and entities of the Islamic Republic to impede their military expansion. Yet, in a condition where the main structures of the national economy are run by state institutions and military organizations, sanctions have effectively become instruments of collective punishment. In reality, the civilian economy and the military economy that supports the Islamic Revolutionary Guard Corps (IRGC) and its extraterritorial operator, the Quds Force, are indivisible.[24] Over almost four decades what started as the United States embargo turned into unilateral comprehensive economic sanctions, cutting the government's lifeline (oil export), financial relations, access to main currencies (dollar and euro), and freezing foreign assets, among other measures.[25] The latter wave of sanctions targeted not just the energy sector and oil exports, but also mining and metal industries, manufacturing, textiles, major petrochemical firms, and enlarged the list of sanctioned banks, institutions, and individuals.[26]

Sanctions have been almost exclusively publicized and justified for ending the Islamic Republic's nuclear enrichment program and extraterritorial support for terrorism, but with the termination of the Joint Comprehensive Plan of Action (JCPOA) also known as the "nuclear deal," by the Trump administration in 2017, sanctions (among administrations' covert operations, cyber warfare, and assassinations) have openly become a weapon of proxy warfare against the Islamic Republic and its allies in the Middle East. The Trump administration's "Maximum Pressure" campaign aimed to deprive the Iranian people by extending previous sanctions as a way to increase political discontent within the country to change the ruling political regime, or at least lead to state bankruptcy and similar destitution experienced by Iraq in the nineties (marked by the notorious "oil for food" program).

Above and beyond the financial and material dimensions, sanctions involve representational politics. They have deprived the Iranian population of self-representation internationally first by limiting access to means of knowledge production in multiple ways, including for instance pressuring publishing houses and grant programs internationally. Second, the name of Iran has been widely erased from the cultural sphere and mainstream media unless associated with certain keywords such as "WMD," "Nuclear Enrichment," "terrorism," and the like. Sanctions render Iran an outcast and have turned the entire multi-ethnic nation into the "enemy" of not only the United States but all nations.[27] Conflating the state and civilians, as a result, have turned people into human shields— represented simultaneously as victims of the autocratic state and potentially justified targets, whether by sanctions or military assault should an open war break out.

Ironically, sanctions have provided a perfect scapegoat for the Islamic Republic's political oppression at home and promoting armed violence across the region. Violence begets violence. As a case, expansion of Islamic Republic's military operations across Iraq and Syria as a direct result of US military invasion of Iraq in 2003 and withdrawal post 2008, is well documented.[28]

Landscapes of Sanctions

To circumvent the pressure of sanctions the Islamic regime and its military arm of IRGC have pursued the establishment of a "resistance economy," emphasizing diversification of economic activities, establishment of new transborder businesses, seeking heavier presence in black market economies, and the pursuit of alternative trade routes.[29] These include circumventing sanctions by exporting oil across the high seas under the flag of convenience that hides the origins of the cargo, among other opaque transactions that are revealed occasionally by accident or reconnaissance.[30] Simultaneously new ventures were sought in geographies that fall outside the US influence, for instance, in Cuba and Venezuela.[31]

Under sanctions, the pathways of illicit market economies (both literally and figuratively) were seen as the most legitimate way to escape the embargo of goods. As foreign markets began to close on Tehran as early as the mid-1990s, they were replaced by new networks, relations, and spaces of movement. The smuggling routes across the Iranian border under the control of the IRGC expanded their traffic and operation. With Dubai closing its gates to Tehran's business elites, Sulaymaniyah, Erbil, and other towns in Iraqi Kurdistan gradually became new extensions of Tehran's bazaar. Reinventing Iraqi Kurdistan as a backyard of the Islamic Republic has turned the mountainous region of Kurdistan across the Iran-Iraq borderline into a new highway of smuggled goods.

Highly organized smuggling organizations are the only means of livelihood for desperate Kurdish locals whose capacities of subsistence have long suffered as a result of underinvestment and neglect by ethnocentric states and pressures of international imperialism. Cartels operate by exploitation of Kurdish koolbars traversing old native routes mainly on foot, passing through land mines (souvenirs of the Iran-Iraq war) and surviving the debilitating topographic and climate conditions, not to mention the unpredictable charge of border patrol that often leaves casualties and permanent fear. It is not without reason that the locals call this mountainous stretch of the border, the "Death Zone."[32]

Koolbars transport cargo such as fuel to Iraq (since fuel price is much lower in Iran) and bring back embargoed items such as spare parts, tires, household appliances, and cigarettes, often carried on their backs, averaging 80-90 pounds per load. This is backbreaking work causing injuries, premature physical problems, disability, and early age retirement, if not death, all for four to 13 dollars per travel. Koolbars are labeled as "economic saboteurs," hunted by the border patrol, get shot and imprisoned for the crime of smuggling.[33] While the network is organized by handlers and middlemen on both sides of the border, the imported cargo ends up in stores across the country and profit goes to unknown figures at the top ranks in the military and state.[34] Like piracy on the high seas, smuggling across borders is not an even social terrain. It comes at a high cost for the dispossessed people of ethnic minorities, deployed in highly risky business by those in positions of power. Once again, marginalized geographies of transborder black market merge old and new social, racial, and ethnic injustices.[35]

The secrecy, the impossibility of tracing money, and the opacity of the state's shadow economies make it impossible to map the extended geographies of the black markets or to know the social networks of illicit trade at the leadership level. However, it is generally known that evading sanctions is possible mainly for people, businesses, and companies close to the state—whether owned by the IRGC and *bonyads* (state corporations) or run autonomously by individuals tied to the state elite.[36] Only those supported by the state apparatus have access to necessary back channels, information, and logistics, and only they can afford the risk of getting caught evading sanctions.[37] As a result, the private sector and independent businesses have been severely weakened. Sanctions enabled the Islamic Republic to achieve one of its biggest dreams, to hold the nation's wealth in the hands of those loyal to the regime: "The sanctions have created the economic revolution that makes those tied to the Revolutionary Guard and Khamenei's [Supreme Leader] inner circle the owners of the vast majority of wealth inside Iran."[38] In the past decades the currency value has depreciated multiple times followed by strangling inflations (in 2023 alone the currency has lost 30% of its value).[39] The middle class has disappeared and the poverty line has been redrawn repeatedly.

Even though from a geopolitical perspective, it may appear that the Islamic Republic has survived the economic pressures by evading sanctions and aligning itself with other superpowers, more notably Russia and China, once seen through the geospatial and environmental lenses, the long-term environmental and biological implications of sanctions and the so-called "resistance economy" become evident and cast a looming threat on all life forms.[40] Under economic pressures, the land and the built environment reemerge as a currency, that is to say, the state has unleashed new ways of exploiting property regimes, construction projects, and resource extraction in wildly diverse ways: land grabs, selling public lands to private entities, unnecessary infrastructural projects and hefty construction contracts benefiting IRGC companies, exploitation of public infrastructure, and seeking incentivized construction contracts in neighboring states, among others. The exploitation of public infrastructure can be exemplified in the deregulation of Bitcoin mining. Bitcoin offers relief amid the shortage of foreign currencies. The mines are fed by the dated public energy grid, believed to have contributed to power outages in populated cities, wreaking havoc on public services. This is when, due to the shortage of natural gas, city power plants were ordered to burn Mazut (heavy-grade fuel oil), resulting in an orange, highly toxic smog filling the air in larger cities and reportedly causing serious health problems.[41]

The exploitation of land is also evident in the sales of resources, deregulation of extraction for foreign companies, and ultimately possession and sale of anything that can be turned into a commodity. These include palm trees, sand from the riverbeds, fish stock in the sea, and the vast pool of minerals that is leading to major geological and hydrological shifts across the country, among others. Accelerated exploitation of land (and people) as resource and real estate has created socio-environmental catastrophes yet to be seen. The necropolitical violence is made not only by dehumanization, assault, pollution, and the collapse of fragile ecosystems but also by cutting the Native's access to their traditional territories, non-extractive forms of livelihood, and interspecies relations at the core of the Native means of subsistence.

Uncertainties

Revealing the invisible landscapes of sanctions—whether the result of embargoed trade, emerging black market geographies, or proliferating extraction sites from the scale of the body to territory—is a crucial step in transcending the propagandist narratives of warring states. As an act of counter-representation, this mapping process offers a grounded perspective on the current realities of sanctions as tools of domination. It provides a narrative from the vantage point of marginalized geographies silenced in the shadows of transnational imperialism and state autocracy. In the current geopolitical uncertainties across the Middle East, looming Trump's presidency, and expansion of colonial violence (e.g., genocide of Palestinians in tens of thousands in Gaza), the historical ground truthing seems as necessary as before. After all, imperial forces build their legitimacy on historical amnesia, invisibility of their inhumanities, and shameless self-victimization. As the most sanctioned country in the world, Iran is not just another outsider in the geography of free trade (a euphemism for neo-colonialism). It is a key to understanding hidden geographies of violence between the financial imperialism of the United States and geopolitical conflict across Western Asia at the turn of the year 2025. This act of counter-representation provides a guide through which we begin to see the shadow side of contemporary spatial history, struggles for justice, and our place in it.

-----

[1] Joy Gordon, "The Brutal Impact of Sanctions on the Global South," *Yale Journal of International Law: Symposium on Third World Approaches to International Law & Economic Sanction*s (28 June, 2023).
[2] Vasuki Nesiah, "The Fog of Peace: Who Profits from Economic Sanctions?" Y*ale Journal of International Law: Symposium on Third World Approaches to International Law & Economic Sanctions* (28 June, 2023).
[3] Woodrow Wilson, *Woodrow Wilson's Case for the League of Nations*, ed. Hamilton Foley (Princeton University Press, 1923), quotes respectively from pages 67, 71.
[4] Nicholas Mulder, *The Economic Weapon: The Rise of Sanctions as a Tool of Modern War* (Yale University Press, 2022), 4.
[5] Nesiah, "The Fog of Peace."
[6] Ibid.
[7] Ibid.
[8] I am using the term "necropolitics" as defined by Achille Mbembe in "Necropolitics," *Public Culture* 15, no. 1 (2003): 11–40. The term refers to the application of sociopolitical and geospatial power to determine who lives and who dies.
[9] See Joy Gordon, *Invisible War: The United States and the Iraq Sanctions* (Harvard University Press, 2010).
[10] According to Nesiah, while there are cases that demonstrate the effectiveness of sanctions in persuading engagement in diplomatic relations—in the case of South African Apartheid and the current Russo-Ukrainian war—these cases should be considered as exceptions to the norm.
[11] Gordon, "The Brutal Impact of Sanctions."
[12] Mohammad Gholi Majd, *The Great Famine & Genocide in Iran: 1917-1919* (University Press of America, 2013).
[13] Patrick Clawson, and Cyrus Sassanpour. "Adjustment to a Foreign Exchange Shock: Iran, 1951 - 1953," *International Journal of Middle East Studies* 19, no. 1 (1987): 1–22, http://www.jstor.org/stable/163025; Mohammad Gholi Majd, "The 1951-53 Oil Nationalization Dispute and

the Iranian Economy: A Rejoinder," *Middle Eastern Studies* 31, no. 3 (1995): 449–59, http://www.jstor.org/stable/4283736.

[14] The word "hybrid war" is borrowed from Vijay Prashad in "Hybrid Wars and US Imperialism" (2019), https://www.youtube.com/watch?v=D-uxISFZbG8.

[15] See John F. Kennedy, "U.S. Overseas Internal Defense Policy," August 1962, Papers of John F. Kennedy. Presidential Papers. National Security Files, JFKNSF-338-010, https://www.jfklibrary.org/asset-viewer/archives/jfknsf-338-010#?image_identifier=JFKNSF-338-010-p0003.

[16] On historical, multifaceted foundations of American financial hegemony see, Michael Hudson, *Super Imperialism: The Economic Strategy of American Empire* (Holt, Rinehart and Winston, 1972); Thomas Polley, "Theorizing Dollar Hegemony: the Political Economic Foundations of Exorbitant Privilege," *Dollar Hegemony*, eds. Thomas Polley, et al. (Edward Elgar Publishing Limited, 2024), 20–56.

[17] Juneau Zhang,"Prospects for the Yuan Unsettling the Dollar," *GIS Reports*, August 21, 2023, https://www.gisreportsonline.com/r/yuan-unseating-the-dollar/.

[18] Jeff Stein and Federica Cocco, "The Money War: How Four U.S. Presidents Unleashed Economic Warfare Across The Globe," *The Washington Post*, July 25, 2024.

[19] Ibid.

[20] Gordon, "The Brutal Impact of Sanctions."

[21] Smart sanctions target selective individuals, corporations, and parties, rather than the entire nation. They are presented as a humanitarian alternative to the full-on embargo.

[22] Gordon, "The Brutal Impact of Sanctions."

[23] FATF is responsible for setting anti-money-laundering standards and determines which countries are considered high risk, likely to evade the standards or evade sanctions. According to FATF, most countries in the "Third World" are "risky." This causes the decision of international banks to provide direct services to national and local banks, as well as correspondent bank relations (CBRs). See Gordon, "The Brutal Impact of Sanctions."

[24] The IRGC was established in 1979 and gained experience during the Iran-Iraq war (1980–1988), amidst international sanctions and maximum pressures on the country. After the war, it advanced its role in civilian space and reconstruction projects while extending its intelligence and military influence across the Middle East. For more see, Hossein Rassam, and Sanam Vakil. "The Iranian Deep State: Understanding the Politics of Transition in the Islamic Republic." *Hoover Institute Essay: The Middle East and the Islamic World* (Hoover Institute Press, 2020).

[25] Narges Bajoghli, Seyyed Vali Reza Nasr, Djavad Salehi-Isfahani, and Ali Vaez, *How Sanctions Work: Iran and the Impact of Economic Warfare* (Stanford University Press, [Kindle Edition] 2024); Clayton Thomas, "Iran Sanctions," Congressional Research Service, Feb 2, 2022.

[26] Bajoghli, et al., *How Sanctions Work*, Chapter 3.

[27] Ibid, 13.

[28] Jeremy Scahill, and Murtaza Hussain," The Change of Overlords: From the Rubble of the U.S. War in Iraq, Iran Builds a New Order" *The Intercept*, November 18, 2019, https://theintercept.com/2019/11/18/us-iraq-invasion-iran/.

[29] The state-sponsored companies and the Revolutionary Guard have been in control of the most lucrative import and exports as well as geostrategic checkpoints, ports, and airports.

[30] Evading sanctions often goes unnoticed unless when revealed by accident or as a political exposé. Yet these fragmented cases signify a system and continuous trend whose full scope escapes the news. Johnathan Saul, et al., "Flags of Inconvenience: Noose Tightens Around Iranian Shipping," *Reuters*, July 26, 2019, https://www.reuters.com/article/world/flags-of-inconvenience-noose-tightens-around-iranian-shipping-idUSKCN1UL0LX/.

[31] Bajoghli, et al., *How Sanctions Work*, esp. Chapter 2.

[32] *They Shoot Koolbars, Don't They?*, film directed by Jamshid Bahrami, produced by Maziar Bahari (Iran Wire, 2021), https://www.youtube.com/watch?v=zxsVx9Ikfo8.

[33] Ibid.

[34] Author's interview with anonymous Koolbars.

[35] Tom Westcott, and Afshin Ismaili, "Sanctions and Smuggling: Iraqi Kurdistan and Iran's Border Economies," *Global Initiative against Transnational Organized Crime* (2019); Emrah Yıldız, "Kaçak | Qaçax | قاچاق : Fugitive Forms of Bureaucracy and Economy across Southwest Asia," *Journal of Cultural Economy* 17, no. 2 (2024): 147–153.

[36] A major part of the country's economy is run by the state (semi-public) corporations called Bonyad. The corporations were created in 1979 by the expropriation of the monarchy's assets namely the Pahlavi Foundation. The leadership of these foundations is appointed by the Supreme Leader often from the ranks of former IRGC commanders. Bonyads are exempt from taxes and their book (records of businesses) are notoriously closed to outsiders.

[37] Bajoghli, et al., *How Sanctions Work*, 52.

[38] Ibid.

[39] Vivian Yee, "Iran's Rulers, Shaken by Protests, Now Face Currency Crisis," *New York Times*, March 6, 2023, https://www.nytimes.com/2023/03/06/world/middleeast/iran-economy-currency-rial.html.

[40] Kaveh Madani, "Have International Sanctions Impacted Iran's Environment?" *World* 2, no. 2 (2021): 231–252. https://doi.org/10.3390/world2020015.

[41] Ershad Alijani, "Gas Shortage Renders Iran's Air Quality 'Unbreathable' Due to Mazut Pollution," *The Observers*, Jan 26, 2023, https://observers.france24.com/en/middle-east/20230126-gas-shortage-iran-air-quality-pollution-mazut.

Designing Within Conflict

(No one asked me to come, but here I am)

Malkit Shoshan

The built environment is both a record and repository of complex personal and cultural histories, capturing the complex narratives of the people and forces that shapes it over time. Moreover, buildings and urban spaces embody the societal contexts from which conflicts emerge, offering a comprehensive understanding of the broader historical, social, political, and economic arcs that create pathways for violence and injustice. Through the tools of architecture and urban design, we can uncover the underlying structures, meanings, and dynamics that shape our lived realities, revealing layers of history, power relations, and cultural expressions that have long been interwoven into our environments.

This essay aims to expand on this understanding by examining how the built environment can be explored through various scales and contexts, incorporating personal narratives and analyses that provide essential tools for deciphering conflict spaces as deep, complex, and multifaceted. These spaces cannot be understood solely as urban and spatial phenomena; they represent the lived experiences of the individuals who navigate them. In the book *Borderlands/La Frontera*, Gloria Anzaldúa's articulates the notion of "the space in between," which illustrates how identity, culture, and geography intersect in regions marked by conflict and emphasizes how borderlands—both literal and metaphorical—serve as critical sites for understanding social dynamics, identity formation, and the experiences of those who exist within these liminal spaces.[1]

As such, the built environment may offer a valuable intersectional lens through which we can understand its shaping influence on its diverse users and inhabitants. Kimberlé Crenshaw, who coined the term "intersectionality," highlights the importance of recognizing how overlapping social identities and systemic forces impact individuals' experiences, particularly for those who inhabit multiple marginalized identities.[2] By employing an intersectional lens, we can make visible the subtle yet profound power dynamics at play within the built environment. When analyzed through this perspective, the built environment becomes a framework for exploring how societal structures and historical legacies create barriers, foster inequalities, and perpetuate injustice.

This essay poses a critical question: How can architects and urban designers use their tools and practices to comprehend, engage with, and intervene in these complex spaces? Moreover, how can they advocate for change that amplifies suppressed voices and promotes counter-narratives and counter-practice centered on social and environmental justice?

By investigating these themes, this essay seeks to make visible that the built environment is not a neutral canvas but an active participant in the shaping of social relations and power dynamics. Ultimately, this understanding can inform practices and policies that foster more equitable and inclusive urban futures. To illustrate these concepts, the essay draws on case studies from the projects I have experimented with the Foundation for Achieving Seamless Territory (FAST), an Amsterdam and NY-based architectural think-tank. These examples demonstrate how spatial design tools can reveal systemic violence while simultaneously challenging existing power structures and advancing social and environmental justice. Furthermore, the essay incorporates examples from my pedagogy at Harvard Graduate School of Design, where I engage students in discussions about the role of architecture and urban design in addressing systemic inequalities.

Invisibility and Ethical Considerations

In teaching, intersectionality helps us instigate critical discussions on justice, equity, and inclusivity, enabling students to understand the connections between site and system while developing strategies to challenge the forces shaping our built environment. In past years, I have taught seminars in collaboration with the United Nations Office for Disarmament Affairs, focusing on the spatial aspects of nuclear technologies, including uranium mines, power plants, and nuclear testing sites. During our sessions, we hosted, among others, Valerie Rangel, a Navajo artist and community activist, who discussed the severe health effects of uranium mining and nuclear testing on her community. The public health consequences of these activities are devastating to human and non-human bodies and to the environment. The Navajo Nation has been particularly affected, experiencing alarmingly high rates of cancer and respiratory diseases linked to exposure to hazardous materials associated with uranium mining (EPA, 2020). Rangel emphasized, "Our land is our identity, and the contamination of our environment strips us of our cultural heritage." This is a critical intersectional perspective, revealing how the environmental and public health crises affect the cultural and social fabric of Indigenous communities.

The systemic neglect of infrastructure within the Navajo Nation further aggravates these health issues. Many communities lack access to clean drinking water and adequate healthcare, which limits their ability to respond effectively to health crises. According to the U.S. Department of Energy, over the years, many Native American communities have suffered long-term health problems and economic disadvantages due to uranium mining.[3] According to Rangel, there is an urgent necessity for policies that address these systemic injustices.

Nuclear infrastructure provides a critical intersectional perspective for understanding systemic injustices in our society, rendering visible the so-called "sacrifice zones."

Destruction and radiation from nuclear testing, mining, and power plants have affected more than just the Navajo community. Karen Barad, a scholar and quantum scientist, discusses the unequal impacts of nuclear testing on Indigenous peoples. She notes that "testing sites are never empty lands; they are always inhabited".[4] She emphasizes the need to recognize that these sites are intertwined with the histories, cultures, and identities of the communities surrounding them and points out that the US has dropped approximately 2,000 atomic bombs on Indigenous lands, illustrating the continuous violence inflicted upon these populations. The consequences of nuclear infrastructure extend beyond immediate health impacts; they reflect a historical disregard for Indigenous rights and sovereignty. Researcher J. Kēhaulani Kauanui underscores this point, stating, "Nuclear colonialism is a form of violence that disrupts Indigenous lifeways and perpetuates socio-economic and ecological harms".[5] The systemic neglect of infrastructure in these communities, including access to clean water and reliable healthcare, exacerbates their vulnerability and resilience.

Visibility and relational accountability are the basic of ethics advocated by Aldo Leopold, who is also known as the "father of ecology." He called in his book *A Sand County Almanac*, for a "land ethic" that expands our moral responsibilities to include the natural environment, encompassing soils, waters, plants, and animals. He asserts that we must "see the land" not merely as a resource to exploit but as a community to which we belong, stating, what we see depends mainly on what we look for.[6] Leopold's philosophy underlined that human activities significantly impact ecological systems, and an ethical relationship with the land requires acknowledging these interconnections. Ultimately, Leopold urges us to cultivate a *vision* of the world that reflects our shared responsibility for ecological well-being.

More than half a century later, Timothy Morton introduces the concept of "hyperobjects," which are vast and complex entities that stretch across space and time, extending beyond human experience and perception.[7] His concept of hyperobjects transcends our typical understanding of space and time. Examples of hyperobjects include climate change, nuclear waste, and the internet, which exist beyond human perception and comprehension, affecting our lives in profound yet often invisible ways. He likens the nature of hyperobjects to "goo," suggesting that these entities are intricate and interdependent, often slipping through our grasp and defying easy categorization. Just as goo is a messy and amorphous substance that can infiltrate and shape various environments, hyperobjects permeate our lives and shape our experiences and actions, complicating our relationship with our surroundings, with time, and space.

With nuclear matter, we realize the consequences of our actions cannot be understood solely through our senses, as argued by Aldo Leopold, who linked ecology and ethical action to the way we see the world. So, we ask what happens when we cease to understand the world and stop perceiving the impact of our actions through our senses? How can we address ethics regarding violence that remains invisible to us?

Invisibility is a space where design can matter.

It is not just the nuclear threat that devastates lives and the environment, in the past year alone, thousands of different types of bombs have been dropped on Gaza—more than in any recent conflict—each creating craters of 12 meters or more. This contamination is neither localized nor temporary. The soil in Gaza is severely contaminated by munitions, with estimates indicating that over 35,000 tons of explosives have been used in recent conflicts, resulting in widespread environmental degradation.[8] This contamination poses significant health risks to the local population, as heavy metals and toxic substances infiltrate agricultural land, negatively impacting food security and health outcomes. The air is thick with unbreathable smoke from ongoing military operations, exacerbating respiratory issues and other health complications. According to a report by the World Health Organization, "the deterioration of air quality has contributed to a marked increase in asthma and chronic obstructive pulmonary disease among residents".[9] Moreover, the aquifer in Gaza, which serves as the primary source of drinking water for the population, is now flooded with toxic materials and seawater due to over-extraction and military activity. The United Nations has reported that approximately 97% of Gaza's water supply is unsafe for human consumption, leading to perpetual public health crises.[10]

Remediation of the soil, air, groundwater, and psyche may exceed human capacity to measure, perceive, or effectively address these issues. Many of these pollution sites are not only difficult to access but also require resources and technologies that are often unavailable to us. As Timothy Morton describes, the challenges associated with such vast and interconnected toxicity can be likened to "goo," substances that resist clear understanding, illustrating the complexities and interdependencies within broader ecological systems. The impacts of this war in Gaza bleed into every aspect of life—beyond the perception of our senses, and beyond time and space.

And of course, it's not just Gaza being bombed, nor is it only Israel that is dropping bombs. The ongoing violence in various conflict zones around the world reflects a broader trend of militarization that significantly impacts global peace and security. Currently, there are more than 100 active conflicts worldwide, highlighting a pervasive state of unrest and violence that affects millions as noted in Uppsala Conflict Data Program. According to the Stockholm International Peace Research Institute, global military spending began to increase during the COVID-19 pandemic and continued to rise, reaching an astonishing $2.24 trillion USD in 2022.[11] [12] This escalation in military expenditures amidst a global health crisis raises troubling questions: Why prioritize military growth during a pandemic that has caused widespread suffering and disruption?

The global shift in priorities during such crises indicates a troubling trend where resources that could address urgent social needs—such as healthcare, education, and infrastructure—are instead allocated toward military expansion. During the pandemic, many governments engaged in substantial military contracts and expanded their defense budgets while neglecting essential public welfare initiatives. As noted by political economist Michael Klare, "The persistent willingness of governments to devote substantial resources to military spending—even during times of global crisis—reflects a long-standing prioritization of military readiness over the needs of the populace."[13] Furthermore, this emphasis on militarization often comes at the expense of addressing critical issues such as environmental degradation, climate change, and social justice. Military activities contribute significantly to environmental destruction, from the pollution generated by military operations to the long-term impacts of warfare on ecosystems. The US military is one of the largest institutional consumers of fossil fuels in the world, significantly undermining global efforts to combat climate change.[14] However, the exclusion of military emissions from the Kyoto Protocol and other global emission accounting frameworks renders many of our mitigation efforts nearly counterproductive, as the primary source of emissions is effectively discounted. This situation exemplifies not only systemic neglect but also the obscuration of power dynamics and control that limits our agency to act. The lack of accountability for the environmental impact of military operations allows these activities to evade regulation, while civilian sectors face stringent emission targets.[15]

This discrepancy highlights a critical inconsistency in our approach to climate policy and environmental justice, wherein military emissions—often associated with conflict and destruction—are exempt from the same scrutiny applied to civilian industries. As noted by the World Resources Institute, military activities contribute significantly to global carbon emissions, creating an urgent need for inclusive regulatory frameworks that hold all sectors accountable.[16] The failure to incorporate military emissions into climate strategies not only jeopardizes global mitigation goals but also perpetuates environmental injustices, particularly in regions disproportionately affected by military actions and climate change, which often intersect.

The Role of Spatial Design in Addressing Systemic Violence

Invisibility is a space where design not only matters but also holds the potential for profound impact. Design helps render visible complex relationships and plays a critical role in producing alternative visions and imaginaries of shared values, spaces, and strategies. By fostering shared goals and missions, design can mirror the economic models used by Mariana Mazzucato to create a common vision for sustainable and equitable futures. Mazzucato emphasizes the need to rethink our conventional models to ensure that innovation serves the public good.[17]

By employing our disciplinary tools, we can illuminate the military's heavy reliance on fossil fuels, showcasing how this dependence contributes significantly to greenhouse gas emissions, exacerbating climate change and acting as a threat multiplier for conflicts worldwide. As Klare points out, this military-first approach not only diverts critical resources but also damages the environment upon which our societies depend.[18] However, design can do more than just critique existing systems; it can envision alternatives and expand the public imagination regarding what is possible.

For instance, what if we redirected $2.24 trillion in military spending toward addressing pressing global challenges such as environmental restoration? Such an investment could restore an area about six times the size of the Amazon Rainforest, which is vital for biodiversity and climate regulation. The United Nations states, "protecting and restoring the Amazon is crucial for meeting climate goals and enhancing biodiversity."[19] Alternatively, this funding could be used to construct 2,500 fully equipped hospitals, build approximately 100,000 schools, or create 20 million homes. In this way, design can make these transformative choices visible and tangible, allowing us to imagine and work toward a future rooted in sustainability and equity.

Applying intersectional design principles fosters inclusive advocacy and collaboration that amplifies diverse voices in the design process, ensuring that the experiences of marginalized communities and environmental concerns are prioritized in discussions surrounding environmental justice and sustainability. This approach empowers communities to co-create spaces that authentically reflect their identities and aspirations while simultaneously addressing systemic inequities. By centering these diverse perspectives, design becomes a tool for social change, enabling the creation of environments that not only meet immediate needs but also pave the way for long-term equity and justice.

Ultimately, integrating intersectionality into design practices offers a crucial opportunity to rethink our strategies for tackling global challenges, helping to rectify historical injustices and promote shared goals centered on social and environmental justice. This intersectional lens encourages a holistic approach, where the interconnectedness of various issues—such as climate change, economic disparity, and cultural representation—is recognized and addressed. As we navigate complex global issues, this inclusive framework not only enriches our understanding but also inspires innovative solutions that resonate with broader publics. By leveraging design in this way, we can envision a future where all more voices are heard, valued, and integrated into the decision-making processes that shape our collective lived environment.

Foundation for Achieving Seamless Territory: Because We Care

> Care is a species activity that includes everything we do to maintain, continue, and repair our world so that we may live in it as well as possible. That world includes our bodies, our selves, and our environment, all of which we seek to interweave in a complex, life-sustaining web."[20]

In her work on the ethics of care, Joan Tronto argues

that care must be a public and societal endeavor characterized by attentiveness, responsibility, competence, and responsiveness, engaging diverse perspectives and experiences. This understanding resonates with the practices of FAST, where we strive to employ design critically and proactively, emphasizing its potential to not only critique but also research and respond to societal needs, ultimately contributing to the shaping and transformation of the built environment—simply because we care.

We started FAST in 2005 in response to a question posed to us by the Ein Hawd community, a village of internally displaced Palestinians in Israel. They sought an alternative and extended masterplan to challenge the one imposed on them by the Israeli government, enabling them to engage in negotiations with governmental bodies and assert their basic rights to essential civic services. Following the completion of the long-term process that is described in the book Village, *One Land Two systems and Platform Paradise*. The process included an international architecture competition, public symposia, local workshops, exhibitions, art installations in public space, an advocacy campaign, and the collaborative design of an alternative masterplan, FAST has continued to pursue a wide range of projects across different scales and contexts. We have published award-winning books, initiated policy papers, curated exhibitions, and engaged in educational initiatives. These endeavors are all driven by a shared mission of expanding the field of architecture and spatial design to shed light on and address pressing public concerns and foster visions that promote social and environmental justice.

FAST's work is often unsolicited and arises from encounters and conversations, such as those we had with the community of Ein Hawd. We employ a variety of research methodologies to understand both the site and the system, taking the time to engage with the issues and places we work with, and considering the diverse constituents that inhabit the spaces we engage with, along with the powers that shape those environments. The methodologies we employ include different forms of documentation, drawing, mapping, photography, and spatial analysis, as well as the collection of oral histories, policy analysis, and the development of strategies for engaging multiple stakeholders.

This multifaceted approach enables the development of collaborative projects encompassing alternative master plans, policy recommendations, archives, protocols, storytelling, and advocacy strategies. The outcomes of our work, along with our findings and alternative visions, are made visible through public events, exhibitions, policy papers, and publications, fostering awareness and dialogue around systemic injustices and potential solutions.

The pedagogical elements of FAST's work include working within design schools, particularly the Harvard Graduate School of Design. Here, with our teaching, we aim to expand the curriculum by introducing intersectional conversations that feature a diverse array of experts including scientists, artists and designers, philosophers, lawyers, activists, as well as policymakers, stakeholders, and representatives from various institutions, such as United Nations agencies and other local and global think-tanks. This engagement not only improve students' understanding of the complex dynamics of the built environment but also prepares them to be informed advocates for change.

As argued by Sara Ahmed that we need to think about the labor that goes into making a world that is accessible; we cannot take access for granted.[21] Our projects typically function as pilots or experiments in design activism, resulting in both measurable and immeasurable impacts that aim to broaden the discourse surrounding design as an intersectional lens through which we can engage with our environment.

Intersectionality and Contingency in Architecture

The concept of intersectionality, coined by Kimberlé Crenshaw, emphasizes the interconnected nature of social identities and their collective impact on experiences of privilege and oppression.[22] Crenshaw articulates that the intersectional experience is greater than the sum of racism and sexism, emphasizing how overlapping identities create unique forms of discrimination that require specific attention.[23] By applying an intersectional lens to architecture and urban design, we can more effectively analyze the complexities of systemic violence embedded within spatial practices and recognize the nuanced experiences of marginalized communities.

Scholarship by Angela Davis and Gloria Anzaldúa further illustrates how intersecting identities influence lived experiences. Davis argues that understanding the intersections of race, gender, and class is essential for the movement toward social justice, stating, "We are not just fighting for the rights of one group or for one issue. We are fighting for the rights of all people, including those who are marginalized and oppressed."[24] Anzaldúa's concept of the "borderlands" serves as a critical framework for examining how physical and metaphorical borders create unique experiences of marginalization and resistance. She asserts, "When we can see the borders, we can begin to understand the struggles," highlighting the importance of recognizing how spaces shape identity.[25] Moreover, Anzaldúa distinguishes between contingent thinking and non-contingent thinking in understanding identity and space. Contingent thinking refers to a fluid and dynamic understanding of identity that allows for the complexities and ever-changing nature of personal and social realities. This approach recognizes that identities are shaped by contextual factors such as culture, geography, history, and interpersonal relationships. For instance, the case studies below illustrate the intersectional and contingent perspectives employed by the projects of FAST. For instance, *Atlas of the Conflict: Israel-Palestine* demonstrates this contingent relationality, showing how the interactions between the two nations are not merely a matter of political rivalry but are deeply embedded in spatial design that marginalizes one group while enabling the other to thrive. The project illustrates how the design of space—through factors like borders, land use, cultural heritage, and resource distribution—contributes to the ongoing dynamics of privilege and oppression, emphasizing that the experiences of both communities are interlinked. Similarly, the project *Village: One Land Two Systems* and *Platform Paradise*, exemplifies this contingent perspective through the focus on the evolving history of the village of Ein Hawd. This long-term project examines the division of one village into two distinct yet interconnected entities and narratives, highlighting how systemic inequities continually shape the lives of its inhabitants within the context of their physical environment.

By exploring the intersectional dynamics of space, the border transforms into a site of possibility and confrontation which serves as the context for our design intervention.[26]

Case Studies and Counter Methodologies

i. Decolonizing the Atlas: Atlas of the Conflict. Israel-Palestine [27]

Atlas of the Conflict: Israel–Palestine utilizes more than 500 maps to visualize the emergence of Israel and the disappearance of Palestine over the past century. For this project, we researched and visualized spatial information that was either classified, inaccessible, or intentionally obscured, much like the reality of unrecognized villages. These spaces, often deemed informal, were excluded from public and formal spatial documentation. It took about 10 years to conduct the research, produce the maps, and publish the work.

As a format of territorial representation, the atlas originated during the age of colonial expansion in the sixteenth century and has never been limited to mere data depiction. Its roots can be traced to cartographers like Mercator, whose *Atlas sive Cosmographicae* of 1595 set the standard for subsequent atlases. These early modern atlases utilized collections of maps to visually depict newly discovered lands (by European nations), trade routes, and territorial claims, facilitating navigation and exploration during European colonization. Atlases played a pivotal role in legitimizing territorial conquests, serving as tools for navigation and shaping perceptions of the world that systematically reinforced Eurocentric perspectives, marginalized Indigenous knowledge, and perpetuated colonial ideologies. The borders, often arbitrarily drawn by colonial powers, were solidified and imposed through atlases, contributing to ongoing conflicts and inequalities.

With *Atlas of the Conflict: Israel–Palestine*, we aimed to reclaim this format and challenge it to depict a different set of perspectives and relational dynamics. Instead of representing a singular nation or perspective, it presents two nations, Israel and Palestine, alongside one another, highlighting their interconnectedness and the complexities of their coexistence. The first chapter, titled "Borders," visualizes the extensive history of colonization in the Middle East and Palestine. It outlines the geopolitical transformations in the region following World War I, where European powers, in planning for the aftermath of the Ottoman Empire's dismantling, arbitrarily divided the Middle East into British and French zones of influence. The legacy of these borderlines remains at the root of many of the conflicts that have followed—conflicts with which we are all too familiar.

Other chapters cover themes such as land ownership, cultural heritage sites and memorials, water, demography, landscaping, and the city of Jerusalem. Thus, *Atlas of the Conflict: Israel–Palestine*, seeks to reveal the complexities and interdependencies of spatial relations in the Israel-Palestine context. By acknowledging the complexities of these relationships, we hope to provide a richer, more nuanced understanding of the ongoing struggles for justice and recognition within these historically fraught landscapes.

ii. Socially Engaged Art and Spatial Design: Village: One Land Two Systems and Platform Paradise[28]

While the Atlas illustrates the transformation of Palestine and Israel on a national scale, our subsequent project, documented in the book *Village: One Land, Two Systems and Platform Paradise*, zooms in on a specific location: the village of Ein Hawd. The book navigates the intricate space between justice and pragmatism, narrating the villagers' ongoing daily struggles and weaving together diverse narratives of forced migration, colonization, and oppression. It also highlights our efforts to design a collaborative engagement process with the community and develop an alternative masterplan to use as a tool for negotiating rights to space and resources with local institutions, including planning authorities. Through these exploratory design methods, we aimed to empower and advocate for the community's essential needs, such as safety and access to basic infrastructure and services, using spatial design and socially engaged art tools.

iii. Making Things Public: Zoo, or the letter Z, just after Zionism[29]

The next project I'd like to briefly mention is the research-based installation "Zoo, or the Letter Z, Just After Zionism." It begins on the last page of the lexicon section of the "Atlas of the Conflict: Israel-Palestine," which includes only two terms: "Zoo" and "Zionism." The term "zoo" describes the struggle of a small private urban zoo in Gaza City to survive, highlighting how Gazan zookeepers painted black stripes on white donkeys to make them look like zebras after losing many of their exotic animals due to ongoing wars and a lack of access to medicine and veterinary expertise. "Zionism" refers to the national ideology advocating for the establishment of a homeland for the historically persecuted Jewish people in Palestine. This last page of the lexicon became the starting point for a year-long study of the two terms, or rather, two inventions—the urban zoo and the nation-state—traced back to the Age of Enlightenment and its fixation on classification. We spent about a year working on the exhibition and researching Gaza from the perspective of this kind of classification gone awry.

We began "Zoo" by sketching maps and sections to visualize the walls enclosing Gaza and its imposed and shifting maritime borders. We studied the development and architecture of the urban zoo and meticulously documented Marahland, the zoo in Gaza City where the donkeys were kept. We examined scientific illustrations of various species and gradually began to mix all these elements, drawing imaginary animals and replacing their backgrounds with elements borrowed from news items about Gaza.

The exhibition space featured a large-scale installation of a cage, an archive, and a lexicon, which we attached to the gallery windows. We designed a hard cage that transforms into a living room and then turns into a soft cage made of macramé. We transformed the architecture gallery into a menagerie hosting donkeys, rats, and pigeons cared for by an activist from the animal liberation front.

A few years later, we created another iteration of "Zoo" to be exhibited at the Tropic Institute in Lisbon, Portugal. By exploring the archive of their colonial remains, we managed to incorporate donkeys, pigeons, and rats to tell the story of the zoo in a context that further expanded the narrative of colonial legacies and the longstanding power dynamics of global extraction, oppression, and dispossession.

iv. Counter Archiving: Border Ecologies and the Gaza Strip

Elements from "Zoo" and the "Atlas" were also embedded in a 7.5-meter weave that we exhibited at the 2021 Venice Architecture Biennale. In 2019, we received an open-ended and unspecified invitation to propose a project for the Biennale. We decided to use this international platform to speak about Gaza and share matters of concern with the public, using the Biennale as an effective stage for public outreach and activism. In our projects, we often work with archives to uncover violence and find creative ways to preserve marginalized histories facing erasure.

"Border Ecologies and the Gaza Strip" explores the emergence of unexpected spaces in response to stresses and war at the Israeli-Palestinian border. For nearly a century, fluctuations in the border's shape and form have affected both human and natural ecologies, leading to the formation of spaces of exception—environments that, at times, seem paradoxically more resilient and sustainable than those with steadier histories. This iteration of the project traces the transformation of a small farm in Khuza'a, a Palestinian agricultural village in the Gaza Strip situated along one of the territory's most militarized borders with Israel. Over the past few decades, the four-dunam (or 4,000-square-meter) farm, owned and managed by Abd el Haleem and Khaldya Qudaih, has been repeatedly attacked, damaged, and destroyed by Israeli air raids, shelling, and patrols.

The project is based on oral histories of daily life on the farm, gathered through ongoing conversations with a family of Gazan farmers. Linking mundane material, such as watermelon, sardines, sand, and sediment, to bureaucratic protocols, Israeli-imposed restrictions, and continued acts of violence, these stories attest to the Khuza'a community's continual engagement in collective acts of survival, resistance, mutual aid, and solidarity.

One such story, "Wheat and Weddings," is centered around wheat, an indispensable crop and staple food in Palestine, and two small wheat fields used to host marriage ceremonies. In Gaza, late spring marks both the celebration of the end of the wheat harvest and the beginning of the wedding season. Unlike other farmland in the area, where farmers rotate crops year-round, these two fields are used only for monocropping to allow space for communal gatherings and wedding parties in the summer.

The installation is centered on a dining table with a custom-made tablecloth featuring interwoven stories of daily life on the farm. Two projections juxtapose short videos showing the daily life on the farm with footage of the perpetual violence the villagers face, all captured on mobile phones by the farmers. The exhibition also includes photographs, short stories, testimonies, and a website that makes the exhibition material accessible online for those who cannot visit in person.

The project "Border Ecologies and the Gaza Strip" is a documentation of multi-year conversations with a community of farmers in Gaza. Through this engagement, we collected oral histories and digital copies of diverse documents and artifacts provided by the community. Using this material, we crafted an initial seven-and-a-half-meter weave, with timelines, drawings, and stories linked through barcodes to a dynamic online platform that we continue to expand. Our conversations are still ongoing. The tablecloth, crafted in collaboration with a master weaver at the Tilburg Textile Museum, serves as an artifact and is preserved in the museum archive. We ensured that it not only showcases a design but also carries stories within it. By leveraging cultural production infrastructure, we have created unexpected spaces for documenting, preserving, and archiving stories.

This project won the Silver Lion at the Biennale. The jury viewed the project as daring and thought-provoking, inviting reflection on divided histories, agricultural practices, daily rituals, and the realities of settlement and occupation.

v. Intervening on protocols and other institutional formats: BLUE: The Architecture of UN Peacekeeping Missions[30]

UN peace missions operate today inside hundreds of cities across the world. Planned and engineered with the logic of security regimes, using single-purpose infrastructure, and dependent on extractive global supply chains, these "Islands of Blue" generate a massive carbon footprint, profoundly impact local livelihoods, and leave mostly waste after decommissioning. Focusing on two missions and four cities in Liberia and Mali, *BLUE: Architecture of UN Peacekeeping Missions* charts and uncovers spatial realities produced by the UN in mission areas. It traces the complex processes and mechanisms behind the conduct of missions and the various spatial tools and architectural technologies that make them possible. *BLUE* questions the international, spatial, and cultural structures we put in place to support communities across the world in times of crisis.

At the intersection of architecture, urban planning, international relations and activism, *BLUE: Architecture of UN Peacekeeping Missions* seeks not only to change UN missions but also to open up and expand the operative realm of architecture. It combines research and projects involving policymakers, military engineers and officers, anthropologists, local inhabitants, activists, rebels, diplomats and ministers, architects and planners. *BLUE* offers examples of how entrenched institutional bureaucracies can be confronted by using more inclusive models of engagement, and it shows how designs rooted in local cultures and empowerment can address a history of violence.

This project began with an encounter in Kosovo and evolved into a decade-long study and collaborative design initiative aimed at challenging institutional protocols by proposing policy recommendations to redirect resources from global supply chains to local inhabitants in conflict-affected regions. This effort directly contributed to a UN resolution in 2017.

Ethical Considerations in Architectural Practice

The built environment is inherently public, representing our lived world—the spaces we inhabit and the relationships we cultivate with one another and the natural environment. This environment is shaped by complex power dynamics influenced by historical processes, ideology, socio-economic factors, and systemic oppression. Thus, the consequences of design reverberate deeply, significantly influencing social relations, environmental health, and individual and collective well-being. When architects and designers fail to consider the broader implications of their work, they risk exacerbating inequalities and perpetuating systemic violence. David Harvey argues that "the built environment is a product of power relations, material conditions, and historical processes." Therefore, recognizing the ethical implications of design is crucial for architects, who have the responsibility to shape spaces that can either reinforce or disrupt existing power dynamics.

Several ethical frameworks can be considered when thinking about architecture and the built environment. For instance, Hans Jonas's Imperative of Responsibility emphasizes our duty to avoid harm for both present and future generations and to ensure the well-being of the planet. This call urges designers to embed responsibility for ecological and societal well-being into their practices, allowing for designs that not only address current needs but also protect the rights and environments of future populations. The imperative of responsibility also comes across in Charlotte Malterre-Barthes provocative call for a collective moratorium on new construction, suggesting that we critically assess current development models, which often prioritize growth at the expense of social equity and environmental integrity. [31]

Expanding the "do no harm" into a more nurturing act and the ethics of care, which underlines our responsibility to maintain and repair the world to ensure the well-being of all its inhabitants as extensively explored by Joan Tronto articulates, "Caring requires a political context that defines the relationship between civil society, the state, and the economy."[32] She argues that care is a species activity that encompasses everything we do to maintain, continue, and repair our world so that we may live in it as well as possible. Her perspective emphasizes that our world includes not only our bodies and ourselves but also the broader environment, which we seek to interweave into a complex, life-sustaining web. Thus, can architecture and the design of the built environment in itself become an act of nurturing. Emphasizing the ethics of care in architectural practices can transform how we approach the built environment, leading to designs that prioritize inclusivity, sustainability, and the health of both people and ecosystems.

There is a deep intersectionality between social and environmental justice, as further explored by Carolyn Merchant, who advocates for a shift from the notion of (hu)man dominion to an ethics of partnership. She emphasizes the necessity of recognizing the interconnectedness of human and non-human lives, which can be explored in depth and practically applied through the design of the built environment, particularly in how we consider and integrate diverse species and ecosystems into this design. Merchant asserts that "an ethics of partnership recognizes that the fate of one is bound to the fate of others, both human and ecological." This perspective compels designers to cultivate relationships that prioritize inclusivity and cooperation, enabling them to effectively address the intricate challenges faced by marginalized voices – human or *otherwise*.

At the Foundation for Achieving Seamless Territory (FAST), we embody these ethical frameworks through our projects. For instance, in the *Village: One Land Two Systems* project, we engaged the Ein Hawd community to develop an alternative master plan, empowering residents to assert their rights and actively participate in negotiations with governmental authorities. This initiative illustrates how collaborative design processes center the lived experiences of communities, fostering agency and dignity.

Through the *BLUE* project, we challenged institutional protocols by proposing policy recommendations to redirect resources from global supply chains to local inhabitants in conflict-affected regions. This effort contributed to a UN resolution in 2017, demonstrating the significant influence that design can exert on policy. Additionally, our *Border Ecologies and Gaza Strip*, which won the Silver Lion at the Venice Architecture Biennale, allowed us to document the impact of militarization and border conditions on more-than-human lives, including other species, materials, and things (Latour), such as watermelons, sardines, and sediments. We experimented with various methods for gathering information from areas under siege, making oral histories visible and public, while creating counter-archives in collaboration with a community of farmers in Gaza.

By integrating these ethical principles and perspectives into our design practices, FAST seeks to empower individuals and collectives and ensure that the spaces we create reflect the identities, histories, and aspirations of those they serve. Bringing together collaborative design, advocacy, and intersectional thinking presents a crucial opportunity to address systemic violence and global challenges. By leveraging our design efforts to expose injustices and promote collective visions, we can contribute to environments that address historical wrongs and advance social and environmental justice.

Conclusion

This essay explores how the personal and cultural histories embedded in our built environment reveal the power structures, history, and cultural expressions that shape conflict-affected areas. By applying an intersectional lens, architects and urban planners can better address the nuanced power dynamics and injustices in these environments. Case studies from the Foundation for Achieving Seamless Territory (FAST) illustrate how design tools can expose systemic violence and collaboratively create spaces and narratives that reflect marginalized voices. Initiatives such as alternative master plans for Ein Hawd and the "Border Ecologies and the Gaza Strip" project demonstrate architecture's potential for intervention, advocacy, and social change. By partnering with diverse stakeholders, these projects challenge entrenched systems and propose policy recommendations, as seen with project BLUE's influence on a UN resolution. These efforts emphasize the ethical responsibility of designers and the potential agency of architecture to advancing social and environmental justice. Integrating intersectionality and care into design practices fosters a more responsive approach, transforming spaces and reshaping narratives to prioritize justice and the well-being of people and the environment.

-----

[1] Gloria Anzaldúa, *Borderlands/La Frontera: The New Mestiza* (Aunt Lute Books, 1987).

[2] Kimberlé Crenshaw, *Demarginalizing the Intersection of Race and Sex: A Black Feminist Critique of Antidiscrimination Doctrine, Feminist Theory, and Antiracist Politics* (University of Chicago Legal Forum, 1989), 139-167.

[3] US Department of Energy, *The Effects of Radiation on Native American Communities: Environmental Justice and Health* (US Department of Energy, 2020).

[4] Karen Barad, *Meeting the Universe Halfway: Quantum Physics and the Entanglement of Matter and Meaning* (Duke University Press, 2007).

[5] J. Kēhaulani Kauanui, "Nuclear Colonialism: Environmental Racism and the Ripple Effects of US Military Policy," *Social Justice*, 43, no. 3 (2016): 1-10.

[6] Aldo Leopold, *A Sand County Almanac* (Oxford University Press, 1949).

[7] Timothy Morton, *Hyperobjects: Philosophy and Ecology After the End of the World* (University of Minnesota Press, 2013).

[8] B'tselem, *Gaza Strip: The Impact of the Gaza War on the Environment* (B'tselem, 2021).

[9] World Health Organization, "Health in the Gaza Strip: A Situation Report," 2021.

[10] United Nations, "Gaza Blockade: A Violation of Human Rights and International Law," 2021.

[11] SIPRI, *Military Expenditure Database* (Stockholm International Peace Research Institute, 2022).

[12] Uppsala Conflict Data Program, "UCDP Battle-Related Deaths Dataset," 2022.

[13] Michael R. Klare, *The Race for What's Left: The Global Scramble for the World's Last Resources* (Metropolitan Books, 2020).

[14] Oxfam, *The Climate Crisis and Militarization: A Deadly Relationship* (Oxfam, 2021).

[15] Angela Friedrich, *The Kyoto Protocol: What It Is, What It Does, and Why It Matters* (United Nations Climate Change, 2011).

[16] World Resources Institute (WRI), "How Military Operations Contribute to Climate Change," 2020.

[17] Mariana Mazzucato, *Mission Economy: A Moonshot Guide to Changing Capitalism* (Harper Business, 2021).

[18] Michael Klare, *The Race for What's Left: The Global Scramble for the World's Last Resources* (Metropolitan Books, 2020).

[19] United Nations, "Protecting and Restoring the Amazon: A Call for Action," 2021.

[20] Berenice Fisher and Joan C. Tronto, "Toward a Feminist Theory of

Caring," *Circles of Care*, ed. Emily K. Abel and Margaret Nelson (SUNY Press, 1990), 40; Joan C. Tronto, *Moral Boundaries: A Political Argument for an Ethic of Care* (Routledge, 1993), 103.

[21] Sara Ahmed, Willful Subjects (italicized) (Duke University Press, 2014).

[22] Crenshaw, "Demarginalizing the Intersection of Race and Sex," 139-167.

[23] Karen Crenshaw, "Mapping the Margins: Intersectionality, Identity Politics, and Violence Against Women of Color," *The Public Nature of Private Violence: The Discovery of Domestic Abuse* (Routledge, 1991), 93-118.

[24] Angela Davis, *Women, Race & Class* (Random House, 1983).

[25] Anzaldúa, *Borderlands/La Frontera*.

[26] Gloria Anzaldúa, *Interviews/Entrevistas*, ed. AnaLouise Keating (University of Texas Press, 1999).

[27] Malkit Shoshan, *Atlas of the Conflict: Israel-Palestine* (nai010, 2011).

[28] Malkit Shoshan and Maurizio Bortolotti, *Village: One Land Two Systems and Platform Paradis* (Damiani Editore, 2014).

[29] Zoo, or the Letter Z, Just After Zionism: https://seamlessterritory.org/zoo-or-the-letter-z-just-after-zionism/

[30] Malkit Shoshan, *BLUE: The Architecture of UN Peacekeeping Missions* (Actar, 2023).

[31] Charlotte Malterre-Barthes, "A Global Moratorium on New Construction" https://www.charlottemalterrebarthes.com/practice/research-practice/a-global-moratorium-on-new-construction/

[32] Ibid.

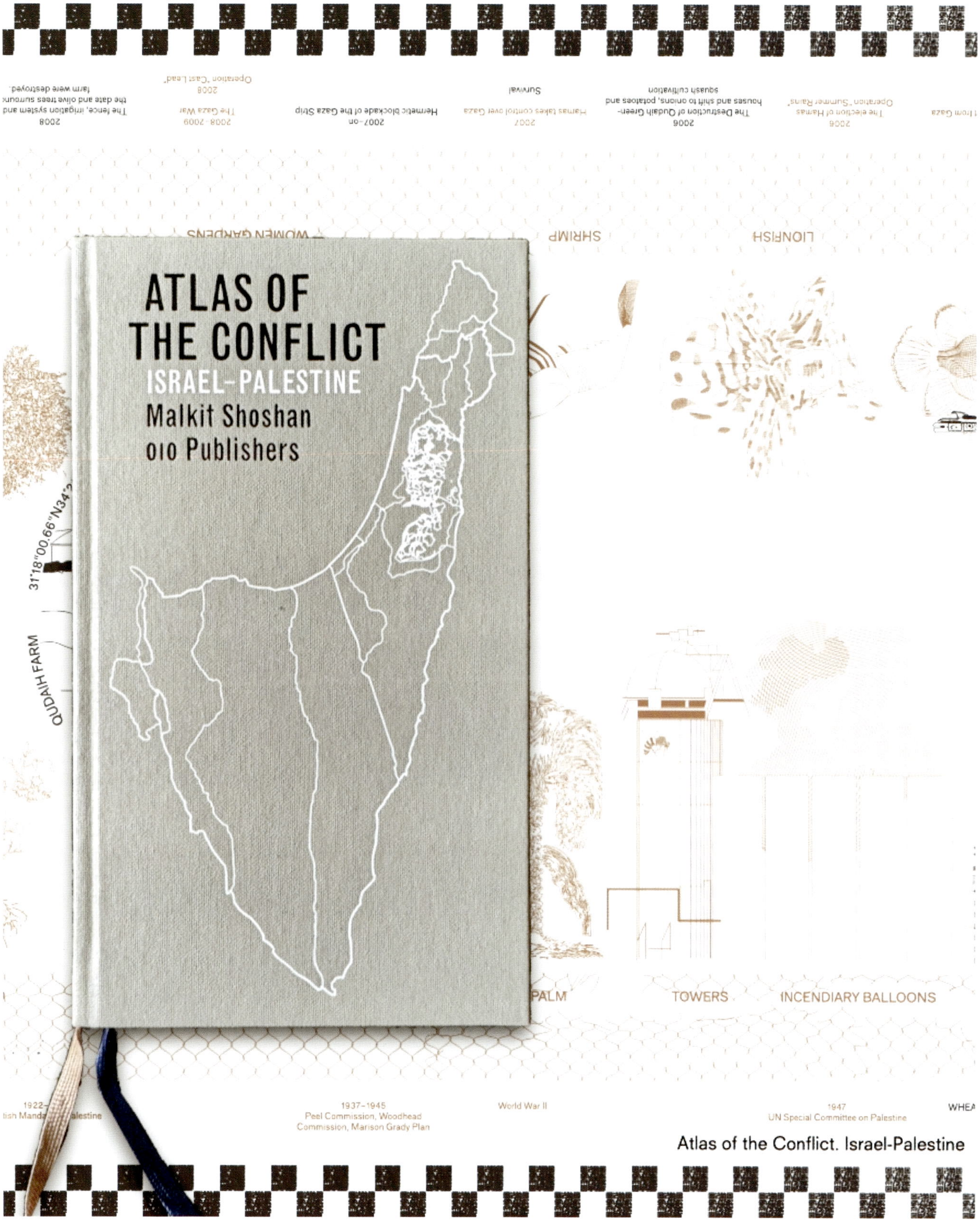

Fig. 1 "Designing Within Conflict: Building for Peace," presentations, projects, and stories, 2024 (images by Malkit Shoshan).

Fig. 2 "Designing Within Conflict: Building for Peace," presentations, projects, and stories, 2024 (images by Malkit Shoshan).

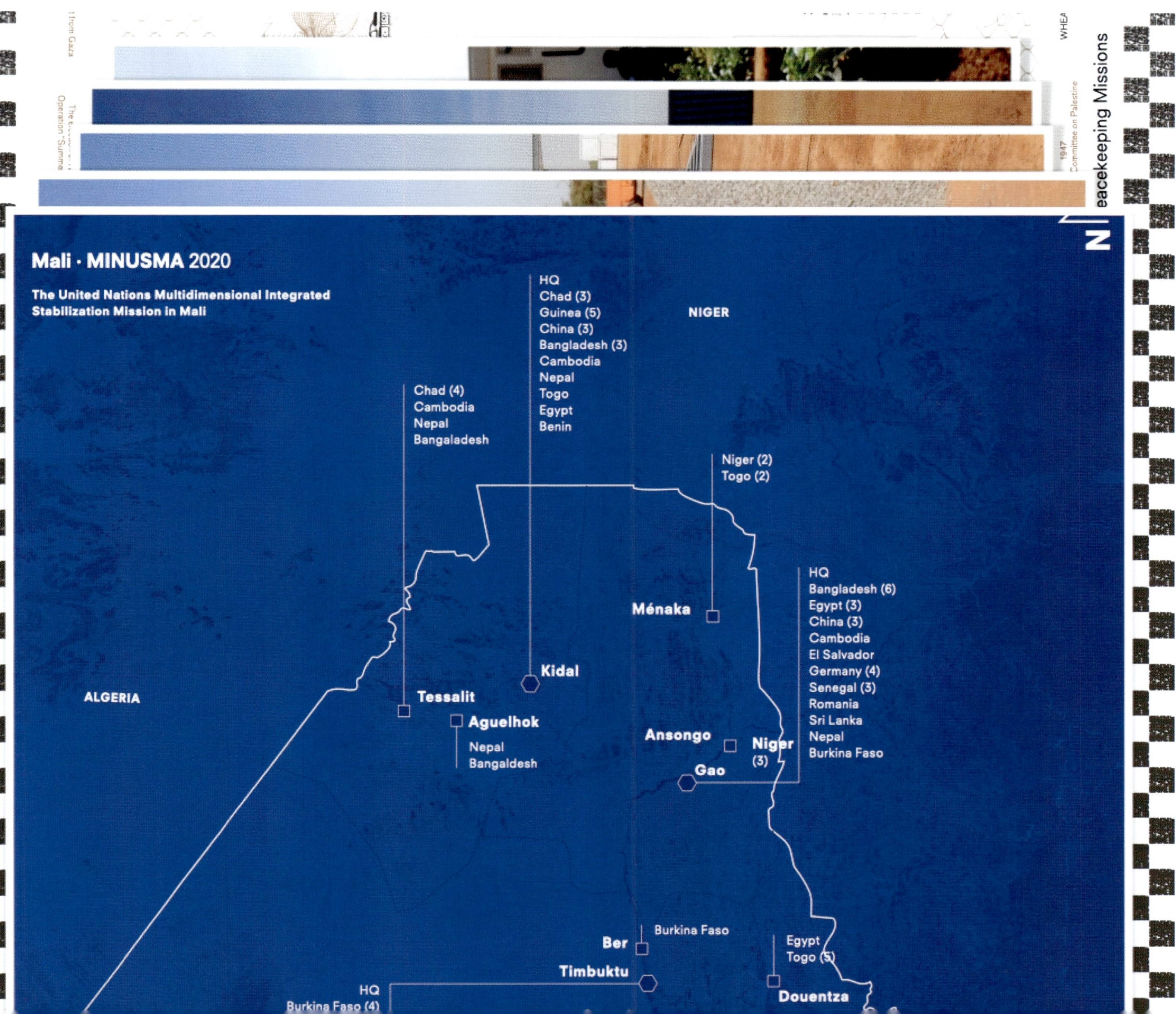

eacekeeping Missions

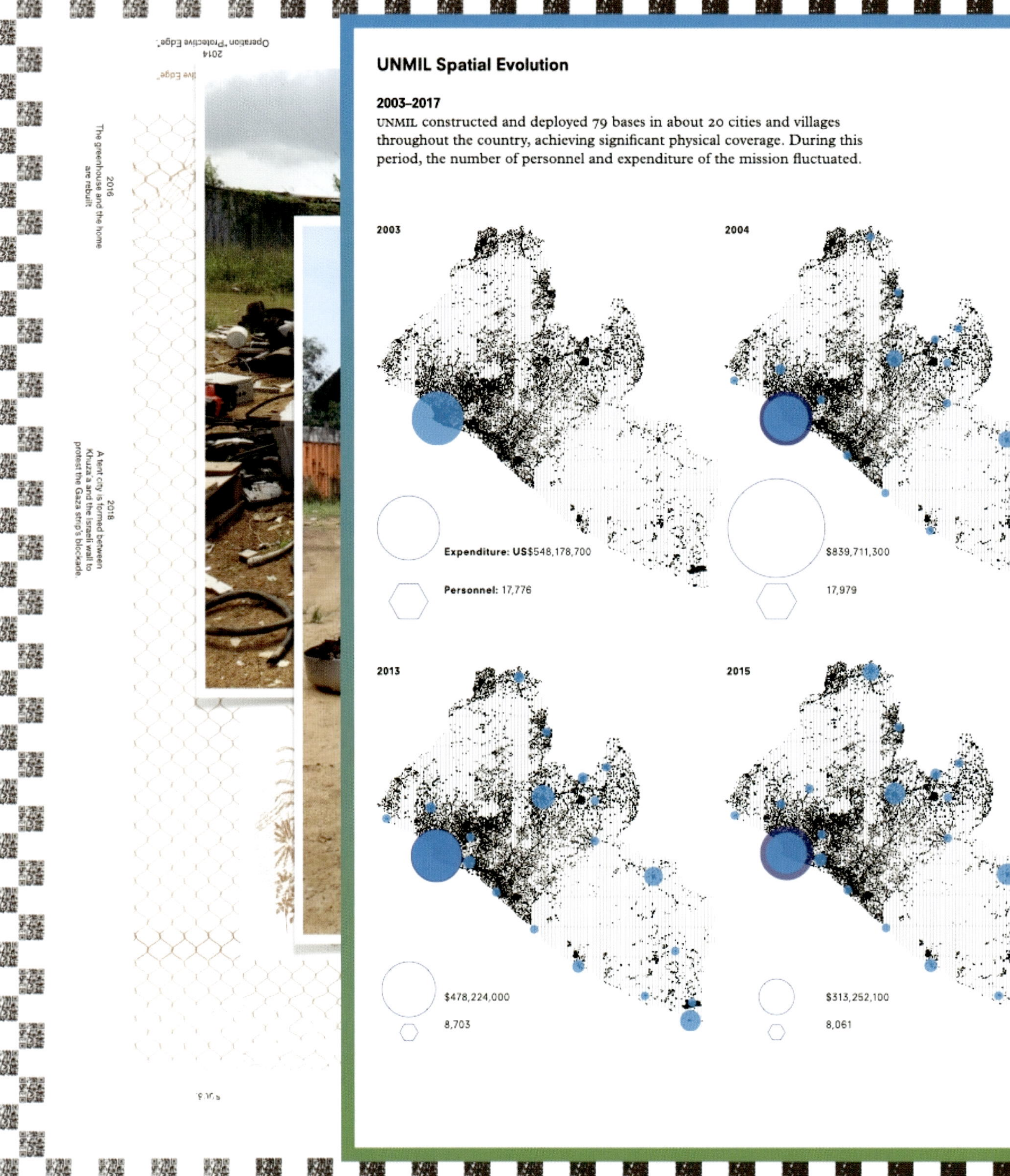

Fig. 3 "Designing Within Conflict: Building for Peace," presentations, projects, and stories, 2024 (images by Malkit Shoshan).

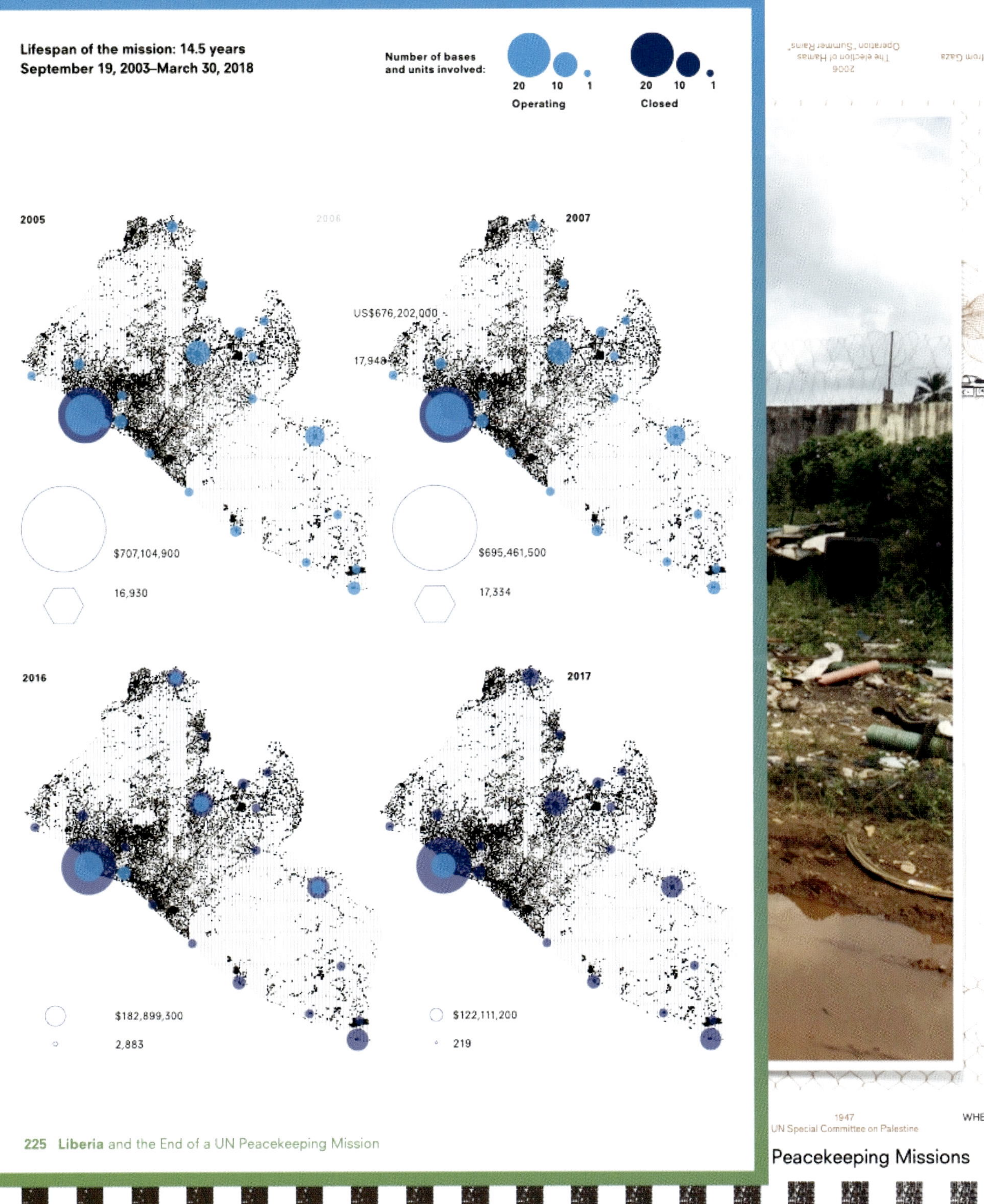

Lifespan of the mission: 14.5 years
September 19, 2003–March 30, 2018
Number of bases and units involved:
20 10 1
Operating
20 10 1
Closed
2005
2006
2007
US$676,202,000
17,948
$707,104,900
16,930
$695,461,500
17,334
2016
2017
$182,899,300
2,883
$122,111,200
219
1947
UN Special Committee on Palestine
Peacekeeping Missions

Fig. 4 "Designing Within Conflict: Building for Peace," presentations, projects, and stories, 2024 (images by Malkit Shoshan).

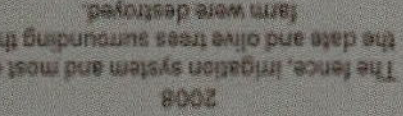

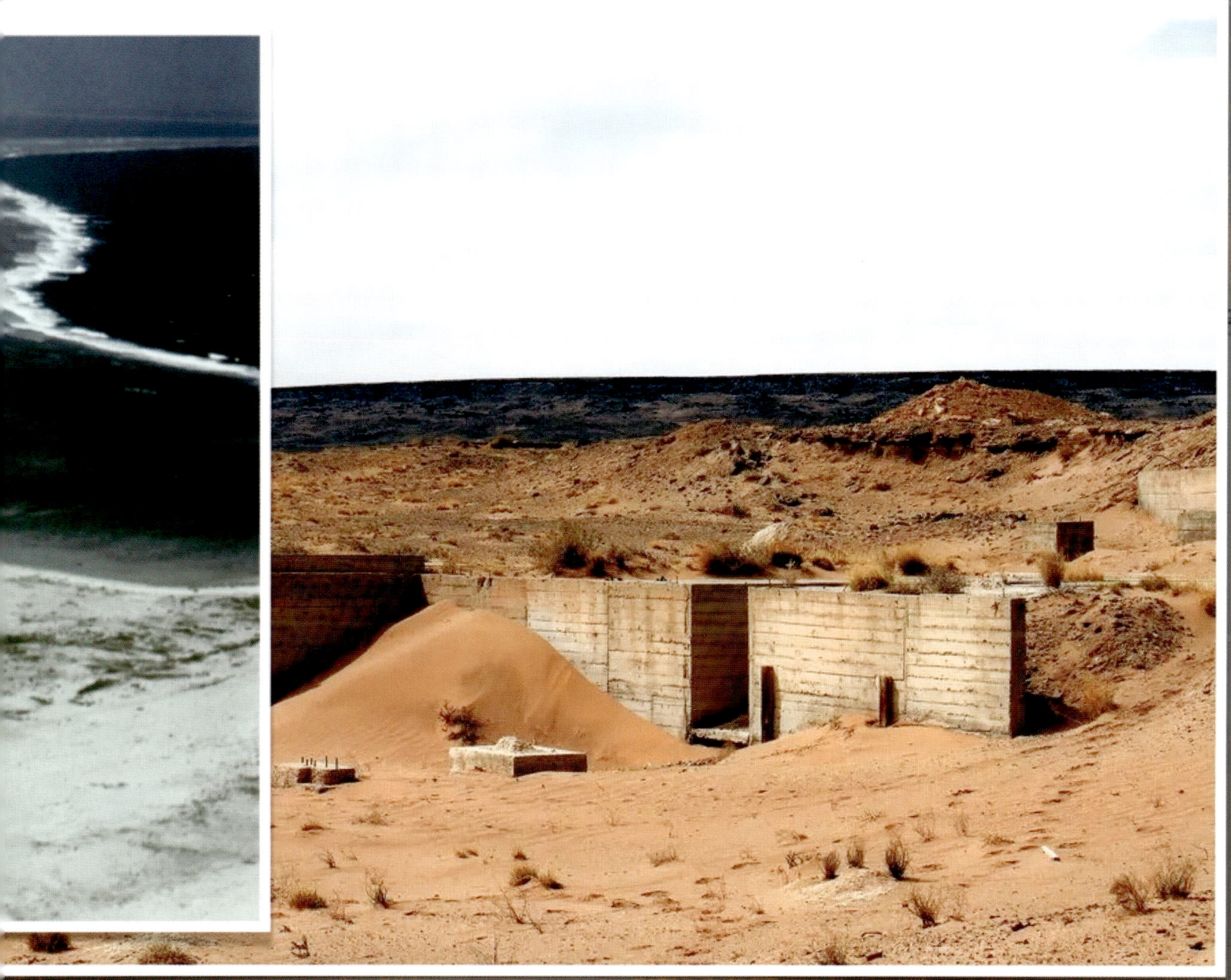

nium mine on the Navajo reservation in Cameron, Ariz., emits dangerous levels of radiation.
tt for The New York Times

IATO GOLD WATER DATE PALM TOWERS INCENDIARY BALLOONS

1922–1948
British Mandate in Palestine

1937–1945
Peel Commission, Woodhead Commission, Manson Grady Plan

World War II

1947
UN Special Committee on Palestine

WHEA

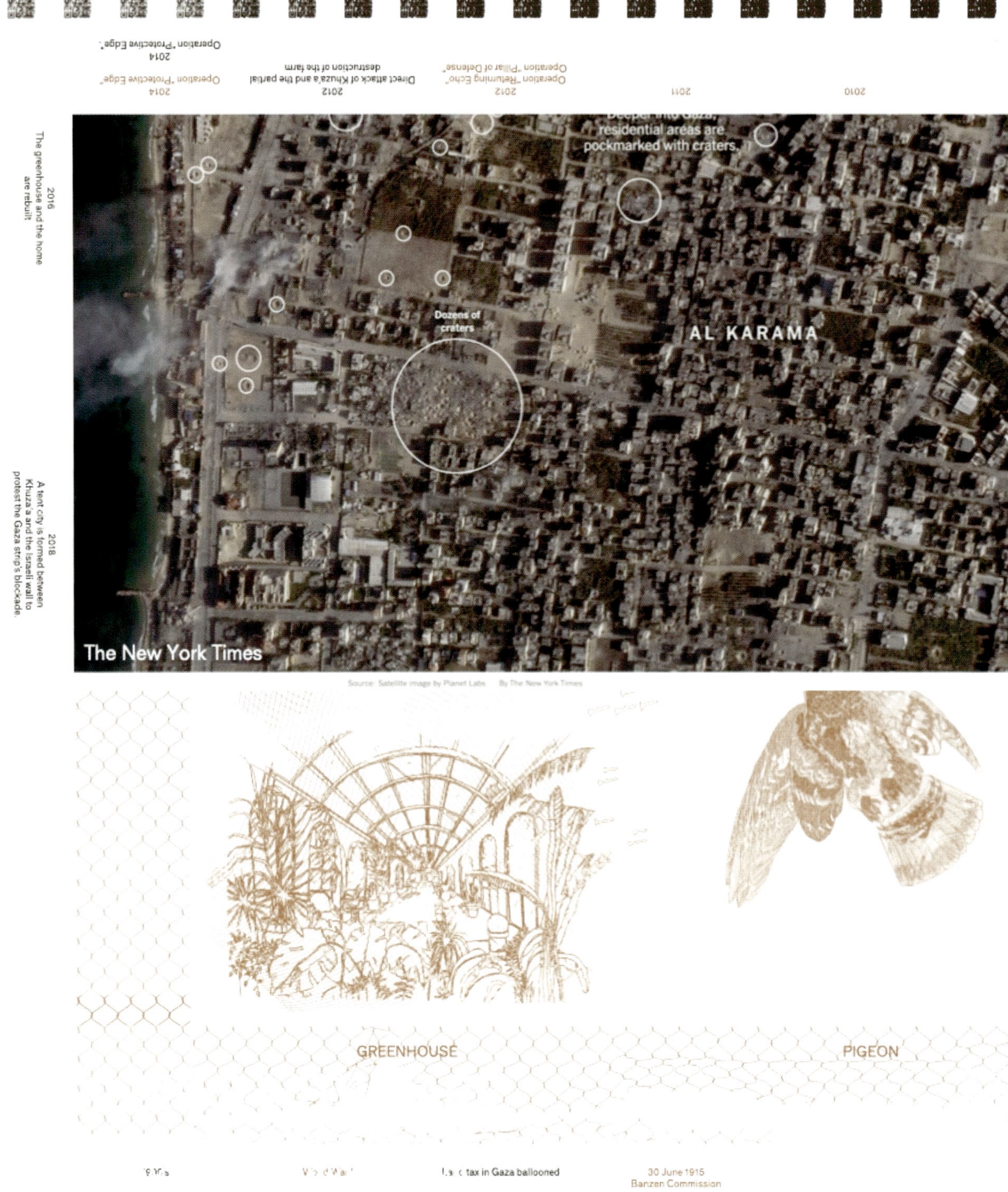

Fig. 5 "Designing Within Conflict: Building for Peace," presentations, projects, and stories, 2024 (images by Malkit Shoshan).

from Gaza

2006
The election of Hamas
Operation "Summer Rains"

2006
The Destruction of Qudaih Greenhouses and shift to onions, potatoes and
squash cultivation

Survival

2007
Hamas takes control over Gaza

2007–on
Hermetic blockade of the Gaza Strip

2008–2009
The Gaza War

2008
Operation "Cast Lead"

2008
The fence, irrigation system and most o
the date and olive trees surrounding th
farm were destroyed.

LIONFISH

SHRIMP

WOMEN GARDENS

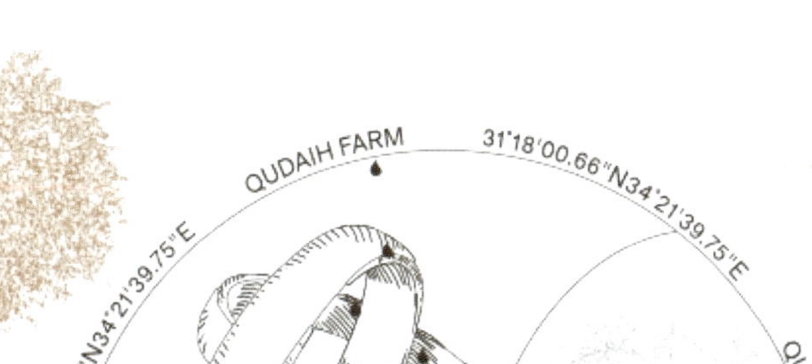

ATO

1922–1948
British Mandate in Palestine

1937–1945
Peel Commission, Woodhead
Commission, Marison Grady Plan

World War II

1947
UN Special Committee on Palestine

WHEA

Fig. 6 "Designing Within Conflict: Building for Peace," presentations, projects, and stories, 2024 (images by Malkit Shoshan).

1922–1948
British Mandate in Palestine
Architecture and Machinery
Indoor Agriculture
Vertical Farms
LED Lighting
Industrial Greenhouses
Agriculture
11%
Monocultures
GMOs
Palm Oil
Corn
Wheat
Soy
Cotton
Irrigation Systems
Pesticides
Industrial Agriculture
Fertilizers
Soil Moisture and Temperature Sensors
Logging Machines
Livestock
60%
Intensive Piggeries
Intensive Feedlots
Enclosed Sheds
Hens in Battery Cages
Net Pens
Humans
36%
Wild Mammals
4%
erated Growth Industry

Core and Coastline

The State of Political Exception in Beirut

May Khalife

The urban environment in Beirut, Lebanon, reflects the invisible politics at play in the public and private realms. In a state of political exception, militarized interventions suspend the conventional rule of law and withhold the state's obligation to universal common good. The militarization of Beirut alters the built and natural environment with the establishment of boundaries around exclusive sites. Militarized interventions reinforce this condition of exception by distinguishing and regulating spaces, resources, and populations. The aim of this chapter is to reveal the spatial conditions and underlying political forces behind these militarized places. The study of two areas in Beirut, its urban core and its coastline, reveals how the militarization of the environment since the early 2000s worked toward the protection of economic interests and financial profits at the expense of defense and security.

The militarization of Beirut manifests through the construction of fences, roadblocks, checkpoints, concrete walls, and the establishment of exclusionary zoning laws and military installations. In a state of political exception, militarized interventions suspend the conventional rules of law. The philosopher Giorgio Agamben refers to the "state of exception" in his discussion of how security becomes the only source of political legitimacy with the birth of the modern state.[1] It also exceptionalizes certain humans and their practices from the rule of law and establishes sovereignty as the making of a space of negativity, a concept Agamben defines as that of groundlessness and nothingness.[2] The suspension of law in modern democracies leads to the destruction or loss of the everyday experience, which marks contemporary age's nihilistic condition.[3] Similarly, the anthropologist Begoña Aretxaga explains how states suspend the rule of law and use military and police violence in a state of political exception to proclaim sovereignty.[4] Measures of security lead to the gradual depoliticization of society and the institutionalization of terror. Instead of focusing on preventing disorder and crisis, the state's main concern works toward the control and perpetuation of such emergencies of political and economic instability.

An understanding of Lebanon's governance system reveals the way in which the military and political realms intersect to express control over territories, people, and economies. The state exercises its power to militarize the environment through the installation of physical barriers in the urban setting, including the fortification of urban areas and the social construction of divisions between the inside and the outside.[5] It materializes how society organizes itself around the production of exclusion and violence. Stephen Graham describes the new military urbanism as one that involves the "normalization of military paradigms of thought, action, and policy," the "disciplining of bodies, places, and identities," the "sanitization and romanticization of violence" to achieve security and maintain peace, albeit a fragile one.[6] By constructing invisibility, authorities control land and people, and neutralize any efforts toward accountability, resistance, or opposition. This dehumanizes the citizens and strips them of their agency in the built environment.

Beirut's urban core and coastline changed constantly in response to fluctuations in militarized control over the past two decades. Since 2005, with the assassination of Prime Minister Rafik al-Hariri and the Syrian military withdrawal, the government has grappled with multiple social, political, and economic crises. Public spaces were significant places of resistance in the post-2005 period, with the emergence of civic activism and growing awareness of the right to inclusive public space, particularly in Martyrs' Square. Within these urban areas, the control of public spaces increased, especially after the 2011 crisis in Syria and the massive influx of refugees. The assassination of a Lebanese politician in April 2024 by a group of Syrians fueled tensions around the presence of Syrian refugees in the country.[7] This tragic incident is one of many that intensified street brawls and increased public restrictions on Syrian mobility in the last decade.

The militarized control of streets and public spaces increased in response to immigration flows and social movements. Governmental institutions like the Lebanese Armed Forces (LAF) and the Internal Security Forces (ISF) substantiate the increasing militarization of spaces in Beirut. Paradoxically, the LAF has played a significant role as an anchor of stability since the country's independence in 1943. Marked by its integrity and honored reputation, this military institution acts as a conciliatory mediator between the citizens, the government officials, the sectarian leaders with their affiliated political parties. It is one of the major agents of militarization within the purview of state-sanctioned operations. In parallel, the army's militarization perpetuates the status quo and political discords. Under the pretext of preserving national peace, it ultimately protects the political interests of government officials and their business partners.

Through its military institution, the state operates, uses, measures, and controls the city's urban core and its coastline. The center and the coastal margins in Beirut emerge as interlinked geographies, working in tandem between the center of bureaucratic planning and the sites of militarized interventions. The center holds the base of governmental and corporate institutions, which coordinate the militarization of the environment in the public and private spheres. The bureaucratic planning materializes in the urban core and coast respectively through the construction of security borders in the central district and the sites of exclusion and extraction on the seafront.

A Controlled District in a Militarized Landscape

The securitization of the reconstructed central district resulted in the emergence of "militarized landscapes" with highly controlled public spaces.[8] There are primarily two factors that explain the militarization

Fig. 1 The securitized entrance to the Parliament block with a view of the clock tower in Place de l"Étoile or Nejmeh Square. Source: Author, August 2024.

of the environment in Beirut's urban core: the need for increased security and control to protect the Parliament block and other institutional buildings like the Government Palace; and the responsibility to defend the privatization and commodification of land and property in the country's neoliberal economy. Officials intensified militarization in Beirut's city center and its public spaces in times of conflict, particularly during the October 2019 protest movement.

This militarized environment sets up highly securitized and invisible places for control and security, which increased since the early 2000s in response to a series of bombings and assassinations, massive protests, blockades, and riots. The presence of other public institutions like the regional United Nations headquarters (ESCWA fortification wall), the planning authority known as the Council of Development and Reconstruction (CDR), the bank headquarters and embassies (British, Australian, Japanese) further exacerbated this military control over the surrounding areas. These buildings are representative of the different forms of control and their implications on the built environment. The local Beaux-arts trained architect Pierre el-Khoury designed and completed the ESCWA building during the postwar reconstruction period in 1997. It occupies a full block facing the Gebran Khalil Gebran Park with its glazed central atrium, prominent entrance, solid side exterior walls, and curved corners. As it stands today, the precast concrete security walls surrounding it turned the nine-story development into a massive fortification. Lift arms and army booths, heavy blocks, and movable security measures reinforced a militarized control of space, particularly in response to sit-in protests and encampments between December 2006 and May 2008.[9] Authorities added barbed wire and heavy security forces around the Government Palace and Bank Street with the advent of the 2019–2020 protest movement.

Militarization also aims to hide lands and construct invisibility around properties to protect investors' private interests. This militarized security further alienated Beirut's residents from the central district. The postwar reconstruction efforts in downtown turned the districts surrounding the Parliament block into a neoliberal safe haven for high-end luxury stores and multinational company investments.[10] Private joint-stock companies such as Solidere took over the reconstruction process of the heavily damaged postwar city center and turned it into a commodified territory regulated by the purchase of stocks and the management of properties with high capital value.[11] The resulting "controlled district" in the business center contributed to the systematic violation of property rights, the exclusion of local communities, and the profiteering of war criminals. The center city is also the locus of decision making in the planning of the acquired and reclaimed lands, a point discussed in the next section of this paper. Solidere acquired Beirut's waterfront. Although open to the public, the sidewalks, deck, and open space in this area are under the constant scrutiny of private guards and surveillance cameras. The spatial planning of this district is a military strategy to protect the investments and businesses and to create an exclusive haven for wealthy upper-class locals, returning expatriates, or foreigners. It perpetuates the stronghold of the neoliberal system of extraction and displacement.

The construction of invisibility here manifests through securitization, commodification, and privatization of the public sphere. The expressions of control within and beyond the boundaries of vision marked these commodified lands and heightened the invisible nature of the forces that dominated them. Hence, invisibility represents the unseen political and economic forces, which perpetuate forms of violence and constantly reshape Beirut's public spaces. It also refers to the conditions of spaces that seem public but are hidden in plain sight. In the marina redevelopment known as Zaitunay Bay and the yacht club, the design of Steven Holl Architects and associate architects Nabil Gholam Architecture creates a publicly accessible deck on the lower level of the seafront. Yet, it disconnects the space from the street side by establishing a hierarchy of controlled ramps and staircases. This securitized area restricts social interaction through rules of conduct limiting the free use of public space and streetscapes, forbidding activities like picnics, music performances, bike rides, or gatherings of foreign and domestic workers. The emergence of such "controlled districts" limits the opportunities for encounters between different communities.

Political and financial crises heightened the prospects of militarization. The October 2019 protest

Fig. 2 The militarized street-level access to the center city's luxury hotels near Mansour Assaf Mosque, with Mohammad al-Amin Mosque's minaret and Saint George Maronite Cathedral's tower in the background. Source: Author, August 2024.

movement most recently attested to the increasing militarization of public spaces in the city's center and on its seashores. The economy suffered immensely and still its impact lingers today from the financial engineering operations of the Lebanese central bank and the country's commercial banks. These corporate and capitalist institutions, directed by the central bank, imposed ad hoc capital controls on their small and medium depositors – the majority of the middle-class citizens and noncitizens.[12] Enraged by such informal financial practices, crowds took to the streets and attacked the accessible Automated Teller Machines (ATMs). In response to this disruption, the banks as well as commercial storefronts and hotels blocked off their street-level façades with plywood boards and barbed wires. The institutional bodies of the LAF and ISF endorsed and maintained this unwarranted militarized control as they did in the crackdown on protesters.

The violent encounters between the demonstrators and the armed forces took place against the backdrop of a highly aestheticized corporate and commercial environment in the city center. Protesters responded with an escalation of resistance. Unable to withdraw money or complete account transactions, the depositors resorted to armed bank robberies to "steal" money from their own financial accounts.[13] Bank authorities shut their doors and called for security support to protect the employees and fend off the hostage standoffs. By demonizing the public interface of the automated machines, the banks' policies and depositors' actions further exacerbated the militarization of the streetscape. These controlled urban conditions represent moments of crisis in which the party in power constructs impenetrable boundaries of forced invisibility to prevent the citizens from rightful access to their own bank accounts.

This violence was representative of more opaque forms of exclusion and oppression. The central district's institutions and businesses used their building enclosures to reinforce such symbols of power and control. In his essay "Through the Looking Glass," Shawn Rickenbacker analyzes how the struggle of social equity and spatial justice in the public realm transformed the nature of building enclosures, particularly display windows and storefronts.[14] Security barriers replaced the commercialized aesthetic of glass and transparency to protect the enterprises of commerce and capitalism. This illustrates the intricate relationship between systems of exclusion and oppression and the built environment. The empty streets and high-end stores, combined with the securitized urban center, enabled a highly controlled and militarized form of neoliberalism.

To further support this militarization, the army and police forces closed off many roads between the center city and its traditional working-class surrounding neighborhoods like Basta and Bashoura, further increasing the gap between the socioeconomic classes. The urban environment conveys and produces new forms of political and military action, similar to the cutting of boulevards in Paris to resist public unrest and protest under the purview of Baron Haussmann. The enforcement of impenetrable boundaries kept out "undesirable" populations, including the angry depositors and protesters. Street militarization hindered people's mobility and segregated them not only based on class and status but also on established "sectarian geographies," which circumscribe the limits of sectarian communities.[15] Major religious-political organizations further contribute to the state-sanctioned militarization by strategically using militia-operated interventions.

Military urbanism reinforces existing inequalities in spatial access and movement, and produces an "uneven and insecure citizenship," according to Kristin Monroe.[16] As Hiba Bou Akar claims in the "logic of the wars yet to come," the militarization of everyday urban life transforms ordinary urban spaces into militarized frontier zones, always in anticipation of future violence and terror.[17] The territorial battles operate along sectarian lines and infiltrate both the public and private sectors. Such conflicts exacerbate the militarization of the built and natural environment.

Fig. 3 The concrete structures of the Military Club's seaside resort connecting to Émile Lahoud's beach house near the Manara lighthouse. Source: Author, August 2024.

This arbitrary construction of invisibility perpetrates physical and psychological violence on the citizens and noncitizens, and ultimately targets the ecological wealth and natural resources of the coastal land.

The Coastline as a Site of Exclusion and Extraction

Beirut's model of neoliberal urbanism undermines the nation's social welfare and its natural ecosystem. This militarized landscape, including the city's contested waterfront, protects the interests of local investors and foreign capital at the expense of people and nature. It engages a process of profiteering urbanization founded on the exclusion and extraction of human and nonhuman resources. Ethnographic researcher Aihwa Ong describes it as the phenomenon of "neoliberalism as exception," which limits the scope of governance to position the state in the competitive global economy.[18] It reduces the capacity of sovereignty and territoriality to exceptional practices of governance and tactics of domination. In this context, the military forces at play recreate the coastline as a site of exclusion and extraction in public and private investments.

The "Central Military Club" on Beirut's coastline, an establishment set up by the French army since 1942, known as the "*Bain Militaire*," or the "Military Bath," enforced the exclusion of social classes and the establishment of social hierarchies between the privileged groups and the working classes. In 1958, this seaside resort was a place of refuge for the US Army during the first US military invasion in the Middle East, known as Operation Blue Bat.[19] In May 1975, the Lebanese government took over the land development

Fig. 4 The securitized borders to the Military Club with a checkpoint, barbed wire, and oversized solar panels. Source: Author, August 2024.

and expanded it into an army tourist facility affiliated with the Lebanese Armed Forces (LAF).[20] Today, the Bain Militaire offers a seaside retreat to the country's military officers, their families, and guests.[21] The militarization of this space is highly contested by the public opinion because of the costly commissions involved in its reconstruction and expansion. The massive project underwent two major reconstruction phases, one in 2005–2007 and another one in 2021.[22] The 2000s redevelopment was funded by then-president and former army commander Émile Lahoud to promote his personal interests and access his own beach house in the military club.[23]

A series of concrete structures frame two coastal bays, protected by a man-made island extending into the sea with sport courts, pools, and piers. It sits on the coastal boulevard of Avenue Général de Gaulle and reserves a strategic corner in the upscale seaside neighborhood of *Ras Beirut* (Tip of Beirut), next to the new Manara lighthouse.[24] A fortification of thick walls and overscaled solar panels fences off the exclusive resort, built into the natural limestone cliffs on the coast. The militarized space incentivizes a selected group of civilians to enter the facility with their affiliations to syndicates and professional orders. The facility accommodates different classes of people, yet it reflects the hierarchical orders of the military institution within segregated areas. This synthetic landscape enables the militarization of the environment by using public monies while obfuscating public access to the beach.

The state-sanctioned militarization of the coastline simultaneously mirrors the militarized interventions of the profiteering higher political-economic classes. Right next to the Bain Militaire, a number of private investments sprang up along the Beiruti coast. Every seaside development established its own boundaries, further reinforcing its invisibility and the process of extraction from nature. The story of Beirut's Dalieh and the fight to save it are representative of yet another attempt to militarize the city's seashore.[25] The peninsula of Dalieh overlooks the officially protected and national landmark of the Raouché (Pigeons' Rock). The land is a natural reserve and a space open for the public, including Beiruti fishermen, local visitors, Iraqi and Syrian refugees. It is also a place for the Kurdish community in Lebanon to celebrate the Nowruz festival, marking the spring equinox.[26] In 2013, the municipality ordered armed forces to install metal fences and barbed wire, and to send eviction notices to the fishing communities who lived there.[27]

The state representatives spearheaded the instant militarization of the site in preparation for a new coastal development. Property ownership of this land varied over time between public domain and private ownership. Yet a change in the legal framework in the 1990s increased the exploitation factor on the coast and permitted private investments on public domain. A new form of ownership by al-Hariri's real estate companies was likely to transform this natural site into a high-end touristic project, allegedly designed by the star architect Rem Koolhaas.[28] Authorities from Beirut's municipality fenced off the area, placed a guard kiosk and large concrete wave breakers, or accropodes, to restrict any public access to the beach. With the deliberate yet stealthy construction of invisibility around this site, the authorities did not expect to draw people's attention to it. Unsurprisingly, a public outcry over this news mobilized a grassroots group and a coalition of individuals and non-governmental organizations to protect the urban commons in Dalieh.[29]

The control of seashores in Beirut promotes different forms of violence, which limits the citizens' agency and subjects them to pollution, displacement, and disempowerment. The development of dumpsites like the coastal landfills of Bourj Hammoud and Jdeideh, on the northeastern side of Beirut, is a symptom of the country's failing neoliberal policies and legislations.[30] The waste management infrastructure is a profitable source of income for many politicians and sectarian parties. They commission private subcontractors and business partners, often affiliated with elite political and sectarian allegiances, and collect rubble and waste in landfills to develop land reclamation projects.[31] Decision-makers transform these waste sites into highly profitable real estate ventures, two cases of which are the reclamation of the Normandy Landfill and the present Linord reclamation project.[32] Solidere's "Waterfront District"—also owned by al-Hariri—is a lucrative real estate development associated with the Normandy private waste management business located on the northern side of the central district.

The waste management crisis in 2015 foregrounds the problem of landfills in the country.[33] Instead of allowing municipal authorities to oversee a safe, workable plan for solid waste collection, politicians monopolize the landfills' development to maximize their profits, and armed forces support their ventures.[34] The militarization of the environment in this case is apparent not only in the control of waste collection and land management, but also in the violence surrounding the creation of these militarized spaces. The waste crisis mobilized the You Stink social

Fig. 5 The natural peninsula of Dalieh marked by large concrete wave breakers near the Raouché landmark. Source: Author, August 2024.

movement to force the government into addressing the environmental and health hazards of landfills.[35] Although these dumpsites were far from invisible, the police brutality and the divisive condemnations of the social movement attempted to stifle the reasonable concerns of the demonstrators. The invisible forces at play here worked toward dehumanizing the most vulnerable populations, particularly those who lived in the affected marginalized areas.

The politicization of coastal lands works in tandem with the militarization of the environment, just as the city's core and coastal margins operate as interlinked geographies. The market-driven capital regulations, compounded with mismanagement and lack of accountability, historically led to disastrous consequences, such as the tragic port blast of August 2020. Militarized interventions in the urban space turn the coastline into a "technical land," to use Jeffrey S. Nesbit and Charles Waldheim's terms.[36] These sites of exclusion and surveillance are rendered invisible in highly aestheticized geographies, despite being geographically close. The state perpetrates ecological violence in anticipation of future real-estate development or so-called technical violence. The limitations, and thus damages, imposed on such sites invoke the relation of capital to nature and the tensions between human and nonhuman places. Religious and political organizations vie to control and militarize these places as tools of power brokerage. This explains the strong relation between the places of administration in the center city and the damaged coastal landscapes. The state normalizes violence through a techno-bureaucratic lens and engineers the damaged landscapes to increase the land's capital value.

Such a state of neoliberal exception keeps citizens and noncitizens on guard, always expecting violent disruptions in the cityscape. The construction of invisibility through militarized landscapes perpetuates the state of precarity and insecurity while the neoliberal capitalist globalization process continues to erode the functions of the governing state. The global neoliberal policies reduce the social safety nets and reinforce the feeling of being unsupported by the state, the feeling of statelessness.[37] The militarization of the environment, coupled with the frail neoliberal system, invokes conditions of precarity and uncertainty, associated with a frail legal and democratic system.[38] By compromising the employment and livelihood of a large group of its consumers, it also disenfranchises vulnerable populations through its fragile exclusionary political, social, and economic system. The exceptional political strategies in Beirut's urban core and coastline reveal the complex nature of Lebanon's governance and how it directs its military urbanization toward a continuous state of exception.

-----

[1] Giorgio Agamben, "Security and Terror," *Theory and Event* 5, no.4 (2001): 1–2. Giorgio Agamben, *State of Exception*, orig. *Il Stato eccezione* (2003), tr. Kevin Attell (University of Chicago Press, 2005), 1–5.

[2] Giorgio Agamben, *Language and Death: The Place of Negativity*, orig. Il linguaggio e la morte: Un seminario sul luogo della negatività (1982), tr. Karen E. Pinkus and Michael Hardt (University of Minnesota Press, 1991), xi–xiii.

[3] Ibid. See also, Giorgio Agamben, *Infancy and History*, orig. Infanzia et storia (1978), tr. Liz Heron (Verso, 1993), 11–64.

[4] Begoña Aretxaga, "Maddening States," *Annual Review of Anthropology* 32, no.1 (2003): 393–410.

[5] Stephen Graham, "The New Military Urbanism," *Cities under Siege: The New Military Urbanism* (Verso, 2010), 60–88.

[6] Ibid., 60.

[7] Maya Gebeily, "Killing of Party Official Fuels Tensions in Lebanon," *Reuters*, April 9, 2024, https://www.reuters.com/world/middle-east/killing-party-official-fuels-sectarian-political-tensions-lebanon-2024-04-09/.

[8] Christine Mady, "The Evolutions, Transformations, and Adaptations in Beirut's Public Spaces," *Urban Planning* 7, no.1 (2022): 116–128, https://doi.org/10.17645/up.v7i1.4724. See also Mona Fawaz, Mona Harb, Ali Gharbiyeh, "Living Beirut's Security Zones: An Investigation of the Modalities and Practice of Urban Security," *City & Society* 24, no.2 (2012): 173–195.

[9] Beirut Urban Lab, "Mapping Security in Beirut: A Decade of Research," https://beiruturbanlab.com/en/Details/620.

[10] Marieke Krijnen and Mona Fawaz, "Exception as the Rule: High-End Developments in Neoliberal Beirut," *Built Environment* 36, no. 2 (2010): 245–59. http://www.jstor.org/stable/23290069.

[11] Owned by the late prime minister Rafik al-Hariri, Solidere expropriated the majority of the land in Beirut's city center in the 1990s. This real-estate company started in partnership with the CDR, the official public planning advisory body. In Saree Makdisi, "Laying Claim to Beirut: Urban Narrative and Spatial Identity in the Age of Solidere," *Critical Inquiry* 23, no.3 (Spring 1997): 665–668, 675.

[12] "World Bank Accuses Lebanese Politicians of Cruelty over Deposit Promises," Reuters, August 3, 2022, https://www.reuters.com/markets/emerging/world-bank-accuses-lebanese-politicians-cruelty-over-deposit-promises-2022-08-03/.

[13] Timour Azhari and Emilie Madi, "On the Run, Lebanese Woman Who Stole Own Savings Says She's Not the Criminal," Reuters, September 22, 2022, https://www.reuters.com/world/middle-east/run-lebanese-woman-who-stole-own-savings-says-shes-not-criminal-2022-09-21/. See also Zach Goldbaum and Todd Bieber, "Meet the World's Most Honorable Bank Robbers," *New York Times* video, 8:39, February 28, 2023, https://www.nytimes.com/2023/02/28/opinion/lebanon-crisis-economy-bank-robbers.html. 28-year-old interior designer Sali Hafiz, who forcefully retrieved part of her family's savings in a bank holdup to treat her cancer-stricken sister, is one of many.

[14] Shawn Rickenbacker, "Through the Looking Glass," in *Nature of Enclosure*, ed. Jeffrey S. Nesbit (Actar Publishers, 2022), 210–212, 216.

[15] Joanne Randa Nucho, *Everyday Sectarianism in Urban Lebanon: Infrastructures, Public Services, and Power* (Princeton University Press, 2016), 11. See also Scott A. Bollens, *Bordered Cities and Divided Societies: Humanistic Essays of Conflict, Violence, and Healing* (Routledge, 2021), 43, 52, 59.

[16] Kristin V. Monroe, *The Insecure City: Space, Power, and Mobility in*

Beirut (Rutgers University Press, 2016), 8, 140–141.

[17] Hiba Bou Akar, "Urban Interventions for the Wars Yet to Come," *Middle East Report* 290 (Spring 2019), https://merip.org/2019/07/urban-interventions-for-the-wars-yet-to-come/. Hiba Bou Akar, *For the War Yet to Come: Planning Beirut's Frontiers* (Stanford University Press, 2018).

[18] Aihwa Ong, *Neoliberalism as Exception: Mutations in Citizenship and Sovereignty (*Duke University Press, 2006).

[19] Zina Hemady, "Operation Blue Bat: The 1958 U.S. Invasion of Lebanon," https://www.photorientalist.org/exhibitions/operation-blue-bat-the-1958-u-s-invasion-of-lebanon/article/.

[20] The Official Website of the Lebanese Army, "The Central Military Club," accessed April 21, 2024, https://www.lebarmy.gov.lb/en/content/central-military-club-%E2%80%93-beirut.

[21] The Lebanese government rebranded it as the "Central Military Club," which is part of a larger military complex with institutions in Jounieh, Yarzeh, and the Cedars.

[22] The first major reconstruction was completed in 2005–2007 by S. Mokbel and Partners with the consultant Samir Khairallah and Partners. The complex was redesigned in February 2021 by Maalouf Contracting. In S. Mokbel and Partners, "Bain Militaire" (2007), http://www.smokbel.com/subpages/description.asp?cat_id=3&pro_id=107; Maalouf Contracting Projects, "Bain Militaire Beirut," http://www.maalouftc.com/Contracting/ProjectDetails/68/Bain%20Militaire%20Beirut.

[23] "Le Chalet du Président," *L'Orient-Le Jour*, May 20, 2002, accessed April 27, 2024, https://www.lorientlejour.com/article/376085/Le_chalet_du_president.html.

[24] The old lighthouse was in operation from 1957 to 2003. It was decommissioned because a residential building was constructed, obstructing its view. The new lighthouse was constructed in the early 2000s.

[25] The author participated in the Ideas Competition proposed by the Civil Campaign to Preserve the Dalieh of Beirut, 2015. The aim of this competition was to protect and reclaim the coastal area of Dalieh through a multidisciplinary collaborative work. It responded to looming threats by private developments that would alienate the shared communal space and obscure both access and visibility to the sea.

[26] Abir Saksouk-Sasso, "Making Spaces for Communal Sovereignty: The Story of Beirut's Dalieh," *Arab Studies Journal* 23, no. 1 (2015): 296–318, http://www.jstor.org/stable/44744909.

[27] Ibid.

[28] Dictaphone Group, "The Sea Is Mine: Sound Piece and Research Booklet on Beirut Coastline," *Jadaliyya*, May 27, 2014, https://www.jadaliyya.com/Details/30708.

[29] Alice Stefanelli, "Contesting Property: Urban Commons, Statecraft, and the 'Tyranny' of Liberalism in Lebanon," *Journal of the Royal Anthropological Institute* 29, no.2 (June 2023): 421–438.

[30] The Bourj Hammoud landfill started as an uncontrolled dumpsite during the Lebanese Civil War. The Bourj Hammoud/Jdeideh site was proposed as a stopgap measure to address the 2015 solid waste management crisis, which hit Beirut and the Mount Lebanon area with the overflowing of the Naameh landfill and the piling up of garbage in the streets. See Global Atlas of Environmental Justice, https://ejatlas.org/conflict/naameh-landfill-lebanon; "Lebanon: Beirut Landfill Near Capacity," *Human Rights Watch*, June 25, 2019, https://www.hrw.org/news/2019/06/25/lebanon-beirut-landfill-near-capacity.

[31] Monica Basbous, "From the Rubble of Beirut," *Architectural Review*, June 9, 2021, https://www.architectural-review.com/essays/city-portraits/from-the-rubble-of-beirut.

[32] Michael Young, "Your Poison, My Profit," Carnegie Middle East Center, August 28, 2019, https://carnegie-mec.org/diwan/79729; Salah Sadek and Mutasem El-Fadel, "The Normandy Landfill: A Case Study in Solid Waste Management," *Journal of Natural Resources and Life Sciences Education* 29, no.1 (2000): 155–161, https://doi.org/10.2134/jnrlse.2000.0155. See also Basbous, "From the Rubble of Beirut."

[33] The Naameh landfill, open since 1997 in the south of Beirut as a temporary landfill despite the residents' opposition, exceeded its capacity in 2015, and the government failed to extend the contract of the only trash collector in Beirut and Mount Lebanon. This led to an environmental disaster, with solid waste piling up in illegal dumpsites on the streets, under bridges, in the valleys, etc.

[34] Ziad Abu-Rish, "Garbage Politics," *Middle East Report* 277, no.1 (Winter 2015), https://merip.org/2016/03/garbage-politics/.

[35] Nisrine Chaer, "The Biopolitics of the Lebanese Garbage Crisis," *Global Dialogue* 6, no. 2 (June 9, 2016): 1, https://globaldialogue.isa-sociology.org/articles/the-biopolitics-of-the-lebanese-garbage-crisis.

[36] Jeffrey S. Nesbit and Charles Waldheim, eds., *Technical Lands: A Critical Primer* (Jovis, 2022).

[37] Monroe, *The Insecure City*, 10–11.

[38] Judith Butler, Precarious Life: *The Powers of Mourning and Violence*, 2nd ed. (London: Verso, 2006); Isabell Lorey, "The Government of the Precarious: An Introduction," in *State of Insecurity: Government of the Precarious* (Verso, 2015), 1–15.

Soviet Telescopes in Latin America's Cold War

Pedro Ignacio Alonso
Hugo Palmarola

Chile is reputed to be the country that received the largest ever Soviet-made Maksutov telescope, the AZT-16 instrument. Aimed at studying the stars of the Southern Hemisphere, it was installed in 1967 as part of a scientific mission led by the Academy of Sciences of the Soviet Union and the National Observatory of Pulkovo. The telescope was designed by Dmitri Dmítrievich Maksútov (1896–1964), and it was a remarkable advancement for optical engineering. The country is also alleged to have one of the world's best astronomical observation conditions in the dry and clear-sky environment of the Atacama Desert in northern Chile. However, despite the international campaign initiated in the 1950s by the director of the National Observatory of the University of Chile, Professor Federico Rutllant, to promote the Atacama location—Rutllant had succeeded in the establishment of the Inter-American Observatory (OICT) on Cerro Tololo in 1965 and the European Southern Observatory (ESO) at La Silla in 1966—the Soviet mission was installed in the less favorable locations of Calán and the El Roble hills, near Santiago. This chapter explores reasons behind selected locations, arguing that the installation of Soviet astronomical facilities in Chile was not driven exclusively by scientific, technological, or practical concerns but by strategic logics associated with Cold War and Space Race geopolitics between the USSR and the USA. Inserting itself into the small but growing literature on Cold War history of technology in Latin America, this article offers a narrative that balances previous studies of US intervention in Latin America motivated by Cold War strategizing in relationship with equivalent Soviet endeavors. Presenting the geographical positioning of imported technologies as the unstable balance between science and politics, and documenting a historically important but lesser studied set of Cold War relationships—those between the Soviet Union and Latin America—this examination of the Maksutov AZT-16 unpacks the frictions between Soviet technical objects and the role of their distribution both in Chile and in the South American context more broadly.

According to one of Maksutov's main collaborators, Yuriy Streletskiy, Maksutov's 1941 modification to Bernard Schmidt's 1930 telescopic system was a remarkable advancement for optical engineering: "By adding a correcting spherical lens that prevented hyperbolic deformation, it was easier to fabricate mirror surfaces, avoiding any optical aberration."[1] The advantage of the Maksutov system lies in its simplicity, as the design avoids the need to manufacture hyperbolic lenses, which are more difficult and expensive to make. In addition, the design is more sophisticated because it achieves a greater range of observation despite being a relatively compact instrument, thus redefining the spatial qualities needed in the construction of astronomic domes. This telescope was considered the most important astronomical instrument resulting from the cooperation contract between Chile and the Academy of Sciences of the Soviet Union. The local press described it as a photographic apparatus "specially built to photograph the stars, with a focal length of 2,076 millimeters, with a mirror one meter in diameter; and a double meniscus (correction lens) of 70 millimeters. After locating a star, the tracking engine can follow it. It moves electronically."[2] The telescope was designed to take photographic plates of 18 x 18 centimeters each, and it proved particularly useful for searching for supernovae in southern galaxies.

The decision by the Soviet Union's Academy of Sciences to install this instrument in Chile was made after a 1959 astronomical mission sent to Chile to measure and evaluate the observation conditions in Southern Hemisphere. As a result, in 1960, an initial agreement of collaboration was signed during the conservative government of President Jorge Alessandri Rodríguez, which was followed by the arrival in the country of first group of Soviet scientists on October 12, 1962. The group was led by chief astronomer Mitrofan S. Zverev.[3] Then it began an initiative with far-reaching consequences in the exploration of sites in the Atacama Desert, due to its high altitude, lack of light pollution, and the thin, dry air made it the perfect place for both optical and radio astronomical observations. In fact, by 2030 the Atacama will contain more than half of the astronomical capacity of the world.[4]

All these extraordinary developments began 70 years ago, in the 1950s, with an international campaign initiated by the director of the National Observatory of the University of Chile, Professor Federico Rutllant, to promote the Atacama as a hot spot for astronomy at a global scale. Roughly at the same time, paradoxically, the Soviet mission led by Zverev decided to install their first-class equipment in the less favorable locations of Calán and El Roble hills, near Santiago, despite the fact that the scientific agreements between the Soviet Union and Chile were administrated through the same National Astronomical Observatory of the University of Chile (OAN for the Spanish Observatorio Astronómico Nacional) run by Professor Rutllant.

During the 1950s and '60s, several technological exchanges between Latin American countries and the United States took place within the context of the political, ideological, and economic disputes of the period. These exchanges included the 1957 installation of a US satellite tracking station in Chile as part of the Minitrack Network, a chain of nine stations along the South American continent intended to track radio signals from what was then the United States' Vanguard project, which included locations in the US, (pre-revolutionary) Cuba, Panama, Ecuador, Peru, and Chile. These installations were developed at the Naval Research Laboratory (NRL). Cutting through South America, this initial north-south line was nicknamed "the fence" by its creators at the NRL. Although it was built and administrated by the US Army, this series of stations was installed in 1957, under the banner of science, in the context of the International Geophysical Year (IGY) celebrated between July 1, 1957, and December 31, 1958. As the IGY was coming to a close, the stations were transferred to a new scientific and civilian agency established on October 1 of that year, the National Aeronautics and Space Administration (NASA).

Even though the whole operation belonged to the US military space program, Eisenhower's creation of NASA allowed government officials and aerospace executives and engineers "to eschew the public rhetoric of war in favour of the language of scientific planning and management."[5] Although the history of NASA has been extensively studied, and it has been widely shown that in the United States space exploration was developed primarily with view to its possible military uses, the creation of NASA uncovers the effort invested by the United States to portray the stations in Chile—and the Minitrack Network in general—as a scientific venture. According to Jennifer S. Light, such activities were established for "diverting attention from the nation's other growing space program dominated by military and intelligence data-gathering concerns."[6] [7] Despite the tangible scientific breakthroughs achieved by these satellite tracking networks, an examination of the actual and rhetorical transition from the military-industrial complex to NASA reveals that its creation was an integral component of a well-staged US strategy to shape the agency's desired image for international promotion.[8]

A site in Peldehue, about 50 kilometers north of Santiago, had been chosen by the US Naval Research Laboratory (NRL) and was granted to the United States in a 1956 agreement with the Chilean government and the University of Chile. This installment would serve as the second of two US Army satellite tracking stations in the country. The other facility, built at the Salar del Carmen in the Atacama Desert, was dismantled in 1963 when the increased capacities of new satellites and of the Peldehue station made it redundant. In fact, Peldehue soon became the largest US base in South America, with a support staff of over 300 people, including 100 resident engineers, occupying an enclosed and self-sustained site of more than 100 hectares. In addition to the various types of antennas positioned in its fields, monitoring equipment and computers were housed in one-story buildings prefabricated in the United States by Armco. The station was also fitted with its own electricity generator, medical facilities, ambulance, petrol supply, and fire station.[9]

In October 1957, a year before the establishment of NASA on October 1, 1958, the Minitrack Network was fully operative. The project had begun in March–April 1955 when, under the direction of Captain Winfred Berg, the senior navy project officer assigned to the Vanguard project, a team of NRL and army personnel traveled through South America to locate possible sites and negotiate the necessary agreements with the various countries involved.[10] This site-selection team picked six initial locations: Havana, Panama City, Quito, Lima, Antofagasta, and Santiago.

On July 28, 1955, the White House press secretary James Hagerty announced that President Dwight D. Eisenhower had approved plans for the launching of small, earth-circling satellites as part of the United States' participation in the International Geophysical Year: "The president expressed personal gratification that the American program will provide scientists of all nations this important and unique opportunity for the advancement of science."[11] This announcement was not surprising given Eisenhower's hesitation about the use of manned high-altitude reconnaissance aircraft like the U-2 and OXCART (a concern ultimately proven correct when the Soviet Union shot down Gary Power's U-2 in 1960). Thus, on September 9, 1955, the secretary of the navy assigned the task of setting up the Minitrack stations to the NRL. One year later, in September 1956, the US Army chief of engineers-initiated construction at the six identified sites at the request of NRL. More specifically, the task fell to the specially created Project Vanguard Task Force.[12] Evidence of their overlap can be found not only in the exchange of personnel between the newly formed agency and the US Army, but also in the working of the SPACECONN Communication Network. A diagram included in NASA's Communication Standing Operating Procedures shows that the information gathered at the tracking facilities in Chile,

Peru, Ecuador, and Panama was first delivered to the Pentagon before being forwarded to NASA's Operations Control Center, at the time located in Washington, DC.[13]

The first-ever signal tracked by the NASA Peldehue station was that of Sputnik 1, the satellite successfully launched by the Soviet Union on October 4, 1957, sparking major concern in US military circles. Fearing that the Russians might have other outposts in orbit that could not be detected by a tracking beacon, the US quickly expanded its network of stations on five continents.[14] [15] Between 1957 and 1972, the US government invested roughly one billion dollars in tracking and data acquisition facilities.[16] From 1957 to 1989, more than 22 stations were placed around the world, from the 75th meridian "fence" to its global dissemination in the enlarged STADAN, SATAN, and NASCOM networks.

Following the successful launch of Sputnik 1, the Soviets began construction of their own facilities for astronomical observation. Not coincidentally, selected sites were in the same geographies where the US previously built, including Cuba, Ecuador, Chile, Peru, and Bolivia, reinforcing a north-south geopolitical hot line along the continent. The Maksutov AZT-16 was installed in 1967 on Cerro El Roble, a 2,200-meter-high peak in the Chilean coastal mountain range, just 65 kilometers away from the NASA station.[17] At the same time, the installation of El Roble station was paired with the design and construction of another dome and smaller telescope, the Grand Passage Instrument on Cerro Calán, in Santiago, under the design and supervision of Yuriy Streletskiy.

In 1968, several reports on the Soviet operations in Chile were sent to the State Department by the US ambassador Edward M. Korry. According to one of these confidential telexes, the USSR activities were apparently limited to astronomy, but they also appeared to be, at least in the public discourse, linked to the space program of the Soviet Union.[18] The report, signed by Korry, highlights the claim by Soviet astronomers that their aim in making observations from Chile was to carry out a meticulous and accurate study of the coordinates of the Southern Hemisphere in order to establish the route of future interplanetary spaceships that would take men to other planets.[19] Korry's concern was understandable, considering that the Soviet activity occurred during the most critical decade of the Space Race and Cold War. *La Tercera* newspaper, in an article dated Saturday, February, 5, 1966, reported:

> Soviet astronomers living in Chile celebrated the triumph of the Moon landing of the first cosmic ship: "The arrival of the Lunik 9 to the Moon has been a great success for us, and was achieved after many failed attempts," expressed yesterday Mitrofan Zverev, Chief of the Soviet scientific mission that in our hemisphere studies the location of austral stars. "This first step will in the near future enable us to send a manned spaceship around the Moon.[20]

Zverev referred to Konstantín Eduárdovich Tsiolkovsky, the "founder of cosmonautics," who "predicted that the Moon could be a good cosmodrome to go to other planets... Another of the excellent conditions that the Moon has is the clarity with which photos taken of other planets come out." In the same press conference, Zverev said, "Soviet scientists were preparing a trip around the Moon with two or three cosmonauts," adding that "the flight was technically ready and that it would be attempted in the next few months."[21] For all these projects, deeper understanding of the Southern Hemisphere was essential.

As pointed out by Loren R. Graham, within the Soviet Academy of Sciences, this overlapping of interests—between the purely scientific aims of astronomical research and the more practical applications to space travel—had ideological motivations behind the push for pragmatic research. The real value of a scientific theory's worth "is the applied science which results from it."[22] The "revolutionaries' belief that the new scientific program in Russia must be oriented towards

Fig. 1 Maksutov Telescope AZT-16 at Cerro El Roble Astronomical Observatory in Chile, late 1960s. Yuriy Streletskiy archive, Pulkovo National Observatory, Saint Petersburg.

practice"was integral to one of Marx's most famous statements: "The philosophers have only interpreted the world in various ways, the point however is to change it."[23 24] With an understanding of the importance of communicating through the mass media, the chief Soviet astronomer would openly discuss space travel in his public appearances. This public-facing agenda was critical since both the Pulkovo National Observatory in Saint Petersburg and the Soviet Space Research Institute ultimately made the decisions to select the El Roble and Calán sites.

In political terms, these choices, and the actual installation of the AZT-16 Maksutov, took place three years before Salvador Allende came to power. Despite Allende's bond with the Soviets, the astronomical collaboration had in fact started during the governments of the right-wing Jorge Alessandri Rodríguez and the Christian Democrat Eduardo Frei Montalva. In this sense, the Soviet astronomical mission was very different from Allende's policies toward the Soviet Union, if compared with other alliances like the Soviet donation to the "Chilean road to socialism," in the form of a factory designed to manufacture prefabricated concrete panels for Chile's then fledgling program of social housing—a system that arrived in 1971 and went by the name KPD after the original Russian acronym кпд, meaning large panel construction (крупнопанельное домостроение).

The higher technology required for the prefabrication of large concrete buildings would therefore contrast with what was doomed to be the "poorly built" facilities in Cerro El Roble. The dome for the Maksutov AZT-16 was designed by Chilean architects Enrique Marchetti and Marcelo Deglin. It was a monolithic concrete structure constructed *in situ* that included an observatory with a sliding roof for the large telescope, a photographic laboratory, an office space, and a small three-room apartment with a kitchen and a bathroom. The facility was secretly criticized by Ambassador Korry for its poor construction, as described in his report for the United States Department of State, in which he pointed out that "although the Maksutov telescope itself was a first-class instrument, one of the difficulties at El Roble has been the primitive facilities in that place, which have generated adversity and affected the spirits of both the Soviets and Chileans."[25] The much-criticized concrete structure made by the Chileans could be the result of the difficulties of bringing workers and materials to a summit at 2,200 meters altitude, including the pumping of water needed for the making of concrete. The evident logistic advantages of being close to Santiago would contrast with equal disadvantages due to poor accessibility and road conditions. After the 1973 coup d'état led by General Pinochet, the Soviet astronomical mission left the country, leaving all their instruments and equipment behind.

The Maksutov AZT-16 telescope at the El Roble

station remained abandoned until 1979, when Professor José Maza, a young Chilean astronomer, returned to Chile after completing his PhD in Toronto and started a program to search for austral supernovas using the Maksutov. Together with a very small team, between 1979 and 1984, he discovered 50 supernovas from El Roble. But "because of very strong rise of the dollar, the difficult situation of the country after the 1982 economic crisis, the endemic lack of resources to operate Cerro El Roble and the conviction that without a telescope to follow the photometry or spectroscopy of our objects we were working so that others obtained the scientific credit,"in 1984 they stopped researching in Cerro El Roble, and once again the station plunged into abandonment. [26] Even without the extraordinary conditions of the Atacama Desert, Maza's discoveries validated the Soviet decision to install equipment there. In this respect, Alexander V. Stepanov, who was part of the mission to Chile, still considers the location "very good. El Roble is an excellent place of course if compared to any other place of Russia."[27] However, at the time, they were sending missions to the Atacama Desert, in 1966–1967 to Chaupiloma, with a second mission in 1971–1973 to explore the locations of Chaupiloma and La Peineta. According to Vladimir Jershov:

The most intensive work was in these two

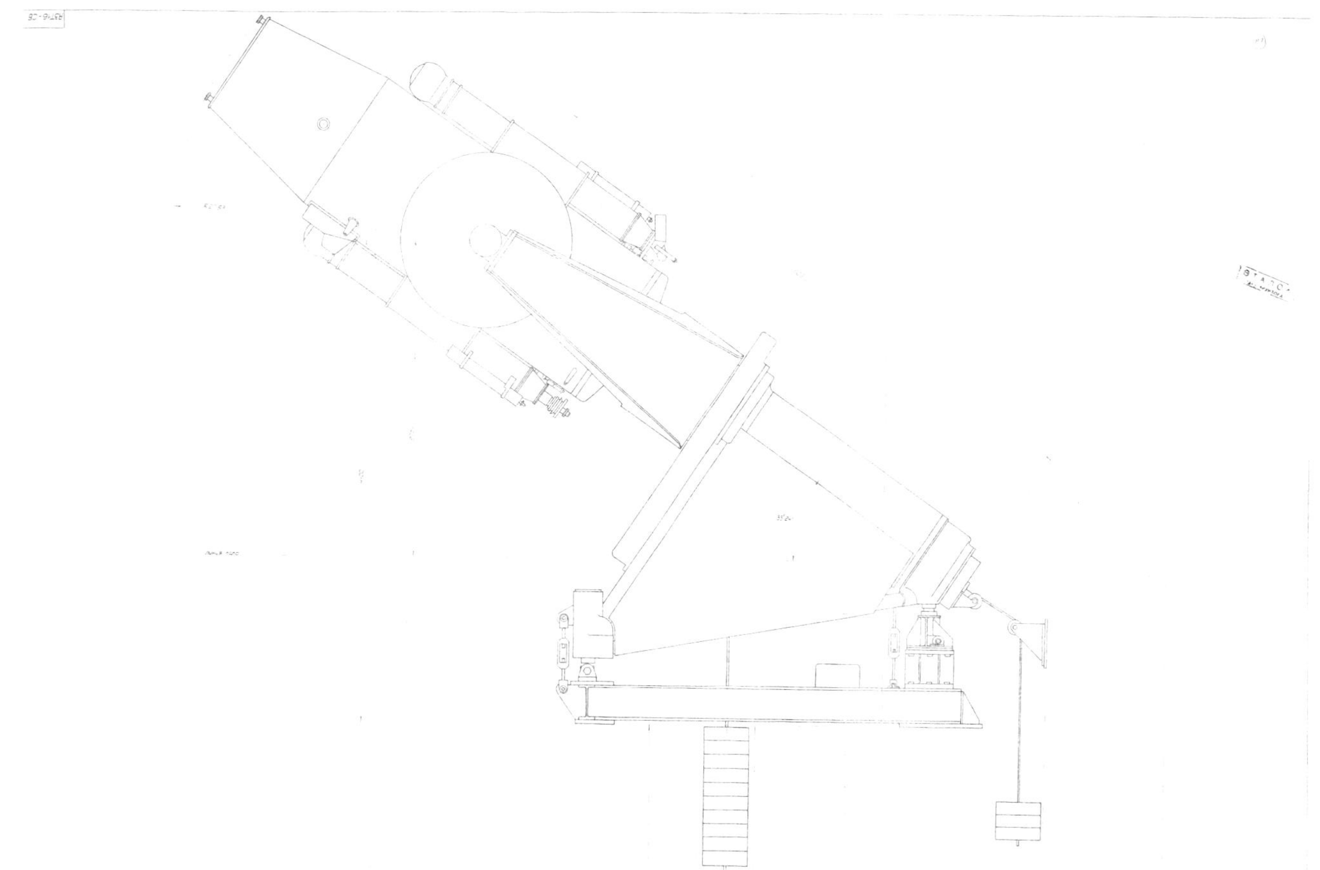

Fig. 2 Planimetry of the Maksutov telescope AZT-16 (elevation detail), Leningrad, mid-1960s. Archive of the National Astronomical Observatory of the University of Chile.

> locations, La Peineta and Chauteloma. There were two Russian expeditions observing astrophysics things. And observing the astroclimate and measuring. The astroclimate is important to choose where you can put the big telescopes. And José Maza told me that La Peineta was considered the best place to put the observatory. But in those years, there was no road to La Peineta.[28]

As a result, by the early 1970s, plans for a prospective site in the Atacama Desert had been prepared, and a new telescope was commissioned. At that time, however, following a process of violent polarization of the country's political factions, General Pinochet led a US-backed coup d'état, ultimately resulting in the tragic death of President Salvador Allende, on September 11, 1973.

While this historical circumstance, significant for both Chilean and international politics, brought the La Peineta prospects to an end, it should be noted that those sites in the Atacama, promoted so eagerly by Federico Rutlland, were the result of explorations and surveys by Jurgen Stock, in the late 1950s and throughout the 1960s. Stock's initial research was commissioned by Yerkes Observatory of the University of Chicago to scout the location for a new 1.5-meter telescope. The sites he discovered in the north of Chile were far too good for a single 1.5-meter telescope, so this eventually led to the foundation of the Cerro Tololo Inter-American Observatory by AURA / NASA. Stock was the observatory's first director (1963–1966) but then moved on to work at University of Chile in 1966. At that time, being functionaries of the same university, he and the Soviet team started communicating.[29]

Mitrofan Zverev mentions in a 1970s article that the Soviet astrophysics work was initially started at Cerro El Roble but subsequently moved to Chaupiloma at the suggestion of Jurgen Stock, whose reports "contain notes on meteorological conditions, wind patterns, seeing, clouds (almost non-existent at night-time, although he worried about haze in some places), as well as other important details, such as water supplies in the region, water quality, estimated costs of constructing pavement roads to the future observatory, surface of the mountains, etc."[30] [31] Yet in 1971, after Allende's presidential victory, Stock's salary at the University of Chile was suspended, and he left Chile for Venezuela. And eventually La Peineta was considered as an alternative site for the Inter-American Observatory.

Jurgen Stock is a figure that helps to qualify the more contrived relationships between the United States and the Soviet Union in their ventures under the spell of science at the University of Chile. At the height of the Cold War, these contesting nations needed to portray their projects as scientific research to be able to install stations and equipment in Chile (and Latin America at large), acquiring access to sites around the world and future orbital space geographies (terrestrial sites for extraterrestrial space). Both Soviet and American agreements with the Chilean government were channeled through the same public academic institution. Rather paradoxically, in administrative terms, the two countries became part of the same Faculty of Physical Sciences and Mathematics. This is visible in a photographic album held in the University of Chile's archives, with US satellite tracking antennas and USSR telescopes appearing side by side.

The tension between the existence of NASA in Peldehue, the scope of a new era of space travel, the good observation conditions in Chile, together with issues of accessibility and funding, show the way these scientific endeavors entailed rather contrived sets of relationships between technology, politics, and culture, often mobilized by a number of not necessarily coordinated agents. Thus neither the NASA station nor the Soviet observatories fulfilled just one mission, but balanced often layered and simultaneous concerns, in between the scientific, the military, and the political.

Fig. 3 El Roble Astronomica Observatory (with the Maksutov telescope AZT-16 inside). Archive of the National Astronomical Observatory of the University of Chile.

[1] Yuriy Streletskiy, interview by Pedro Ignacio Alonso and Hugo Palmarola, Pulkovo National Observatory, Saint Petersburg, March, 1, 2015.

[2] *El Siglo*, August 12, 1967, quoted in "Science: Soviet Astronomy Activities in Chile," unclassified confidential airgram no. A-673 from the embassy in Santiago to the Department of State, June 19, 1968, 4.

[3] Philip C. Keenan, Sonia Pinto, and Hector Alvarez, *The Chilean National Astronomical Observatory*, 1852–1965 (University of Chile, 1985), 6.

[4] A glimpse at the economic scale of these infrastructures is provided by the two largest projects now under development: the Extremely Large Telescope (with a mirror 39.3 meters in diameter) at Cerro Armazones, a US$1.16 billion project led by ESO, and the Giant Magellan Telescope (with a mirror 25.4 meters in diameter) at Las Campanas Observatory, a US$1 billion project led by the US, in partnership with Australia, Brazil, and South Korea. Other multinational conglomerations already in place include the Atacama Large Millimeter Array (ALMA).

[5] Light, *From Warfare to Welfare*, 96.

[6] See Adam Yarmolisnky, *The Military Establishment: Its Impacts on American Society* (Harper & Row, 1971); Walter A. McDougall, *The Heavens and the Earth: A Political History of the Space Age* (John Hopkins University Press, 1985) and Jennifer S. Light, *From Warfare to Welfare: Defense Intellectuals and Urban Problems in Cold War America* (John Hopkins University Press, 2003).

[7] Light, *From Warfare to Welfare*, 102.

[8] The network was initially employed for such physical research as the Lyman Alpha experiment, the cosmic-ray experiment, and environmental studies like temperature, pressure, and surface erosion measurements. NRL Report 4700. Project Vanguard Report No. 1: "Plans, Procedures and Progress," unclassified secret document (Washington, DC: Naval Research Laboratory, January 13, 1956), 48–50.

[9] "Proposal for U.S.-U.S.S.R. Cooperation in Outer Space," confidential memorandum from John Foster Dulles to Dr. James R. Killian, Jr., Special Assistant to the President, the While House. Washington, DC, July 23, 1958. Unclassified document no. 911.802/7-2358. Source: National Archives and Records Administration (NARA), Washington, DC.

[10] Operating for more than thirty years, it was finally closed in 1989, when US strategic satellite tracking needs could be commercially outsourced or possible without the aid of earth-bound facilities. The site was then donated to the University of Chile, becoming the Centro de Estudios Espaciales (Center for Space Studies) until it was sold to the Swedish Space Corporation (SSC) in 2008. The Swedish Space Corporation holds stations in Chile, Australia, and Canada. It is engaged in all business areas related to satellite management, development of rockets and balloons, launching services, and flight tests.

[11] William R. Corliss, *The Space Tracking and Data Acquisition Network* (STADAN), *the Manned Space Flight Network* (MSFN), and *the NASA Communications Network* (NASCOM) (NASA, 1974), 23.

[12] Ibid., 121.

[13] Ibid., 20–23.

[14] Document in the John T. Mengel Papers, held at the NASA Historical Archive, Washington, DC.

[15] Corliss, *The Space Tracking and Data Acquisition Network*, William R. Corliss, op. cit., 33.

[16] In order to count the initial set of Minitrack stations, we shall refer to those that were already built and in operation by October 1957, namely: Blossom Point (Maryland), 1956–1966; Coolidge Field (Antigua Island), 1957–1961; Batista Field (Havana, Cuba), 1957–1958; Pampa de Ancón (Lima, Peru), 1957–1969; Paramo de Cotopaxi (Quito, Ecuador), 1957–1981; Salar del Carmen (Antofagasta, Chile), 1957–1963; and Peldehue (Santiago, Chile), 1957–1988. See Corliss, *The Space Tracking and Data Acquisition Network* and Sunny Tsiao, *Read You Loud and Clear!: The Story of NASA's Spaceflight Tracking and Data Network*, part 1 (National Aeronautics and Space Administration, 2008).

[17] Corliss, *The Space Tracking and Data Acquisition Network*, 3.

[18] The dome for the Maksutov AZT-16 on Cerro El Roble was designed by the Chilean architects Enrique Marchetti and Marcelo Deglin.

[19] "Science: Soviet Astronomy Activities in Chile,"1.

[20] "Science: Soviet Astronomy Activities in Chile," 2.

[21] *La Tercera* newspaper (Santiago), February 5, 1966.

[22] *Las Ultimas Noticias* newspaper (Santiago), February 5, 1966.

[23] Marx and Engels, *Werke* (Berlin, 1962), 3: 276.

[24] Loren R. Graham, *The Soviet Academy of Sciences and the Communist Party*, 1927–1932 (Princeton University Press, 1967), 41.

[25] Marx and Engels, *Werke*, 3:7.

[26] "Soviet Astronomy Activities in Chile," unclassified confidential airgram no. A-673 from the embassy in Santiago to the Department of State, June 19, 1968, 3.

[27] José Maza, "El pan amazado de Juan Parra y el Premio Novel" (unpublished manuscript, 2011).

[28] Alexander V. Stepanov, interview by Hugo Palmarola and Pedro Ignacio Alonso, Saint Petersburg, 2015.

[29] Vladimir Jershov, interview by Pedro Alonso, London, January 2014.

[30] A. K. Vivas and M. J. Stock, "Jürgen Stock: From One End of the Andes to the Other," in *Fifty Years of Wide Field Studies in the Southern Hemisphere*, ASP Conference Series 491, ed. S. Points and A. Kunder (Astronomical Society of the Pacific, 2015), 17.

[31] Mitrofan Zverev's summary on the five years' work of the Pulkovo team in Chile was published by *News of the Main Astronomical Observatory of Pulkovo* magazine in 1970. Strangely, the article was three years overdue when published, as the five-year anniversary of the mission had been in 1967. The article is the most comprehensive report on the mission's work, including the detailed timeline of the preparations, organization, and setup of the Chile mission, notes on climate and observation conditions, scientific findings and data. Apart from making full-page photos of the text, I also rephotographed all photos in the article so they could be printed large.

[32] Vivas and Stock, *Jürgen Stock*, 20.

Border Blimp Bomb

César A. Lopez
Jeffrey S. Nesbit

Deep in the desert of the southwestern United States and northwestern Mexico, two technical objects appear: a border patrol observation blimp, tethered to the ground by a coiled steel cable, and an unarmed atomic bomb shell, sitting modestly on a truck trailer. Both are smooth, white masses, curved and shaped like water droplets, sitting on their side and slightly lifted off the desert ground. The blimp and bomb are painted stark white, shimmering brightly from reflections of sun rays, and can be seen from long distances against the seemingly passive desert backdrop. They are not "hiding in plain sight"; on the contrary, their presence and power are demonstrated through what they make visible or invisible about the desert. Beyond their shared aesthetic, these objects intentionally mark geopolitical territories for national defense and military strength—ostentatious reminders that broadcast a national presence and world power. This essay explores how the history of productions, imaginations, and aesthetics purposefully constructed the American desert, and access to territories of visibility, through the border blimp and atomic bomb.

The Chihuahuan and Sonoran Deserts span and set the extreme environments of the American southwestern and Mexican northwestern region. It is a space of political production and imagination as the politics of declaring the Mexico–United States border began over 200 years ago at the end of Spanish governance in North America. Since then, the political boundary has undergone five major transformations, starting east of the Mississippi, before the Louisiana Purchase, to the Gadsden Purchase, of 1854, which placed the boundary

Fig. 1 "Fatman" Atomic Bomb Replica, White Sands, New Mexico. Source: US Army Archives.

Fig. 2 Air and Marine Operations Tethered Aerostat Radar System "TARS." Source: US Customs and Border Protection.

firmly in the Sonoran and Chihuahuan Deserts. The characterization of the Mexico–United States border desert region is dominated by the visible and invisible operations that sustain political geography and national security while crafting the representation of an American landscape. This essay explores the events, narratives, and operations that remain contingent on the region's rendered emptiness, and the objects, both active and defunct, that give us new insight into our past, present, and future conception of the territorial desert.

The border region is a product of the 1848 Treaty of Guadalupe Hidalgo, which forced Mexico to drop any claim to Texas territory and authorized the United States to capture land comprising much of the present-day Southwest. As the border shifted south, Mexican people living on the newly claimed territory were given a choice between US citizenship or segregation as foreign aliens. In contrast, the Indigenous Camanche, Apache, Seri, Coahuiltecan, and Kiowa people were forcefully relocated from their ancestral lands.[1] These policies instigated by the new border formation fueled the Mexican-American race, created a dominant minority population in the American Southwest desert, and simultaneously continued the practice of marginalizing Indigenous groups across the region. The border was more than an abstract line on a map. It was always meant to be an evolving, nation-building project that deployed ethnic cleansing tactics in the desert imaginary in pursuit of political interests over land.

The Mexico–United States border line we see on maps today was surveyed by a boundary commission that navigated the region in the 1890s. The desert's environment was a constant challenge, as the heat and dryness hindered the surveying party's travel. The constant fear of being attacked by Indigenous peoples, whom they referred to as "desert people," stoked fear and disdain for the desert region among members of the party. Historian and researcher C. J. Alvarez summed up their attitude in the book *Border Land, Border Water*: "The desert was an awful place inhabited by awful people, economically worthless and aesthetically hideous."[2] Much of the 1,220 square miles surveyed were made up of "valleys, mesas, and deserts," in which the flatness of the terrain was perceived as the "absence of civilization" since, at the time, mountains and hills were integral imagery of European societies.[3] Moreover, the desert's extreme heat distorted and often warped their equipment—as if the land resisted being measured and commodified. Mirages continuously fooled travelers with illusions in the distance. It's not difficult to imagine that these characterizations and experiences were one of many accounts that began to stir a narrative of the American desert as a place without order. An image promoting a consciousness of the region that has led to the systematic exploitation of the land, ecologies, and people.[4]

The Mexico–United States border settled in its current configuration by the twentieth century, and the desert landscape surrounding it continues to be one of the most contested regions in the Americas. Not because the region became a static barrier for claiming border territory. Instead, the Mexico–United States border evolved into a policy and infrastructural mechanism and military activities filtering capital, material, law, and labor into a constant state of political alterity—ultimately positioning the border as an evolving national project. The Mexico–United States border wall only symbolizes the boundary between the two nations. Despite early security concerns about illegal immigration, migrations into the United States proved to be as equally opportunistic as different national laws between the United States and Mexico positioned the border to be a popular destination to participate in illegal and illicit activity.

The border and the desert are entangled in a complex narrative of a nation's imaginary over land and stimulate projections of a world view.[5] When the United States entered World War II, in December 1942, the secretary of war, Henry Stimson, ordered the director of the Los Alamos Ranch School in northern New Mexico to shut down its school without warning or explanation.

Secretary Stimson wrote in a letter that land was being acquired simply for "military purposes." As noted in the local *Durango Herald* news, the "school officials were forbidden from saying why the school closed on Feb. 8, 1943, and all records of the condemnation proceedings were sealed."[6] The school was seen by the United States government as dismissible, remote, and distinctly "sealed"—a landscape of enclosure.

At 5:29 AM on July 16, 1945, a single military experiment in the New Mexican desert changed the worldview forever. Detonated by the United States Army, the world's first nuclear weapon erupted on the Trinity Site, about 70 miles north of Alamogordo. The colossal blast sent shock waves across incredible distances, over 160 miles, and launched radioactive fallout found more than 250 miles from the detonation site. This first nuclear event instantaneously produced a wasteland wilderness.[7] The desert is described by the state as remote and distant yet instantaneously, immediately upon the nuclear blast, the land and its impacted adjacent communities are made a wasteland of hazardous chemicals lifting into the atmosphere and spoiling the soils below. Perhaps such a moment elevates the profile of the desert from a national or military perspective to a global one. The desert is now seen as a threat: a place militarized through scientific advancement for global destruction.

Power was demonstrated on August 6 and August 9, 1945, in Hiroshima and Nagasaki, respectively, less than three weeks after the first test. The world was instantaneously ever changed. The world threat and boundaries of power were now entangled with the technical object produced by the American image of the militarized desert landscape. The other existed in the desert—both as the place for perpetuating nuclear deterrence and for increasing border security. In both forms of national infrastructure, the desert landscape strategically became the place "on the ground" counter to its orbital infrastructure network in space.

It's misleading to continue thinking that the boundary between Mexico and the United States is strictly a boundary between the two nations. Instead, the region marks a geographical *space*, not a just line, from which Mexico and the United States interact with the rest of the world. The Mexico–United States border is a space of global production, collaboration, and deterrence. As a thickened border and restricted military testing site, the desert tends to align in the imagination with lawlessness. The desert radiating from the border is a filter through varying degrees of bordering, such as testing the levels of security, including scale, distance, and "hardness" of the desert as a boundary. National imaging becomes a mechanism of thickening the threshold of the nation-state and continues to render the desert remote, placeless, and empty intentionally.[8] Desert is intentionally rendered as having no place to establish and designate a national image of control and expand territorial politics—where empty remoteness is the measured outcome of Indigenous resettlements, land thefts, and ethnic cleansing.

Border security redefined the desert as a condition of US infrastructure—an operational wilderness—broadening and decentralizing its geography.[9] Advanced scientific technology of the bomb and interests in securing a national border are strangely implicated in a place often perceived as a remote wilderness where the operational territory of proving grounds advances science and military technology. Such test sites and border monitoring are intentionally located far from large populations for reasons of safety and security, thereby allowing the military to deploy secret, classified, and hazardous activities.[10] Rural communities likely never envisioned the vast defense spending in their own "backyards," while most of the United States understood decentralization as a core principle in Cold War tactics for defending against nuclear warfare. From scientific instruments and the manufacturing of launch complex infrastructure to networking distributions across the continent (and across the globe), military infrastructure allowed decentralization to take place. The atomic bomb and the desert became entangled with interests of national decentralization for defense, and thus infrastructure enabled such practices, linking vast desert landscapes of power. While the memorial bomb serves as a reminder to the world that the US is prepared to use extreme force to safeguard its land and interests. The border blimp extends this authority into the unordered and vast desert, exerting power over neighboring countries as well as the populations and environments within its borders. In other words, the blimp and the bomb are visible expressions of the US's efforts to command this—claimed to be—unordered space of the desert and thus exert power over enemies, over neighbors, and over the natural world.

Just before the United States entered World War II, the government became increasingly concerned with the shortage of food production during the war. In 1942, the US formed the Braceros Program with Mexico, providing "job opportunities" for millions of Mexican nationals, who migrated north and provided agricultural labor to meet the rising need. It was at this point that foreign labor and border security operations were entangled, as the US Border Patrol agency was then overseen by the US Department of Labor. Since the border marked a difference in law, currency, and cost of living for populations in the region, border enforcement and unilateral economic and security policies became critical frameworks in regulating labor and capital. The primary port of entry and the recruitment center were in El Paso, Texas.[11] This agricultural program, along with the increase of military-industrial activities and scientific research in the desert, was thought to be critical for success in the war.

In her book *Border and Rule*, activist Harsha Walia refers to the Mexico–United States border as a "testing ground for security" provoked by a combination of exclusionary structures and commodified inclusion strategies.[12] On the one hand, the United States military and border security apparatus manages and governs the desert region through a 500-billion-dollar industry that deploys everything from physical barriers, cargo scanners for commercial flow, surveillance towers and ground sensors for human movement, drones, and other aerostats.[13] On the other hand, industrial stability programs such as the Bracero Program pull workers across the Mexico–United States border from around the world. What compels these workers to navigate the physical and political terrains of the United States immigration crisis is hope for a better life, despite pathways to citizenship falling further out of reach.

The security infrastructures and economic policies and programs described above give way to the realization that the border is, in fact, nebulous. It's not just a wall because the border doesn't just format land; it racially sorts people for political and economic gain. Therefore, the border appears in various forms and can exist everywhere and anywhere, leveraging military and policing structure, tethering our sense of security to the alterity of others.

Geographic arrangements of techno-scientific military practices and the expanding geographical perspective of human settlement across the globe begin to break down the boundaries between disparate territorial legibility. Political and ideological controversies surrounding extreme scales of human inhabitation—such as the lack of human occupation in the remote desert or Arctic landscape—offer another kind of illumination into new geographical boundaries, vis-à-vis planetary urbanization. With the creation of the North American Free Trade Agreement (NAFTA), the world's most expansive free-trade agreement, the American Southwest also saw the emergence of border militarization in the region. This mirrors Mexico's Border Industrialization Program (MBIP), which addressed high unemployment rates in northern Mexican cities experiencing a rise in crime and civil unrest in the 1960s. NAFTA and the MBIP formatted the Sonoran Desert into logistical and military territories. While these industrialization projects created more government, programs like NAFTA loosened the border and the desert region surrounding it, rendering it defenseless—which encouraged more elusive borders beyond the construction of walls.

In the early 1980s, the US Customs and Border

Protection Agency launched a program that deployed a tethered aerostat radar system (TARS) to counter the rising number of unauthorized low-flying small aircraft. The first of these blimps was installed in Cudjoe Key, Florida, to track and limit potential narcotrafficking from Cuba and other Latin American countries. Following the TARS blimp's success, six more blimps were installed in the deserts along the American Southwest and southern Texas region to provide overlapping radar coverage of the entire length of the Mexico–United States border from Yuma, Arizona, to Rio Grande City, Texas. These *border blimps* are 210 feet long and float up to 12,000 feet in the air.[14] While the border blimps only monitor suspicious flight activity, their presence, hovering in the sky over communities, has been controversial. To this point, the border blimp provides a layer of surveillance that places communities beneath in a constant state of danger and fear. As recently as 2022, residents in Nogales were startled by the installation of a border blimp that now hovers over their homes. The blimp came with no prior warning, convincing residents of the border region that they were increasingly living in a police state.[15]

While the blimps have aided the border patrol in monitoring unwarranted air traffic, their cost compared to their performance has not convinced even some of the staunchest supporters of border security in the United States Congress. Although the border blimps are relatively lower in operational cost than other surveillance infrastructure, their constant exposure to ultraviolet radiation, extreme desert heat, dryness, and winds thrusting with sand causes significant wear and tear. Typically, each border blimp has to be replaced every five to six years, costing the United States government 8.9 million dollars each time. Coupled with the five-million-dollar annual cost for maintenance and technical expertise, which border patrol agents are not inherently trained to have, it's no surprise that the border blimps have been decommissioned over time.[16] However, the fear is that something more intrusive to communities and invasive to the land will replace them.

It has been stated that "military occupancy of land is a critical issue almost because of its relative invisibility," and it should be understood as a process of operational control.[17] If military geographies in the assumed remote desert have historically been operationalized, marginalizing local communities, and tend to define perimeters of control, then what can be said of the discrete objects employed throughout the operationalized desert that are used to monitor migrations of people and the place for global defense and surveillance? In other words, the desert has an aesthetic that is made to appear invisible. The American image of the desert is made to appear as an empty, lawless wilderness, while the image of military occupancy of the desert is meant to construct itself as a deterrence of invasion by foreign military or people.

The TARS border blimp installation in Deming, New Mexico, is just over 110 miles southwest of the infamous Trinity Site where the memorialized bomb is sited. It's difficult to truly know why these two objects, from two different eras of the national insecurity crisis, share so many aesthetic and formal properties. But these similarities certainly contribute to a representation of the American landscape as a place for military testing and border production. The "military imagination of landscape" contributes to the shaping of both its coordinates, literally its place on the globe, and its technical objects embedded in its place. The bomb and blimp are objects of military and immigration deterrence in the desert, penetrating a new virtual wall, what Paul Virilio calls the "wall of Atlantis."[18] The US Customs and Border Protection Agency marks the blimp as the "frontline" for deterring activity on the ground and in the air.[19] As mentioned before, these objects are not hidden in plain sight—the TARS blimp and the nuclear bomb replica are just as important as the systems of surveillance and military defense themselves—a strange reminder of anti-remoteness. And therefore, the images mediated by visualizing the objects in the desert produce an accelerated awareness of land monitoring and the power of scientific militarization.

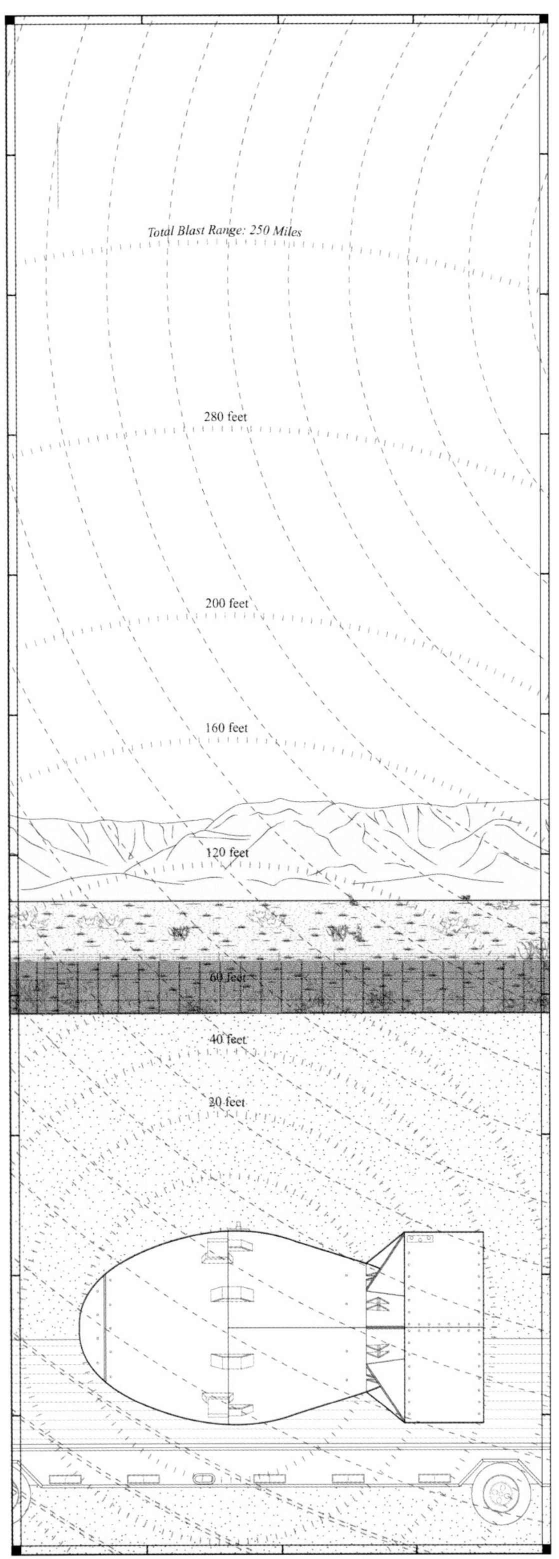

Fig.3 Geographic Elevation, "Fatman" Atomic Bomb Replica (Drawing by Author).

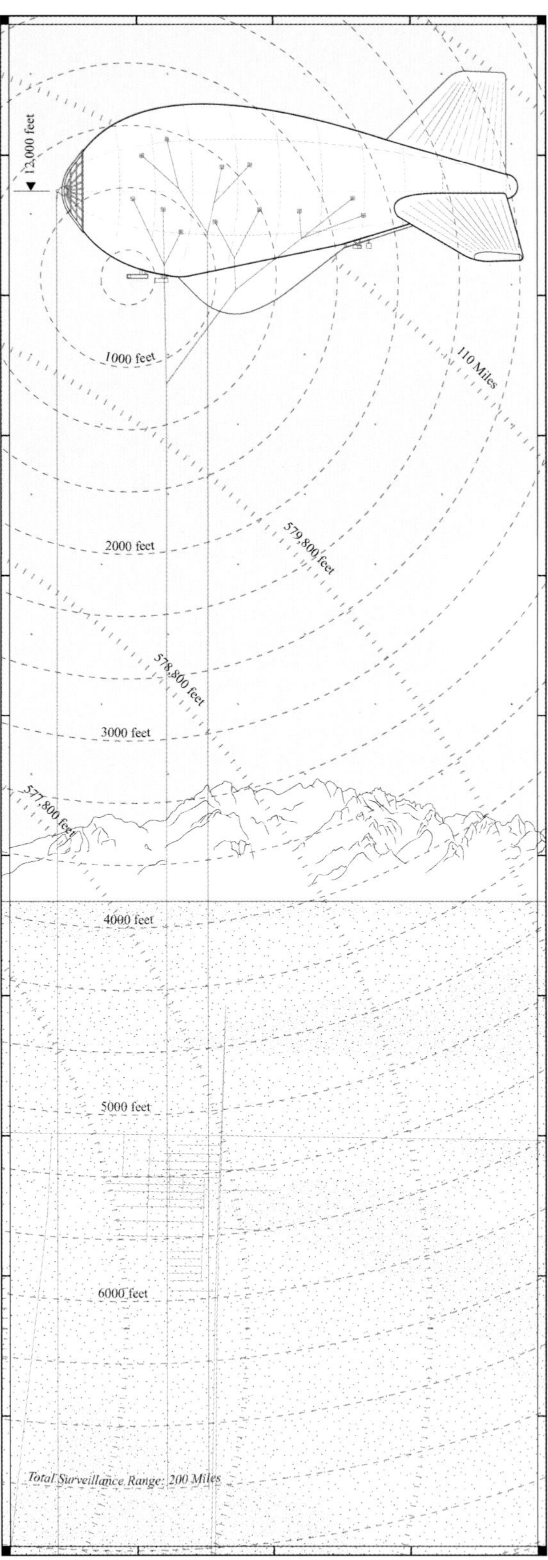

Fig.4 Geographic Elevation, Air and Marine Operations Tethered Aerostat Radar System "TARS" (Drawing by Author).

Modernity, as an obsessive form of progress over nature and control over land, requires its mediated object: the border and the bomb.

Such monitoring and surveillance continue today across the world. Even though we seem to be embraced and influenced by the most innovative technologies, such as facial recognition, advancements in closed-circuit television (CCTV), and the rise of drone networks, it's the "balloon" and blimp that seem to be the legible versions of sustained national interests and military presence. In recent news, a Chinese balloon was shot down near the coast of South Carolina.[20] These surveillance balloons have a long history and remain a national security threat. A *New York Times* article mentions that the Pentagon has noted that even though Chinese balloons have flown over the United States numerous times, it is not until the media places particular pressure on the topic that it must be addressed. For Chinese surveillance over distant global territory, the balloons are launched from the South China Sea and float over international waters until nearing the US Eastern Seaboard. Balloon launches have been reported in many places worldwide, including the Korean Peninsula, where they are used to broadcast information and political propaganda across the Demilitarized Zone (DMZ). Though such reports have been received with much scrutiny in the domestic news, the US, too, has a long history of using balloons for military practices and documentation of territory, including balloons issued by President Dwight D. Eisenhower in the early days of the Cold War. With new technologies in military equipment, we tend to think that the world is quickly dematerializing and border walls are being replaced by other forms of intelligent surveillance. But then we are quickly reminded by the appearance of surveillance blimps and balloons floating over our heads that these practices are likely not to dematerialize anytime soon.

Today, the bomb is a tourist attraction, ultimately reminding us of a troubled era that prompted the irreversible creation of the world's first atomic threat. At the same time, the border blimp is one of many operations in the region that place mixed-status populations in a constant state of fear. The desert is the site of an evolving project of spatial and territorial transformation. After all, the Mexico-United States border is relatively young compared to others worldwide. It has time to change. Yet the border blimp and the memorial bomb are products of the United States' insecurities, not the establishment. They are inadequacies that have grown to overwhelm the landscape and imagination of the desert. As the desert continues to be a zone of experimentation, just like the border infrastructures deployed to innovate the United States Homeland Security and defense systems of surveillance, we also see another territorial transformation rising. The departure from terrestrial grounds to the occupation of aerospace as a three-dimensional domain of restricted national control. From this standpoint, the desert is the space of past, present, and future militarization and establishment of malleable borders.

-----

[1] Harsha Walia, "The Historic Entanglements of US Border Formation," *Border & Rule: Global Migration, Capitalism, and the Rise of Capitalism* (Haymarket Books, 2021).

[2] C. J. Alvarez, "The Border in the Nineteenth Century," in *Border Land, Border Water: A History of Construction on the U.S.-Mexico Divide* (University of Texas Press, 2019), 24–27.

[3] Ibid.

[4] Ibid., 32.

[5] For more on the border wall controversy, see Michael Dear, "Why Walls Won't Work," in *Borderwall as Architecture: A Manifesto for the US-Mexico Boundary*, ed. Ronald Rael (University of California Press, 2017).

[6] Sue McMillin, "Atomic New Mexico: Exploring the Origins of America's Radioactive History," in *Durango Herald*, June 24, 2018.

[7] Peter Galison, "Wastelands and Wilderness: Nuclear Lands," National Humanities Center lecture, Research Triangle Park, North Carolina, February 8, 2018.

[8] For more on "military geographies," see Rachel Woodward, *Military Geographies* (Wiley, 2004). Professor of Human Geography Rachel Woodward describes the global extends of military geographies unseen and invisible as part of "overseas sovereign territory."

[9] Scott Kirsch, *Proving Grounds: Project Plowshare and the Unrealized*

Dream of Nuclear Earthmoving (Rutgers University Press, 2005). Geographer Scott Kirsch posits proving grounds of military weaponry and scientific possibility aligned with remote territories where "geographical limits" are most threatened, particularly in the context of late 1950s military simulations.
Kirsch argues Project Plowshare attempted to radically use nonmilitary lands in Alaska for a scientific experiment but failed because of opposition by the public and the scientific community in the region. Earthmoving tests by nuclear power for Plowshare returned to the already owned and operated property in the Nevada Test Site by 1962.
[10] For example, places selected for missile silos were buried in the remote American landscape, hidden from a national view. See Gretchen Heefner's book *The Missile Next Door* (Harvard University Press, 2012). Paradoxically titled, Heefner, describes the significance of communities living among buried Intercontinental Ballistic Missiles (ICBMs). Yet, at another, more intimate perspective, Gretchen Heefner shows us a rural America and its ambivalent lifestyle with ballistic missiles at our doorsteps. Gretchen Heefner identities military activities actively hidden across broadly dispersed regions in the mid-west United States.
[11] Library of Congress, "1942 Bracero Program," *A Latinx Resource Guide: Civil Rights Cases and Events in the United States: Research Guides*, https://guides.loc.gov/latinx-civil-rights/bracero-program.
[12] Walia, *Border Regimes*, 77–87.
[13] Bonnie Berkowitz, Shelly Tan, Kevin Uhrmacher. Things Used to Secure the Border," in *Washington Post*, February 15, 2019.
[14] United States Customs and Border Protection, "CBP Completes Upgrade of Aerostat Surveillance System" (2014, October 3). Retrieved December 9, 2022, from https://www.cbp.gov/newsroom/national-media-release/cbp-completes-upgrade-aerostat-surveillance-system
[15] Jonathan Clark, "Border Blindsides Community with 24-hour Surveillance Blimp" in *Nogales International* (2022, June 29). Retrieved December 10, 2022 from https://www.nogalesinternational.com/news/border-patrol-blindsides-community-with-24-hour-surveillance-blimp/article_33b2ea5c-f7dd-11ec-8a0d-63dd4bedc311.html
[16] David Long, "CBP's Eye's in the Sky," in *Frontline November Aerostats*, April 11, 2016. https://www.cbp.gov/frontline/frontline-november-aerostats.
[17] Woodward, *Military Geographies*, 12.
[18] Paul Virilio, *Desert Screen: War at the Speed of Light* (Continuum, 2002).
[19] Dave Long, "CBP's Eyes in the Sky," *Frontline Magazine*, US Customs and Border Protection (US Department of Homeland Security, 2016). https://www.cbp.gov/frontline/frontline-november-aerostats
[20] For more on the Chinese balloon surveillance, see David Sanger, "Balloon Incident Reveals More Than Spying as Competition with China Intensifies," *New York Times*, February 6, 2023, https://www.nytimes.com/2023/02/05/us/politics/balloon-china-spying-united-states.html.

Part 3

Urbanisms and Defenses

Engineering the Underworld

Gretchen Heefner

The subterranean world was built on contradiction and paradox, to be sure. It was there, in the 1950s and 1960s, that the United States military sought to hide its growing strategic infrastructure. Military engineers created a vast subterranean world of missile silos, survival bunkers, communication centers, and even bases. It was a place where high-tech capabilities met Stone Age fears. Where proof of strategic know-how sat uneasily alongside a preoccupation with vulnerability. Security and insecurity were hidden away together under the surface of the earth. Here was one answer to the nuclear age. As a 1959 US Army Corps of Engineers report explained, "Only underground installations provide maximum possible protection" against nuclear weapons, from the initial blast to the resulting "nuclear radiation, heat, and fallout."[1] In the event of thermonuclear war, the engineers were certain, survival would depend on the construction of a parallel netherworld.

There was nothing new about using the underground as refuge. Humans have long done so to hide, to protect, to preserve.[2] But the Cold War took things to new extremes. Not only in the sense engineers imagined, at some point, seemingly everything could be buried. But also, because the US military was intent on burying its materials everywhere it went, from the Great Plains up to the Arctic Circle, from tropical island bases to testing areas deep in the Sahara. Hiding thus meant digging holes in places few Americans had ever thought about, let alone been to.

It was this global geography of modern war that concerned military engineers as they thought about building bases and burying things. They had plenty of experience building military facilities at home, so they knew that creating a subterranean bunker outside Washington, DC, was not the same as doing so in Alaska. Any engineer could explain, of course, that the materials you planned to dig into influenced what could be done there. But Cold War technologies upped the stakes. As Engineering Intelligence Guide Number 30 explained, sending things under the surface of the earth required new ways of knowing and seeing, new types of knowledge. The Cold War underground was not just a series of pits and holes, it was to be a world where people could work and exist, much like they did aboveground. These facilities would contain high-tech weapons and communication centers, concrete bunkers, and blast doors. The netherworld needed electricity and ventilation, cooling and heating systems, plumbing. If not competently done, a lot could go wrong.

Think of it this way: if you were going to bury nuclear-tipped intercontinental ballistic missiles in concrete silos two stories underground, you would want to make sure no dripping water, moles, or insects could get in and mess up your systems. Thermonuclear war started by a cockroach might have a certain serendipity to it, given that cockroaches are often presented as the one organism that might survive Armageddon, but it was not a joke worth countenancing.

If the weapons and systems had to be insulated, so, too, did the men sent down to monitor them. Even as popular magazines in the early 1960s informed readers about civil defense plans to shield them from nuclear weapons and the possibilities of building home fallout shelters, the military was already sending its own to live underground. The nation's missile facilities required teams of missileers to rotate through shifts in launch capsules buried 30 feet down. The capsules were suspended on giant springs so that, should a nuclear weapon explode nearby, the men and equipment inside could survive long enough to launch the missiles under their command. In addition to comfortable chairs (with seat belts), computer consoles, a bathroom and a shower, the capsule contained a small shovel so the missileers could dig themselves out after Armageddon. "To dig or not to dig?" *Business Week* queried its American readers in a 1961 article.[3] Not in reference to digging out after nuclear war, but in their own preparation for it.

Around the world the military engineers, largely through the Army Corps of Engineers, had been digging for some time. Not just missile sites in the Great Plains and US West but around the world.[4] In doing so, the engineers began to amass ever more information and expertise about the material conditions—the dirt, soil, sand, ice, and snow—that covered large swaths of the earth. The Cold War underground meant that hitherto marginal processes and materials had to be scrutinized, churned through tests, reports crafted. Not only did dirt and rock come into new focus, but so too did materials like crystals of ice and snow, patches of permafrost. Burying things in places considered "extreme" meant getting intimately acquainted with previously unimaginable bits of information. Burying things in little-known places thus revealed new worlds full of unknown materials and processes.

"Engineering the Underworld" highlights three levels on which Cold War invisibility was constructed. The most obvious, of course, was burying things below ground. But that was not terribly novel or impressive. The US military also took the idea of subterranean survival to hard-to-reach places, which upped the stakes of what could be done—and what could go wrong. In the 1950s, for example, the Arctic became of considerable strategic, and thus scientific, interest. Here was an environment that required new forms of knowledge and expertise, new skills so that materials could be manipulated in novel ways. In trying to master the Arctic, US military engineers thus acquired a covert form of expertise that allowed them to conceal even more.[5]

Fig.1 Aerial photo of Camp Tuto, June 4, 1961. This was the research camp created about 17 miles to the southeast of Thule Air Base in Greenland. It was active from 1954-1966. Hundreds of research programs were launched from the camp. NARA-111-SC-592972, box 1359, no. 12

Go North

By the late 1940s, US strategists looked to the top of the world and saw a front line in a future war against the Soviet Union. It was, after all, the most direct path between the two adversaries and thus the most likely route for bombers and later missiles. As a result, US military activities and facilities crawled up and out. The air force requested the construction of bases in Alaska, Greenland, and Iceland for its bombers, which could be ready to take off and deliver ordinance behind the Iron Curtain. Radar facilities, too, were planned. Working with the Canadians, the US military built the Distant Early Warning Line, aimed at providing advanced warning of a Soviet attack. It included a few dozen remote, manned facilities in the High Arctic.[6]

As these projects got started, however, the Army Corps of Engineers was keenly aware of the limited information available not only about specific places, but about the materials they would find across the far Far North. To be sure, they knew snow and ice, but not in the ways they would need to know it to build modern military facilities. In response, the corps created new and upgraded old research centers and facilities. An institutional apparatus was created and strengthened to grapple with constructing military facilities around the world. The Snow, Ice, and Permafrost Research Establishment (SIPRE) was created in 1949 (it was renamed Cold Regions Research and Engineering Laboratory [CRREL] in 1961). The engineers also leaned on the Frost Effects Laboratory and the Arctic Construction Task Force (the latter was based in Greenland), as well as older centers such as the Engineering Research and Development Center and the Waterways Experiment Station. All turned their attention to the nuances of building in extreme and previously invisible places.

In 1951, the Corps of Engineers pulled as much information together as possible as they headed up to build the northernmost air base ever: Thule Air Force Base in northwestern Greenland. Over two summers the engineers worked to prepare a small city on the coast of Greenland, where five thousand men would live. The base is still open today, though much smaller, and has been renamed Pituffik Space Base.

From the air base, research activities spun out along the edge of the ice and then up on top of it. 80% of Greenland is covered with a giant dome of ice, some of it thousands of feet deep. Until the Cold War it had been little studied. To U.S. military planners and strategists, the harsh and unyielding environment—seemingly perpetually cold and inhospitable—was an ideal place to test out maneuvers and cold-climate operations. Temperatures plunged well below zero, winds could be fierce, and ice and snow were a constant.[7] So active were the research programs that in 1954 the Corps of Engineers created a research facility, Camp Tuto (short for Thule Take-Off), seventeen miles southeast of the base. From this camp on the edge of the ice cap, research teams could more easily spend summers moving along the edges of and up onto the ice, experimenting with vehicles, drilling techniques, survival training, and more.

Permafrost: A Shape-Shifter

Digging began in June 1959, first with pickaxes and handsaws and later with electric drills and some well-placed explosives. The goal seemed simple enough: to excavate a 300-foot-long tunnel, 10 feet high and nine feet wide. But it was the material they hoped to tunnel through that was unique: permafrost.[8]

From their base at Camp Tuto, Greenland, the engineers wanted to know a few things about working in and with "perennially frozen ground." Of primary concern was whether the material itself would be an insulator, both against the extreme environmental conditions where it was found (cold) and against potential bomb blasts from either conventional or atomic explosives. Would digging into permafrost mean that military shelters (such as missile launch capsules) might not have to be built on springs? Or that men in combat situations could be well protected in trenches and bunkers excavated out of the permafrost? Was permafrost a potential construction material? This last point was important because most of the places with permafrost lack timber, a basic building material. What if you could make a beam out of frozen dirt?

By 1959, when they started the permafrost tunnel, the military engineers had been studying permafrost for over a decade. Tunneling was a culmination of many years of preparation. During World War II, for example, the engineers had been called to build military facilities in Alaska and Canada. They had done so in great haste, which taught them that not attending to the oddities of permafrost could have devastating consequences. The Alcan Highway (a road connecting Alaska and Canada for long supply runs) was listing and buckling in places. A post office was splitting in two. The urgency of war and the modern infrastructure that it required had not been carefully enough calibrated to the shape-shifting material that was permafrost. Perfectly stable looking buildings could—months or years after being constructed—slump on one end.

In the years after the war, then, the engineers doubled down on the study of permafrost: why did it melt? Could this be stopped or ameliorated somehow? These were vital questions given the amount of construction that was to be undertaken in cold places. Big construction. Roads, runways, large hangars, and buildings. There had never been so much construction in the North American North.

The engineers defined permafrost as ground that had been frozen for two or more years, but most of the world's permafrost is thousands of years old. How, then, to best match the needs of modern military technologies to ground that had been frozen before humans walked the Earth?

Early military studies of permafrost were concerned mostly with mobility and operations. How could engineers get equipment across the stuff and build in and on it? Through their research centers, the engineers

Fig.2 Column and furniture made out of permafrost in the permafrost tunnel, Greenland. Source: George K. Swinzow, "Tunneling in Permafrost, II" Cold Regions Research and Engineering Laboratory, Technical Report 97, January 1964, p. 12.

studied best practices for creating foundations and insulation layers that would separate human activities above from what was frozen below. In other places (like Thule) the engineers vaulted building up on stilts to keep them from changing the thermal balance below. Engineering teams experimented with painting pavements white to better reflect the sun. The best strategies required knowing what sort of ground you were dealing with. Permafrost is a mixture of soil, rock, and frozen water, but it behaves differently based on its content. Further, not all permafrost contains water and ice: "dry" permafrost is just soil and rock frozen tight. Sometimes the engineers would dig down and realize that ice formed in wedges, needles, or veins—any number of arrangements depending on the ratio of water to other materials in the ground. The formation of permafrost depended on natural surface features of the area – vegetation, drainage, valleys, bodies of water, and so on. The size and shape of soils and granular materials mattered as well. To understand what they might find when they began to dig, engineers' reports emphasized knowing all that was above ground.

What mattered most was what they could not usually observe: how the land thawed or how it would thaw once disturbed. The engineers acknowledged that they had no trouble building things on frozen ground. It was the thaw that mattered: it is what, over time, might make railroad ties separate or asphalt crack. To really grapple with modern construction on permafrost, which the engineers estimated covered 20% of the earth's terrain, they had to study processes and materials they could not see.[9]

Given all of this, tunneling was quite new and rather daring. Not only would the research teams get to see what the stuff looked like—how the ice was suspended in wedges and veins, what else got frozen down into the hard morass—but also how permafrost behaved as a construction material. In fact, so interested in the latter question were the teams in Greenland that, as they dug out their tunnel, they brought molds inside. There they melted some of the permafrost and mixed it with other materials (sawdust and silts), poured it into their molds, let it refreeze, and tested out the efficacy of what they could make. Beams, a few chairs, a table.

Early tests were positive. The chairs held, the table was useful. The weak spot in their tunnel, however, was the entrance (and thus their exit). It was the opening that seemed to melt and deform the fastest, disturbed by the warmer, fresh air that swooped in. So the engineers shored up the opening with metal beams (hauled to northwestern Greenland from the States) and tresses so that it would not cave in. And then they kept digging. They were in part experimenting with an eye toward mining – how could people best dig into the material for the purpose of retrieving things that they might want to sell? But the engineers were also thinking strategically about hiding things. How far could they dig? Could the walls be kept frozen even with men working and possibly living within the permafrost? Or would the equilibrium shift, leading to a sudden, disastrous thaw? It is hard to imagine a man digging down into material that he knew could change with little warning. What if the ceiling caved in?[10] It was the Cold War version of Edgar Allan Poe's "The Premature Burial," the 1844 short story that popularized the buried-alive motif. Could you dig your way out of permafrost? Given how hard it was to dig into it, that seemed unlikely.[11]

Nevertheless, the potential benefits of exploiting the material's properties outweighed the bad. Engineers understood that permafrost was shockingly strong, stronger even than concrete, but also more elastic. That is why they hoped it might be good at absorbing shocks, insulating what was inside from the violence above. In Greenland, they angled a room off to one side, chiseled pits out of one section that they planned to fill with diesel and jet fuels to see how well they could be stored there. A man living underground would need fuel, perhaps a cache of food. They experimented with storing that down there as well.

Fig.3 Using string and pegs to measure ice movement. Source: Donald Rausch, "Ice Tunnel, Tuto Area, Greenland, 1956," Technical Report 44, Wilmette, IL: SIPRE, 1956, ERDC;p 15

Cold Storage

The permafrost tunnel was just one way that the engineers thought about burying things. Throughout the 1950s and into the 1960s, Greenland became a laboratory for US-based cold climate environment studies. Sensational engineering projects were undertaken on top of the ice. The most famous attempt was Camp Century, a subglacial army base where two hundred men could live year-round.[12] While the base was publicized at the time as a research and scientific station, it is now known that Camp Century was built in service of something called Project Iceworm, an army effort to shuttle nuclear missiles around under the ice. While Century was built and occupied for a few years, Iceworm never took shape.

Given the absurdity of Camp Century, dozens of projects that were undertaken in conjunction with that base have been long overlooked—things like the permafrost tunnel. Camp Century was far inland and created by digging deep trenches in the ice cap, which were covered with processed snow. But along the edge of the ice, near Camp Tuto, dozens of tunnels and shafts were excavated out of permafrost and ice to explore alternate ways to manipulate and utilize the materials found in the Arctic. As they had done with the permafrost, the engineers excavated a handful of ice tunnels from the glacier. They drilled back hundreds of feet and—as in the permafrost tunnel—created rooms and pits, imagining the ice cap as a place to live. A 25-five-man camp was planned, complete with latrines, a mess hall, and a recreation building. A diesel generator would keep the lights on and the plumbing working. A reporter who visited in 1959 explained that the ice tunnel glowed blue when the lights were on. The heat of the lightbulbs melted small pits in the walls, creating a lanternlike glow. Another report explained that a team of distinguished visitors had been served a meal in the tunnel and spent the night on cots stored there. The meal was intentional, spending the night was accidental: a sudden storm prevented them from leaving. Some of the men stationed in the area had carved a small altar out of one of the ice walls. They called it the "blue ice chapel."[13]

The ice tunnels were not conceived of as spiritual places, though for a time it does look like the army planned to have men live there. Like the permafrost tunnel, they were carved as subglacial prototypes and possibilities. How could this little-studied material be used for strategic ends? Might the nation rely on such caverns to store food supplies and fuel? As in the permafrost tunnel, things were left in the ice for months on end (usually over the winter, when Camp Tuto was closed and the men returned home). The tunnels were rigged with lights and ventilation shafts. Each year they were lined with wooden pegs and wires, pulled taut so that the rate and direction of the deformation of ice and snow could be measured. How fast was the tunnel caving in?

The warping and slumping were important to understand because one of the primary reasons for the tunnels was yet another utterly fantastic and absurd Cold War construction project: a subglacial subway. This was linked to Project Iceworm, but it was bigger than that. If you could create under ice railways and stations, you could supply massive bases around the ice cap, doing away with the need for surface travel, which was dangerous and time-consuming: It took no less than four days to go one 100 miles across the top of the ice. The idea of sending trains and roads under the frozen earth was a captivating Cold War concept. Such networks would be invisible from above, able to withstand nuclear blasts, and sheltered from the terrible climatic conditions above. Why not give it a try?

Summer was construction season at Camp Tuto and in the Greenland tunnels. Each summer men would return to dig and measure: each winter they closed the tunnels and left, boarding over the entrances so they would not fill with blowing ice and snow. The next year the researchers would return, usually in June, when Camp Tuto reopened, to take measure of what had happened when they were gone. Testing the strings for movement. They did this year after year until one year they did not. By 1963 no one was coming back. Everything was left back in the tunnels, boarded over.

Cold War Thaw

In 1963, the corps started digging a new permafrost tunnel, this one at Ladd Air Force Base in Alaska. Research in Greenland was costly and difficult, and the short construction and research season made those projects seem unnecessary. Alaska, a state with a large military presence, could function in a similar (if less consistently cold) way. The first tunnel was dug straight back 120 feet into the permafrost and was used to study Cold War concerns: how to excavate and work with permafrost. Samples were taken from various places and depths and examined for tensile strength and creep. What were the geotechnical qualities of this odd stuff?

More recently, the tunnel has been expanded and revamped. The type of science and research done there has shifted as well. Since the early 2000s, the engineering focus on strategic concerns has been supplemented by "studies focused on climate change and paleoclimatology." That is because within the walls of the tunnel are organic remains, including plants and bones. Whatever was frozen thousands of years ago has stayed frozen, intact. Visitors to the tunnel remark that, though it is cold, it smells earthy, like things rotting. One item of particular interest is a baby mammoth tooth.[14] Cold-adapted fungi grow down there. NASA has used the tunnel to test equipment meant for Mars.

Cold War strategic priorities—absurd, irrational, fantastical—led to the creation of tunnels and research centers still in use today, albeit for a different purpose. Climate change research is the new strategic, not to mention existential, threat. The melting of ice and snow and permafrost is thus of primary importance. Scientists now know that permafrost stores carbon dioxide and methane, and that its melt releases those greenhouse gases into the atmosphere. The questions are, How much And how fast might it melt? What else might be stored there and released? Some worry that thaw will release microbes foreign to the modern world.[15] And ultimately, of course, the researchers who spend time in the caverns must wonder how long the tunnel itself will last—even with the refrigeration system piped through it. No one wants to be buried in permafrost.

For a long time, strategic questions and military needs drove questions about and research into these extreme materials. So much so that questions of climate systems and climate change were ignored. The men (there is no record of women being involved) who went to Greenland to excavate and study tunnels in the 1950s and early 1960s did so using military infrastructure and resources; they pitched all their questions to strategic ends. Even while they accumulated information that would later be of use to civilian research projects, their efforts drove a particular way of seeing the world and its environments: operational and practical.

These were the prices of building a corpus of secretive expertise about hidden places. To construct invisibility, the US engineers went to faraway places, tried to bury things under the surface of the earth, and in doing so, amassed expertise that itself was kept secret. This hidden knowledge had power, which is what made it so useful. But burying it for so long in military reports and secret plans meant that what might have been most useful of all—the significance of permafrost to earth systems and regulation of climate and this life—remained a question whose answer might only come when it is already too late.[16]

-----

[1] U.S. Army Corps of Engineers, "Collection of Information on underground Installations," Environmental Intelligence Guide no. 30 (1959), Box 20, Records of the Office of the Chief of Engineers (RG77), National Archives and Records Administration, College Park, MD. On the Cold War underground more broadly, see Gretchen Heefner, *The Missile Next Door: The Minuteman in the American Heartland* (Harvard University Press, 2012) and Tom Vanderbilt, *Survival City: Adventures among the Ruins of Atomic America* (Princeton Architectural Press, 2002).

[2] Rosalind Williams, *Notes on the Underground* (MIT Press, 2008), 190–191.

[3] Quoted in Kenneth D. Rose, *One Nation Underground: The Fallout Shelter in America Culture* (New York University Press, 2001), 1.

[4] On the construction of Minuteman missile sites, Heefner, *The Missile Next Door*.

[5] For more on this, see Gretchen Heefner, *Sand, Snow and Stardust* (forthcoming).

[6] On the Cold War Arctic, see Stephen Bocking and Daniel Heidt, eds., *Cold Science Environmental Knowledge in the North American Arctic during the Cold War* (Routledge, 2019); Kristian H. Nielsen and Henry Nielsen, *Camp Century: The Untold Story of America's Secret Arctic Military Base under the Greenland Ice* (Columbia University Press, 2021); Ronald E. Doel, Kristine C. Harper, and Matthias Heymann, eds., *Exploring Greenland: Cold War Science and Technology on Ice* (Palgrave Macmillan, 2016), 75–98; Ronald E. Doel, Urban Wråkberg, and Suzanne Zeller, "Science, Environment, and the New Arctic," *Journal of Historical Geography* 44 (April 2014): 2–14; Matthew Farish, "Frontier Engineering: From the Globe to the Body in the Cold War Arctic," *Canadian Geographies* 50, no. 2 (June 2006): 177–196; Matthew Farish, "The Lab and the Land: Overcoming the Arctic in Cold War Alaska," *Isis* 104, no. 1 (March 2013): 1–29.

[7] On Greenland, see Jon Gertner, *The Ice at the End of the World: An Epic Journey into Greenland's Buried Past and Our Perilous Future* (Icon Books, 2019); Janet Martin-Nielsen, *Eismitte in the Scientific Imagination: Knowledge and Politics at the Center of Greenland* (Palgrave Macmillan, 2013); Ronald E. Doel, Kristine C. Harper, and Matthias Heymann, eds., *Exploring Greenland: Cold War Science and Technology on Ice* (Palgrave Macmillan, 2016).

[8] On Greenland permafrost tunnels, see John F. Abel, Jr., "Permafrost Tunnel, Camp TUTO, Greenland," Technical Report no. 73, Snow, Ice and Permafrost Research Establishment, hereafter abbreviated as SIPRE (October 1960); George K. Swinzow, "Permafrost Tunneling by a Continuous Mechanical Method," Technical Report no. 221, Cold Regions Research and Engineering Laboratory, hereafter abbreviated as CRREL (November 1970); "Review of Certain Properties and Problems of Frozen Ground including Permafrost," Report no. 9, SIPRE (March 1953); "Under Ice Mining Techniques," Technical Report no. 72, SIPRE (January 1961).

[9] Research Report no.10, SIPRE, 16 ; "Permafrost and Related

Engineering Problems in Alaska, " *Geological Survey Professional Paper* 678 (1969); U.S. Army Corps of Engineers, "CRREL's First 25 Years, 1961–1986" (1986). For state-of-the-art thinking at this time, see https://collections.dartmouth.edu/arctica-beta/html/EA02a-07.htm.

[10] For permafrost research, see "Review of Certain Properties and Problems of Frozen Ground Including Permafrost," SIPRE Report 9 (1953); "Some aspects of snow, ice, and frozen ground,: SIPRE Report 10 (1953); "Under Ice Mining Techniques," Technical Report no. 72, SIPRE (January 1961).

[11] Edgar Allan Poe's "The Premature Burial," of 1844, is considered the classic of the genre of man being buried alive.

[12] Nielsen and Nielson, *Camp Century*; Gertner, *The Ice at the End of the World*.

[13] On ice tunnels, see "Ice Tunnel, Tuto Area, Greenland, 1956," Technical Report no. 44, SIPRE (1958); "Grid Technique for Measuring Ice Tunnel Deformation," SIPRE (1959); Theodore R. Butkovich, "Some Physical Properties of Ice from the TUTO Tunnel and Ramp, Thule, Greenland," SIPRE (1959); "An Under-Ice Camp in the Arctic," Special Report no. 44, CRREL (1961).

[14] Paul S. Sellmann, "Geology of the USA CRREL Permafrost Tunnel," Technical Report no. 199, CRREL (July 1967); Margaret Cysewski, Kevin Bjella, and Matthew Strum, "The History and Future of the Permafrost Tunnel near Fox, Alaska," U.S. CRREL, https://pubs.aina.ucalgary.ca/cpc/CPC6-1222.pdf; Madeline Ostrander, "In a Tunnel beneath Alaska, Scientists Race to Understand Disappearing Permafrost," *Smithsonian Magazine* (2020), https://www.smithsonianmag.com/science-nature/tunnel-beneath-alaska-180974804/.

[15] "In a Tunnel beneath Alaska," *Smithsonian Magazine* (2020).

[16] On relationship between US military and climate change, Neta Crawford, *The Pentagon, Climate Change, and War* (MIT Press, 2022). The irony that US military projects have morphed into climate research centers should be front and center in readers' minds. The US military has been a major driver of the processes that have led to global warming, and current attempts to mitigate that cannot and should not erase this long and violent past.

Atlantic Networks and Geometries

Visualizing Military New York (1783–1815)

Victoria Sanger

"Let us recall that the art of drawing towns is in the hands of military engineers and that urbanism in the classical age is in some ways born of military urbanism."[1]
– Pierre Pinon

The geometry of war is inscribed on the plans of most cities planned by Europeans in the Early Modern period.[2] This chapter renders visible the functional and spatial interdependence of civilian and military planning through the case of study of Joseph-François Mangin (1758–ca. 1818). Mangin's story traces how a persistent European military urban approach ultimately undergirded the geometrical configurations of New York City.[3] Despite his difficulties assimilating as a French émigré from Lorraine by way of Saint-Domingue, he transcribed on New York City old world spatiality of defense, colonialism, and territoriality. The historical period of his turbulent career spanned a particularly intense period of military and civilian planning in New York City and its region: the years between the British evacuation on November 25, 1783, and the end of the War of 1812 in 1815.

New York City's planning by Europeans has balanced military urbanism with commercial directives since the Dutch colonists ordered the construction of an expandable, gridded settlement and a star-shaped Fort Amsterdam in Lower Manhattan in 1626.[4] By the mid-1790s New York became the nation's busiest port, surpassing Philadelphia. Repairs were made after the British left, and the Common Council commissioned plans for gridded large-scale real estate development in northern Manhattan. In 1785 and further in 1796, Casimir Goerck subdivided the Common Lands mid-island from today's 23rd-90th streets, from 1797-1803 Goerck and Mangin added a plan of lower Manhattan almost touching 23rd street, and finally in 1807-1811 John Randel Jr. completed the grid up to 155th street.[5] But New York's success made it a target and a player in international conflict. In these interwar years its shipping ambitions were choked in the conflict between England and France, and both countries seized American ships, goods, and sailors in retaliation for double-dealing.[6] From 1806 to February 1815, the city was blockaded from the Lower New York Bay, causing great distress. In 1814 rumors of a new attack triggered a new set of forts, fanned by the news that the British had seized Washington, DC, in August 1814.[7] And so a system of coastal harbor fortifications and land fortifications was an inherent part of New York's design. Where historians have not studied the interdependence of civilian and military projects in New York, this chapter seeks to weave together grid and fort.[8]

Mangin's Colonial Training

Mangin's life and career navigated and transmitted the military and urban culture of the Atlantic world through the late eighteenth century revolutionary storm cloud of France, America and Saint-Domingue/Haiti. In 1784 he emigrated, an ambitious 28-year-old middle-class lawyer from the small town of Dompaire in the Lorraine region of eastern France, eager to make his fortune in the French colony of Saint-Domingue, at the time the richest and most productive colony of any empire.[9] He spent his first year as a steward overseeing the slaves on a sugar plantation. Soon, he moved into the more lucrative field of the military. He was hired by the army first in the militia around 1785 and then as draftsman for headquarters of the army.[10] Working as a mid-level employee on a team of 39 basic surveyors under Naudet, one of eight regional directors reporting to the Grand Voyer du Cap, from November 26, 1788, his duties included "planning roads, levelling, cartography, designing canals, adjudicating properties." In so doing, he amassed a fortune and boasted to his mother of a lavish lifestyle.[11] Joseph-François was joined by his younger brother, Charles Nicholas Mangin (1769–1821) in 1788. In their last two years before emigration in 1793 their responsibilities increased with military tensions as they fought with the French for the continued control and exploitation of its slave population.[12]

The Mangin brothers' experience testifies to their approach that conceived multiple facets of a city on an urban, regional, and global scale. Although little of their work in Saint-Domingue remains in the archives, one remaining example is from 1802, when Charles Nicholas returned to Saint-Domingue and wrote the initial report on the founding of a new town later called Port Napoléon.[13] Built on the Samana Peninsula in the formerly Spanish part of the island, it aimed to be a kind of Cap Français or Port-au-Prince but this time facing east. Charles Nicholas summarizes the conditions of the Samana Bay, its favorable winds for sailing and for healthy air, the depth of its water, the fertile region rich in coffee and sugar plantations, mahogany and cocoa. Its harbor was large enough to berth and repair the biggest ships. It could be reached by a canal and protected by batteries placed on islands and points along the coast. Port Napoléon almost seemed like a version of New York with its harbor, protected by coastal and island batteries, with international trade, and an inland canal.[14] A plan from 1806 by Lieutenant Colonel Bron in a different location may have built following his ideas.[15]

Port Napoléon was typical of the gridded, military towns of Saint-Domingue mainly urbanized in the eighteenth century, the French colony with the most cities, all of them military.[16] Their sites were chosen by a governor or intendant with information from engineers' surveys and planned and executed by a military engineer. The ports tended to forego city walls but rather be protected by coastal batteries where inland towns were fortified against internal rebellions. All but one port was built *ex nihilo* (out of nothing) on a grid plan. Urban extensions and often the dimensions of blocks varied, and at times streets were put at an angle relative to the original grid—the most elaborate being Le Cap, which had five extensions over the course of the eighteenth century, a sign of its economic vitality. The towns were populated by "petit blancs," white commoners such as merchants, artisans and laborers who were tasked with defending the town against inland rebellion.

Eventually, both brothers fled the revolutionary violence in Saint-Domingue in 1793 and immigrated to New York.[17] Although they lost their fortunes, their experience in Saint-Domingue had given the Mangin brothers their means of employment. Within a year of their arrival in New York, the brothers, especially Joseph-François, seemed to have great opportunities. But, caught between their national allegiances, they were never able to secure stable positions of status for more than a few years within either French or American networks. Charles Nicolas retained his French nationality and thought it more promising to return to Saint-Domingue, departing New York in 1798 to launch several failed trading ventures and help the fruitless reconquest campaign for Napoleon before sailing home to France in 1810. His brother, now a naturalized American citizen with a growing family, decided his best option was to enrich himself in New York and later return to a comfortable retirement in France.

Mangin's Vision for New York

Joseph-François Mangin had both large-scale synthetic French visions for New York and ambitious career aspirations. Yet to succeed, he needed to wrestle with an unsympathetic New York where he struggled to assimilate both professionally and conceptually. In January 1796 he wrote a letter to Alexander Hamilton explaining the all-encompassing view of a multifaceted French engineer. The need for him to do so after his being actively involved in New York for three years shows a tepid interpretation into the New York establishment.

> I do not believe it is being arrogant to assure you sir, that I have always been considered a good builder mostly due to my correctly combining and applying reason to all of these works, joining as I do my knowledge with a theory which does not allow me to be wrong. I also believe, sir, that I know how to combine all kinds of defenses and that I know how to adapt them to local and other various conditions: just as I know how to approach all types of construction, I have the ability to present my projects in a clear manner to allow managers to examine them, to respect or accept them on the basis of my knowledge.[18]

In the years afterwords, he continued to solicit Hamilton for more powerful positions in the military, arguing that his bigger ideas were worthy of a higher status and a military rank.[19] The following month, in February of 1796, he wrote a lofty preamble in a proposal for a system of inland canals linking the Hudson and East rivers with two large basins that would sanitize and drain Fresh Water Pond (Collect Pond) while promoting shipping and transporting goods to the city center. He contextualized his project in a vein that showed his French engineer's assessment of the total value of a city, like projects in Saint-Domingue such as Charles Nicolas's Port Napoléon, produced five years later.

> The city of new York appears to be designed as the future center and metropolis of commercial world; as lying at the mouth of two large and Beautiful rivers, on which are imported from the remotest interior parts the productions of fertile and improved countries, and commanding an extensive Bay the Safest and most strongly defended in the union. . . . such advantages as we have shortly Related are deserving of the most serious attention; and the expenses the project will occasion, can not counterpoise its immense utility for in that hippothesis [sic], new York could Boast to unite all conveniencyes [sic] for an immense trade, private manufactories to carry it on, other public and military to afford whatever is

necessary for navy, war, and fortification....[20]

Overall, Mangin's input was both solicited and yet held at arm's length by the establishment. The political context was not favorable. Over the course of the 1790s an initial Francophilia, in gratitude for aid during the American Revolution, had dimmed and for a time America was turning back to England. At the time of the Hamilton letter and canal project, there was a "quasi-war" against France, and New York was fortifying against a potential French invasion.[21] He suffered setbacks: although he was the architect in full partnership with John McComb, he was absent at the ceremony laying the first stone of City Hall in May of

Fig. 1 Lionel Pincus and Princess Firyal Map Division, The New York Public Library. Casimir Goerck and Joseph-François Mangin, "Plan of the city of New-York" *The New York Public Library Digital Collections*. 1803-11. Digital image: https://digitalcollections.nypl.org/items/510d-47da-efa8-a3d9-e040-e00a18064a99

1803, and his name was erased from the record.[22] Most likely his associations with slavery in Saint-Domingue were distasteful to many: Benjamin Latrobe, learning he had lost the City Hall competition to the Mangin-McComb team, disparaged the former as that "St. Domingo Frenchman."[23] Several months after the City Hall disgrace, in November 1803, Mangin's map of New York was rejected.[24] Both Koeppel and Leroy hypothesize that he was discredited for political reasons not substantive ones since his map was largely accepted. Despite his pleas to Hamilton, he was not given a military position in the United States Military Academy at West Point, founded in 1802. It could have been because of Jonathan Williams, first superintendent of West Point, who mistrusted foreign engineers in the current political environment.[25] Although the strong presence of Frenchmen and a Francophile curriculum at this military academy beginning in 1816 calls the lasting impact of this turn of the century francophobia into question.[26]

His later work continues to attest to his multiple competencies in town planning, surveying, engineering, and architecture. By 1816 he was sickly, supporting a family of five children, and out of work. He applied to the City of New York for alms of 50 dollars.[27] There is no further trace of him after 1818. The odds had not been in his favor. Whether for espousing slavery, being French, or having an allegiance with Hamilton, his ideas were not formally accepted. Yet they were so much of his time, and so well presented graphically that they were impactful nonetheless as we will now see.

Mangin's Plan for Manhattan

The most famous work by Mangin is a "regulating plan of the city" for the Common Council. On December 11, 1797, Joseph-François Mangin got the commission in tandem with accomplished surveyor Casimir Goerck, but Goerck died in a yellow fever epidemic in 1798 and Mangin solo completed a six-foot-square manuscript on April 10, 1799 (now lost). In July, the Common Council commissioned an engraving of it by Peter Maverick at half the size and completed in 1803 known as the Mangin-Goerck plan (fig. 1).

By now it is clear that Mangin's comment explaining his intentions to present "not the plan of the city such as it is, but such as it is to be" is part of his synthetic engineer-planner's delineation of the city.[28] Yet this quote is often cited as proof of its his perceived arrogance, his plan's impracticability and an explanation for why it was rejected.[29] In fact, Koeppel's analysis demonstrates how Mangin grappled with landowners and recorded and projected redesigned streets below the base of the Commissioner's Plan.[30] His flaw was not having authorization to open streets. Moreover, Koeppel points to how Mangin planted the seeds for a large vision of New York, the idea of having a planning document to project the city into the future "captured an enduring legacy."[31] Although Mangin's map was recalled in 1803, it was preempted by the even vaster projected grid Randel proposed in 1811.[32] But this time the plan was fully backed with the legislature. As for the colonialist-style land-grab of the enormous grid, Mangin and Randel had a common culture in tacitly continuing the institution of classism and slavery and saw no obstacle to dispossessing Blacks and other marginalized populations in the northern extension of Manhattan's grid.[33] Just as the French towns in Saint-Domingue were part of a military and state sponsored network of racial oppression so were Mangin's and Randel's grid structures for Lower and Upper Manhattan. The 1811 Commissioner's map was met by attack and litigation. Where on the one hand it provided wealthy individuals "equal opportunity" to buy land and commodified real estate in New York, on the other hand many landholders virulently opposed the gridding of their land, and it set the groundwork for how squatters were displaced and a whole vibrant mixed race and class community, Seneca Village, was erased from the map later in the century.[34]

The Goerck-Mangin map emphasized and extended the built parts of Manhattan of its day,

Fig. 2 Attrib. Mangin and his circle? “A Chart of New York harbour”, National Archives, College Park Dr. 142 Sht. 92. Ca. 1803-6. 28 x 19.5” 102279922. Digital image: https://catalog.archives.gov/id/102279922

forging it in the language of military urbanism of the Atlantic World. It proposed to continue the network fringe grids, Bayard in the center, Delancey to the east, and Stuyvesant in the north. The north-to-south streets of extensions were so plausible that they eventually were built. Mangin's map stops just short of the Common Lands, a critical part of the island that had been surveyed and subdivided by his partner, Casimir Goerck.[35] This two-mile area from 23rd to 90th street had first been mapped in 1785, with extra avenues added in 1796. Goerck's map of the Common Lands is considered an important kernel in the later plan of the city. Its avenues became the city's backbone, today's Park, Fifth, and Sixth avenues. The land parcels in this subdivision became the five-acre blocks of the Commissioner's Plan of 1811 reaching to 155th Street. In the Mangin-Goerck plan a new grid at the east side and oriented north-south has the same block dimensions. So, although Mangin's stopped at 23rd Street, it originally referred to another map that went as far as 90th.[36]

Mangin's plan creates axes to circulate around the island. Greenwich Street runs along the Hudson, linking the battery to the new state prison, also designed by him. A canal runs along the base of a grid linking Fresh Pond to the Hudson River, possibly part of the abovementioned canal project. In an undated map, most likely from 1803–1806 (Fig. 2), he supported this idea in an arc traced from Corlear's Hook to the Hudson, suggesting a link between the rivers at about the area of Fresh Pond and the canal.[37] In the Mangin-Goerck plan, Grand Street joins the new canal to complete a triangle around the edges of what was then the city, with West Street and Pearl Street running just inside the docks. He defined the edge along the East River as South Street. Such peripheral circulation routes are typical of military planning from the Renaissance, when they were called the *pomerio*.[38]

Mangin's vision is hardly a Baroque plan such as L'Enfant's for Washington, inspired by Le Notre or Christopher Wren. Even the theory that its colliding grids are elements creating nodal points and visual "urban delight" seems overstated.[39] His influence is more likely military colonial designs from the mid-eighteenth to early nineteenth century, such as French Le Cap and French, Spanish, and American New Orleans. His planning is similar to the contemporary American Sector (Faubourg St. Mary) developed just outside the Vieux Carré to the south of a newly planned Canal Street whose waterway linked Lake Pontchartrain to the Mississippi River (1792-ca. 1810).[40]

Programmatically, Mangin's buildings are prominently featured in the plan: in addition to the state prison mentioned above, he designed the Park Theater.[41] City hall is labelled "New Court House," one part of its tri-partite program.[42] It adds a structuring classical architecture to the preexisting park. Stylistically, it is a mixture of French and English influences. The resemblance to the Louis XV detailing of the façade (channeled rustication, arched windows, swags, balustrade…) and volumes of the stair hall of the Nancy town hall of Mangin's native region of Lorraine is striking.[43]

The coexistence of a levelling grid with the underlying hilly topography points to the dual military and civilian conception of the site of New York that I will now elaborate. On the one hand, there was a civilian residential and commercial grid devoid of any topographical qualities, leveled and crisscrossed with roads for circulation of traffic and healthy air. On the other hand, hills and depths were featured and engineered following a military geometry of defense. The city embankments have been filled in to make of Manhattan an angular, sword-shaped polygon (Figs. 1 and 3). On closer inspection, Mangin uses clear graphic language to indicate the existing topography, shaded beneath the grid with diagonal hatching and the unbuilt areas with either trees at ground level or stippling where leveling or infill was required.

A project begun slightly later lends insight into how Mangin's grid erased topography when not needed for military reasons. He mapped Paulus Hook in New

Fig. 3 Joseph Fr. Mangin, *A Chart of New-York Harbour*, National Archives, Record Group 77 FORTS-D642-8, ca. 1801.

Jersey in 1804, overlaying a developer's grid on a marshy former Revolutionary defense point facing Manhattan.[44]

Mangin's Shared Vision for Harbor Defenses with Jonathan Williams

Just as the Common Council had requested from Mangin a map of Lower Manhattan only, so did his projects for defense focus on this part of the island. The earliest known chart by Mangin of New York Harbor (fig. 3) here follows military cartographic convention and is depicted as flat, shaded red with the same polygonal outline as his civilian plan. By contrast, the site surrounding the urban core is portrayed as unbuilt and natural with all its marshes, hills, and rocks. It shows parts of lower New York Bay and all upper New York Bay without fortifications and with a bathymetric chart of depths in fathoms of navigable channels. Although these points had been fortified in the past centuries by Dutch, English, and Revolutionaries, Mangin presents the site as a *tabula rasa*. Sometime before 1806, Mangin mapped out a military vision of mutually reinforcing harbor batteries (Fig. 2), noting distances between the batteries to demonstrate their effectiveness and showing the paths of cannonballs radiating their deadly crossfire. Mangin's reliance on a network of coastal batteries would be enacted by the establishment engineer Jonathan Williams, who agreed with this approach.

Unlike Mangin who had trained in the field, France-trained Colonel Jonathan Williams was at the center of the American military establishment. He had accompanied his great-uncle Benjamin Franklin in France (1776–1785) and had trained at the Ecole Militaire.[45] He was later appointed by Jefferson as first inspector of fortifications in 1801 and superintendent of West Point in 1802. Williams imported and fused in West Point the educational model and theorists of two key French military and civil institutions: the Ecole Militaire and the Ecole Polytechnique.[46] There,

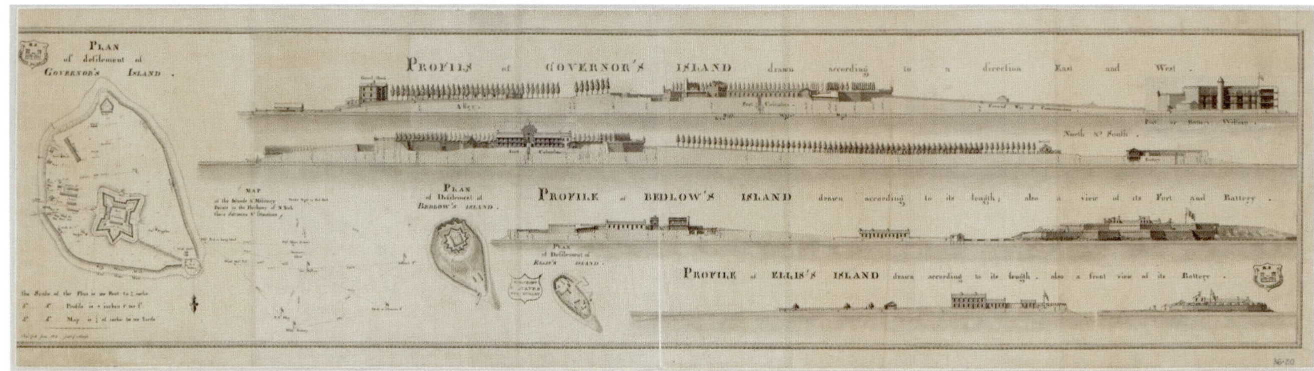

Fig. 4 Joseph-François Mangin, Plan of defilement of Governor's Island. / Profils of Governor's Island drawn according to a direction East and West. / Map of the Islands & Military Points in the Harbour of New York their distances and situations. / Plan of Defilement of Bedlow's Island. / Profile of Bedlow's Island drawn according to its length; also a view of its Fort and Battery. / Plan of Defilment of Ellis's Island. / Profile of Ellis's Island drawn according to its length, also a front view of its Battery, June 1813, NARA, Drawer 036, 77-Forts-36-20, Digital image: 102280039. https://catalog.archives.gov/id/102280039

he founded the United States Military Philosophical Society (1802–1813). This overlooked organization was a keystone to the military planning of New York.[47] The minutes from the meetings emphasize interdisciplinarity in both theory and practice. He promoted the study of the latest military science from Europe, specifically the work of the marquis de Montalembert, whose round coastal battery and star-shaped designs Williams emulated in Castle Williams and Bedloe's Island (Liberty Island).[48]

In 1807, Williams prepared a report surveying the coastline and the charts of the harbor. Like Mangin in the prior year (Fig. 2), he concluded that a great force of batteries in a narrow passage was the solution. By 1812, Williams's (and partly Mangin's) vision was largely built.

By far Mangin's most striking military map is the graphic presentation which celebrates William's similarly conceived harbor defenses. June 1813 (Fig. 4).[49] It celebrates Williams's harbor defenses as those made by a kindred spirit. The map is rendered in wash and ink, and its forms are crisply shaded: bastions, merlons, flags, and trees stand at attention, war-ready. Mangin emphasizes the importance of precise height measurements in several ways. First, with the overall title "defilement," which indicates the height advantage from raking fire of cannons atop forts that are carefully staggered and shown in elevation as well as measured sectional views. The key forts in Williams' project were on Governor's, Ellis' and Bedloe's islands and are also produced in plan with spot highlights in red showing their heights. Mangin shows off the structure of the forts. Fort Columbus (today Fort Jay) had been improved by Mangin but still follows the form of the Vauban-style bastioned star fort, which combines masonry with earthworks. It is higher than the other forts on the island, and the three forts on Governor's Island are shown to be complementary. Highlighted is Jonathan Williams' "Fort or Battery William" (Castle Williams) whose Montalembert influenced design produced dense fire from cannons in stacking gunports. Arches provide extra strength for the fort, which is all masonry. This structure became a prototype for American coastal batteries.[50]

On the left sheet is a fascinating plan of the harbor system of forts as an ensemble, produced on a smaller scale with Mangin's typical mistakes in English ("1/4 inche to 100 Yards"). Fort William is at the center of an irregular pentagon made up of nine forts, and Mangin has measured the distance between them. He is emphasizing that the forts are all well within the effective shooting range of one mile (5,280 feet). At half that distance from one another, their crossfire would be deadly to ships attempting to pass through. Mangin has thus traced an invisible geometry of ballistics shot from man-made forts atop the harbor topography. It is this geometry, invisible to the untrained eye, that allows for the open gridding of Manhattan. Whether or not the whole system of forts he depicts was his idea alone, he makes the most forceful cartographic presentation of the geometrical configuration in both two and three dimensions.

Conclusion

The seeds for New York's future were planted in the years between 1783 and 1815. Seeing the absence of an overall scheme, Joseph-François Mangin opportunistically stepped in, showcasing the multifaced and geometrical vision of the French military engineer. Established Williams may have domesticated French military theories and practices, but Mangin taught New York to think big; his mistake was not thinking big enough. William's protégé and successor, Joseph Gardner Swift's larger territory in his plan to fortify New York in 1814 corresponded to the greater area of the Commissioner's Map of 1811.[51] Swift and Randel eclipsed his projects to the north of Manhattan by extending the terrain to the whole island to 155th Street. However, Mangin defined the Southern part of Manhattan and the harbor defenses. I have demonstrated how Mangin's plan was firmly embedded in the pragmatic French and European colonial planning culture seen in Saint-Domingue and New Orleans. When Mangin's different maps are seen together, they present a total vision for Manhattan: a leveled, gridded open city for circulation, commerce, and habitation and radial permanent harbor defenses reaffirming natural features in the topography.

Today, a visitor standing atop Castle Williams can palpably feel Mangin's legacy, the geometry of the harbor defenses that defines the panorama, the motorist can traverse his circulation patterns on the West Side Highway and Canal Street, and a visitor to City Hall can experience its nod to Lorraine and the tradition of French aristocratic architecture.

-----

[1] Pierre Pinon, "Saint-Domingue: l'île à villes," eds. Emilie d'Orgeix and Laurent Vidal, *Les villes françaises du Nouveau Monde* (Somogy Editions d'art, 1999), 112.

[2] On military urbanism, see Victoria Sanger "Vauban Urbaniste," eds. Warmoes and Sanger, *Vauban, bâtisseur du Roi-Soleil* (Somogy, Cité de l'architecture, Musée des Plans-reliefs, 2007), 214–225, 259–265. Martha Pollak, *Cities at War in Early Modern Europe* (Cambridge University Press, 2010).

[3] On the urban culture and institutions of French engineers, see Antoine Picon, *French Architects and Engineers in the Age of Enlightenment* (Cambridge Studies in the History of Architecture, Cambridge University Press, 1992).

[4] Christopher P. Heuer, "Delirious New Amsterdam" eds. Piet Lombaerde and Charles Van den Heuvel, *Early Modern Urbanism and the Grid. Town Planning in the Low Countries in International Context. Exchanges in Theory and Practice 1660-1800* (Brepols, Turnhout, 2011), 177-186.

[5] Gerard Koeppel, *City on a Grid. How New York became New York* (Da Capo Press, 2015), chap. 3 and 4; Hilary Ballon, ed., *The Greatest Grid. The Master Plan of Manhattan 1811-2011*, (Columbia University Press, 2012), 17-47.

[6] Steven H. Jaffe, "Hot Shot and Heavy Metal," in *New York at War: Four Centuries of Combat, Fear, and Intrigue in Gotham* (Basic Books, 2012), 111–138.

[7] Ibid. See also Isaac Newton Phelps Stokes, *The Iconography of Manhattan Island* (R. H. Dodd, 1915–1928), 3:505.

[8] Jaffe does not refer to civilian planning, for example: Steven H. Jaffe, ibid., 111–138 nor do the authors including Ballon in *The Greatest Grid*. While Koeppel in *City on a Grid* admirably discusses at length Mangin's oeuvre without seeing it as a system.

[9] For a fascinating biography in its historical context based on family archives and the correspondence of Joseph-François and his brother Charles-Nicolas, see Thibaud Leroy, with Edmond Varene, *Joseph François Mangin, L'homme qui imagina Manhattan* (Kindle edition, 2019), chap. 1, "Le départ." This book's materials are a significant rectification of Mangin's biography in the otherwise solid Gerard Koeppel, op. cit.

[10] *Dessinateur de l'état major général de l'armée du corps français à Saint Domingue*. Service Historique de la Défense (SHD) GR2 YE 2669/2670 Etat de service militaire. Cited by Leroy, *Joseph François Mangin*, chap. 2, "Splendeurs et misères de la colonie (1784–1785)."

[11] Leroy, op. cit., letters to Marie-Anne Milot, from Jean-François, February 26, 1788, and from Charles-Nicolas, January 4, 1789.

[12] SHD Etat de Service GR2YE2669 Mangin, Charles Nicolas.

[13] SHD, GR1 m 1669, July 31, 1802, Charles Nicholas Mangin,

"Reconnaissance faitte dans la baye de Samana, par les ordres du citoyen Desfourneaux General de division Commandant en chef la ci devant partie Espagnole, par Nicholas Mangin arpenteur du département de Samana accompagné du citoyen Poulharnier capitaine aide de camp du dit General."

[14] Ibid.

[15] SHD GR1VM 99, pièce 38bis, Colonel Bron, "Carte de l'entrée de la Rade et du port Napoléon dans la Baye de Samana relative au mémoire de Mr. Lieut. Colonel Bron ».

[16] Pierre Pinon, op. cit., 108–119. Gauvin Alexander Bailey, *Architecture and Urbanism in the French Atlantic Empire: State, Church, and Society,* 1604–1830 (McGill-Queen's University Press, 2018).

[17] Leroy, op. cit., chap. 4, "La spirale des désordres (1789–1793)."

[18] Letter from Mangin to Hamilton, January 11, 1796, in Gerard Koeppel, *City on a Grid*, 31–32.

[19] Ibid., 32, *Papers of Alexander Hamilton*, mss. LOC, January 11, 1799.

[20] Joseph-François Mangin and Charles Nicolas Mangin, "Sketch of a Project to Construct Docks in the Interior of the Town, in New York" February 22, 1696. For the memorandum, see Stokes, *The Iconography of Manhattan Island*, 5:1328. Minutes of the Common Council, 2:218. He does not reprint Mangin's drawing, cited in metal file no. 17 of the City Clerk's record room.

[21] See François Furstenberg, *When the United States Spoke French: Five Refugees Who Shaped a Nation* (Penguin Press, 2015). Koppel, *City on a Grid*, 31.

[22] Historians have proven beyond a doubt that it is his design. See Koeppel, *City on a Grid*, 41–42, 61–62; Clay Lancaster, "New York City Hall Stair Rotunda Reconsidered," *Journal of the Society of Architectural Historians* 29, no. 1 (March 1970): 33–39. Leroy, op. cit., chap. 7, "Espoirs et déceptions, 1798–1805."

[23] "City Hall, First Floor Interior" Landmarks Preservation Commission report, January 27, 1976, p. 2. https://s-media.nyc.gov/agencies/lpc/lp/0916.pdf. Also cited by Koeppel, *City on a Grid*, 42.

[24] Leroy, op. cit., chap. 7.

[25] Sidney Forman, "The United States Military Philosophical Society 1802–1813, Scientia in Bello Pax," *William and Mary Quarterly* 2, no. 3 (July 1945): 273–285.

[26] Victoria Sanger, "L'influence française et la genèse de l'enseignement du génie militaire à l'Ecole de West Point," in Emilie d'Orgeix and Isabelle Warmoes, eds., *Les Savoirs de l'ingénieur militaire et l'édition de manuels, cours et cahiers d'exercices* (1715–1914), 5e journée d'étude du Musée des Plans-Reliefs, INHA (Paris: Ministère de la Culture et de la Communication Direction des Patrimoines, Musée des Plans-Reliefs, 2013), 127–138.

[27] Leroy, *Joseph François Mangin*, "Toujours espérer."

[28] Koeppel, in *The Greatest Grid*, 24.

[29] Paul E. Cohen and Robert T. Augustyn, "Fanciful Projection of the Future," *Manhattan in Maps* (Rizzoli, 1997), 96–99.

[30] For the delineation of the streets, see Koeppel, *City on a Grid*, 61 (diagram) and 85.

[31] Koeppel, in *The Greatest Grid*, 24.

[32] See "Remarks of the Commissioners of the 1811 Plan," cited in Ballon *op. cit.*40–42.

[33] Mapping the African American Past, Columbia University, map. columbia.edu

[34] Ibid.; *The Greatest Grid,* 57, 87, 98-100.

[35] Koeppel, *The Greatest Grid*, 22–23.

[36] Koeppel, *The Greatest Grid*, 22–24.

[37] Attributed to Mangin and his circle, National Archives, College Park Dr. 142 Sht. 92. Ca. 1803-6. 28 x 19.5". The dates proposed reflect that the unstraightened edges of the city no longer follow the Goerck-Mangin plan, rejected in 1803. But the fort of Governor's Island shows Mangin's ravelin from 1806 but does not yet reflect the design of Castle Williams. Although the map is unsigned, the handwriting is very similar to a signed map by Mangin ca. 1801 (fig. 4).

[38] This route is still the main freeway for cars linking to the bridges and tunnels of the five boroughs and New Jersey.

[39] Koeppel, *The Greatest Grid*, 24.

[40] See Samuel Wilson Jr., "Early History of Faubourg St. Mary," in *Friends of the Cabildo, New Orleans Architecture,* vol. 2, *The American Sector (Faubourg St. Mary)*, (Pelican Publishing, 1972), 3–11.

[41] Thomas Eddy, *An Account of the State Prison or Penitentiary House, in the City of New-York* (New York, 1801).

[42] Stokes, *The Iconography of Manhattan Island*, 5:1393–1394.

[43] "City Hall, First Floor Interior" Landmarks Preservation Commission report, p. 3. The Nancy Town Hall was designed by Emmanuel Héré de Corny (1752-1755).

[44] This project has not yet been mentioned in discussions of Mangin's work. Joseph-François Mangin, A map of that part of the town of Jersey commonly called Powles Hook. Actually known as Paulus Hook, a section of Jersey City. The map shows a table of rental rates for lots on each land tract and a description of the elevation of the sections of the land, P. Desobry's Lithography, NY, 1804. Powles Hook (Paulus Hook), Jersey City, New Jersey, 1804. Retrieved from https://doi.org/doi:10.7282/T3FN16SV.

[45] Marian Betancourt, "Jonathan Williams Keeping Us Safe from Enemies," in *Heroes of New York Harbor: Tales from the City's Past* (Globe Pequot, 2016), chap. 1. A portion of Williams's archives is at the Lilly Library Manuscript Collection, Indiana University, Bloomington.

[46] Jon Scott Logel, *Designing Gotham: West Point Engineers and the Rise of Modern New York 1817–1898,* (Louisiana State University Press, 2016). Logel discusses this phenomenon for the period starting in 1817.

[47] Forman, op. cit.

[48] Extracts from the minutes of the United States Military Philosophical Society at a stated meeting, held October 6, 1806 (1806-1809). Early American Imprints, series 2, no. 14101. "Summary of Transactions during the year 1806."

[49] Joseph-François Mangin, Plan of defilement of Governor's Island… June 1813, NARA, Drawer 036, 77-Forts-36-20, Digital image: 102280039.

[50] Barbara A. Yocum, F*ort Jay, Governors Island National Monument. National Parks of New York Harbor, New York, New York* (National Park Service, Historic Structure Report, 2005), and Barbara A. Yocum, *Castle Williams: Historic Structure Report, Governors Island National Monument National Parks of New York Harbor, New York, New York* (National Park

Service, 2005).

[51] J. G. Swift, Report on the *Defence of the City of New-York, Accompanied with Maps, Views, and Topographical Plans*, 1814, Ebenezer Stevens Papers, New-York Historical Society, Museum & Library, digital collections, https://digitalcollections.nyhistory.org/islandora/object/nyhs%3Aswift.

Basements as Invisible Defense

Dongwoo Yim

In the summer of 1983, I ventured into the forbidden basement of our apartment building for the first time. As a timid six-year-old, I had never dared to explore this space on my own; it was usually locked and appeared dark and humid. However, when a Communist Chinese pilot crossed the South Korean border in his MiG-21 jet, an air-raid siren shattered the silence. Panic swept the nation, and everyone in our building, including my family, hurriedly descended into the basement without even pausing to gather belongings. This was the only instance when the basement was used as a wartime shelter. Following that initial entry, the basement became one of my favorite playgrounds, a place where I spent countless hours with my friends. The entire apartment compound's heating system was centrally controlled, with pipelines running through the interconnected basement spaces. Originally constructed as an emergency shelter in the 1970s, the basement was designed for such contingencies, but for us children, it transformed into an adventurous and intriguing playground.

Indeed, numerous defensive structures in South Korea were constructed in response to military threats from North Korea. Given the country's devastating war with its northern neighbor—a conflict that claimed over two million lives, approximately 10% of the population, and remains officially unresolved—it is not surprising to find such artifacts integrated into the built environment.[1] For example, hundreds of anti-tank roadblocks have been installed on every road leading to Seoul from the north, designed to delay the advance of North Korean tanks toward the South Korean capital. One particularly notable example is the Dobong Civic Housing, a four-story apartment building constructed in 1969. This building serves a dual purpose: its first floor functions as a military bunker capable of hiding tanks, complete with openings for tank barrels, while the upper floors provide residential units for 180 families.[2] Spanning

300 meters, this structure exemplifies how wartime defensive measures have been seamlessly woven into the fabric of everyday urban life.

In addition to localized defensive artifacts, South Korea also planned infrastructural-scale defensive measures within urban settings. The Jamsu Bridge, constructed in 1976 beneath the Banpo Bridge, was designed to facilitate military movements across the Han River while remaining hidden from North Korean satellites and reconnaissance planes. Another significant example is the Bupyeong Underground Shopping Mall, built in 1978. This extensive underground mall, one of the largest in the world with the longest linear pathways, doubles as an emergency shelter.

Perhaps the most iconic example is Yeouido Park. Developed in 1970 on Yeouido Island in the Han River, this 56-acre area was originally an expansive asphalt plaza, intended to serve as an emergency airstrip in times of war, despite its misleading name. Beneath this plaza, a secret 600-square-meter bunker was constructed as a control center for emergencies. The existence of this bunker was so well concealed that it remained undiscovered until 2005, when it was accidentally found during the construction of an underground terminal. These examples underscore the extent to which wartime preparations have been integrated into South Korea's urban infrastructure, often hidden in plain sight.

Fig. 1 Underground network that connects multiple apartment buildings. Interestingly, there is an exit sign towards the basement space.

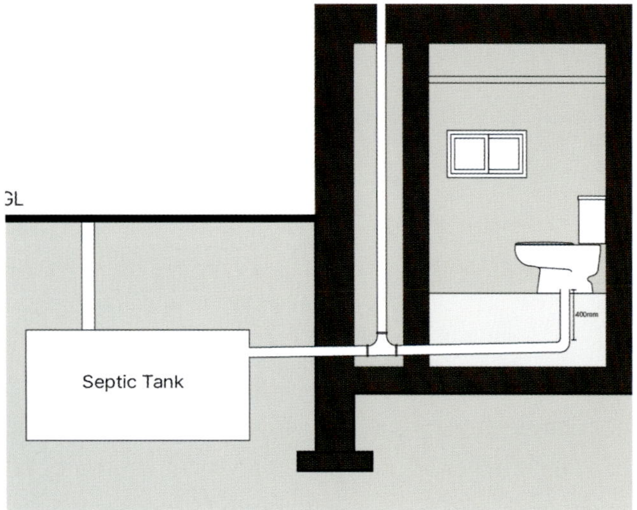

Fig. 2 In order to connect the waste pipe to the existing septic tank, the toilet of semi-basement unit has to be raised.

Although these artifacts are individually massive, it is not just the large-scale structures that have shaped the urban landscape of South Korean cities, particularly Seoul. A piecemeal aggregation of smaller war artifacts has also played a significant role. The ongoing tensions between North and South Korea have influenced architectural legislation, leading to the development of unique architectural typologies and an urban landscape reflective of these security concerns. These laws have ensured that buildings and infrastructure incorporate defensive features, creating a cityscape that is both functional and fortified, blending everyday urban life with preparedness for potential conflict.

The Emergence of the Semi-Basement

The basement I ventured into in 1983 was constructed in accordance with a 1970 architectural code that required any building over 200 square meters to include a basement floor.[3] Political and military tensions between the two Koreas escalated during the 1960s, particularly after North Korean terrorists attacked the Blue House, the South Korean president's residence, in 1968. This heightened the perceived risk of another war on the Korean Peninsula. In response, South Korea mandated the construction of basement shelters to ensure readiness in the event of conflict. Consequently, it wasn't just large-scale apartment complexes that incorporated basements; even smaller multifamily houses began to include basement floors. This widespread adoption of basement shelters highlights the pervasive impact of geopolitical tensions on South Korean architecture and urban planning.

The 1972 architectural code required that more than two-thirds of a basement's floor-to-ceiling height be below ground level, a stricter guideline compared to the 1960s, when only one-third needed to be below

Fig. 3 Elements in semi-basement unit, such as entrance zone, doors, and windows, are often minimized in scale.

ground. This change reflected the shift in the basement's primary function from storage to shelter. Additionally, a new provision allowed for "rooms" in basements, which had not been permitted under the earlier codes. This adjustment was understandable, given the need for basements to serve as emergency shelters for people.

However, this new regulation significantly transformed residential development in South Korea, marking the advent of semi-basement housing, famously depicted in the movie *Parasite*. This type of housing, initially designed to provide safety during emergencies, gradually became a common feature in South Korean cities, illustrating the long-term impact of military tensions on urban architecture and living conditions.

When small single-family and multifamily residential buildings were permitted to have basement floors, and the use of these floors as rooms became allowable, people began to occupy these spaces as residential units. Since the end of the Korean War in 1953, Seoul's population has experienced continuous growth: from around one million in 1953, it increased to 2.5 million in 1960, 5.4 million in 1970, and 8.3 million in 1980.[4] This explosive population growth led to a significant housing shortage in Seoul for several decades. Until large-scale apartment developments became predominant in the late 1990s, the burgeoning population was largely accommodated by low-rise housing types, including semi-basement units.

Although it was technically illegal to have residential units in basements, the government chose to overlook the proliferation of semi-basement residences. In 1984, a new code was introduced, stipulating that only half of the floor-to-ceiling height had to be below ground level for a space to be considered a basement. This change marked the government's tacit acknowledgment that basements, initially mandated as shelter spaces, were predominantly being used as living units. Consequently, the code was relaxed to allow more natural light into these semi-basement residences, improving their livability. This adaptation not only reflects the practical needs of a growing urban population but also underscores the dynamic interplay between regulatory frameworks and urban development in response to socioeconomic pressures.

The fall of the Berlin Wall in 1989 had far-reaching implications that went beyond Germany and Europe, significantly influencing the Korean Peninsula's political climate. Amid a global wave of reconciliation, South Korea, which had already surpassed North Korea economically and militarily, began to move past the constant threats from the north. Reflecting this shift, in 1999, the South Korean government removed the basement-floor requirement from building regulations.

This change interestingly coincided with a period when most of Seoul's population began living in apartment buildings. Consequently, the city no longer needed semi-basement units to address housing demands. These units had been widely constructed under the guise of military threats, but as South Korea's housing landscape evolved and stabilized, the necessity for such accommodations diminished. This regulatory adjustment marked a significant step in South Korea's journey toward modern urban living and away from the war-driven architectural practices of the past.

Physical Aspects of Semi-Basement Units

Although the government legalized semi-basement units as registered housing units in 1975 with the aim of increasing housing accessibility, the actual living conditions in these units did not see significant improvement. Due to regulatory requirements mandating that certain portions of the units be buried underground, semi-basement units lacked sufficient height to allow exposure above ground level. Additionally, these units were typically constructed as part of small multifamily houses, primarily owned by middle-class individuals and rented out to lower-income groups. Consequently, semi-basement units were often built on tight budgets, resulting in minimal ceiling heights, a lack of floor

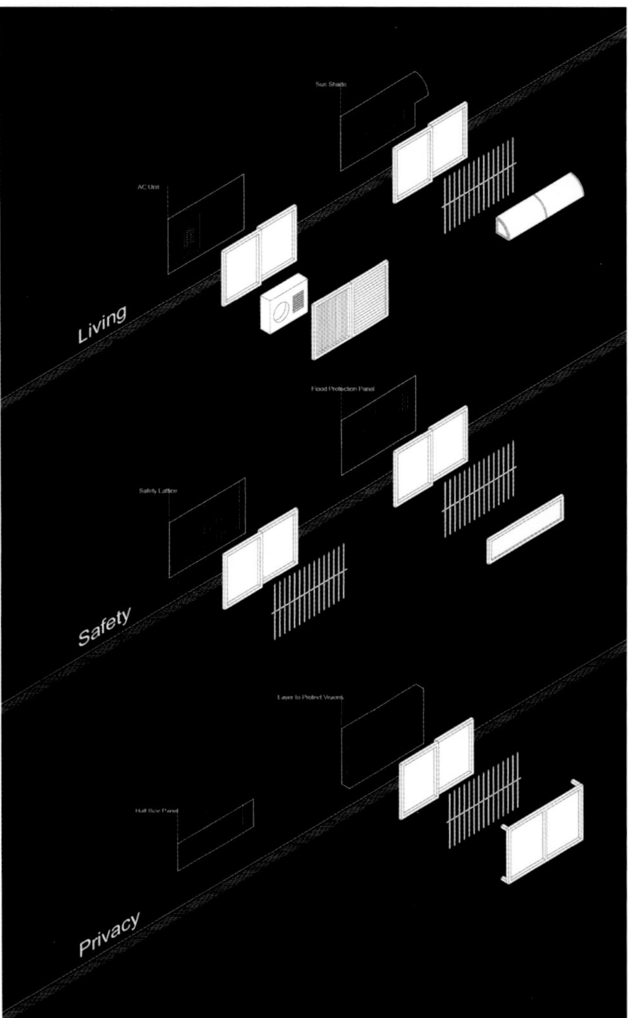

Fig. 4 Windows in semi-basement units, serve as underground intersect the aboveground activities in Seoul.

heating systems, and poor floor and wall insulation. These substandard living conditions underscored the socioeconomic disparities prevalent within South Korean urban housing developments.

The Raised Bathroom

The raised bathroom is indeed a memorable and unique aspect of semi-basement units, as depicted in the movie *Parasite*. Prior to the legalization of basement units in 1975, installing a bathroom in these spaces was impractical because the basement floor was designated as storage and emergency shelter. After obtaining approval for residential use, however, owners began installing bathrooms in semi-basement units to rent them out. This required raising the bathroom from the floor level so that toilet plumbing could be connected to the main building line. Often, toilets were elevated significantly to accommodate connections to septic tanks buried below the ground surface (Fig. 2). Fortunately, the posture required for using a toilet does not necessitate full ceiling height, allowing for this spatial adaptation within the limited ceiling height of semi-basement units.

This innovation represents a significant departure from traditional Korean architectural norms. In Korean culture, bathrooms are typically dug below floor level to contain water, reflecting the importance of maintaining dry living spaces. However, in semi-basement units, this cultural convention had to be reimagined. As a result, a new spatial articulation was necessary, marking a departure from traditional architectural practices in response to the exigencies of urban housing.

Multifunctional Windows

In semi-basement units, windows serve as the interface where the unseen lives of the underground intersect with the bustling activity of the city aboveground (Fig. 4). As such, these windows incorporate multiple functional layers to address the inherent conflict between these two worlds. For instance, while windows allow for limited natural light and fresh air to enter the semi-basement units, they also present a vulnerability, as passersby on the street can easily peer inside. Unlike units located above ground level, which may have buffer areas such as balconies to enhance privacy while still facilitating airflow and daylighting, semi-basement units lack such spaces due to spatial constraints. Consequently, the window in a semi-basement unit must serve as a multifunctional element, simultaneously addressing privacy concerns, regulating airflow, and maximizing natural light intake. These windows represent a crucial design element in semi-basement living, embodying the intricate balance between the need for connection to the outside world and the desire for privacy and security in an underground environment.

Initially, window lattices were developed primarily for security purposes in semi-basement units. However, they also evolved into aesthetic elements of the building, featuring various styles such as art nouveau, traditional, or modern minimal, crafted from different materials. These lattice designs not only enhanced security but also contributed to the overall architectural character of the building. To address privacy concerns, translucent sheets were often applied to the window glass of bedrooms, while solid panels were installed on bathroom windows. While these measures did enhance privacy, they also inadvertently reduced the amount of natural sunlight entering the semi-basement units, leading to issues such as poor hygiene and diminished overall living quality.

Additionally, flood protection panels were installed on semi-basement windows to mitigate the risk of flooding. Given their lower elevation and vulnerability to water ingress, semi-basement units are situated in weak points within the city. Statistics indicate that over 7.5% of all semi-basement units are at risk of flooding during heavy rainfall events exceeding 100 mm per hour, with some districts facing even higher rates of up to 9%.[5] Unlike other architectural types or housing units, windows in semi-basement units serve as the primary

Fig. 5 Semi-basement units are the foundations of low-rise urban context in Seoul.

Fig. 6 A variety of items are used to keep the privacy, safety, and security of semi-basement units..

means to implement flood protection measures, underscoring their critical role in safeguarding against natural disasters and ensuring the habitability of these unique living spaces.

Minimized Elements

When semi-basement units were legalized, they underwent further minimization, as they were no longer required to be inspected as storage or shelter spaces. This extreme condition necessitated the accommodation of highly minimized elements within these units. Moreover, the systematic layout of these units, mandated by the requirement for official registration, further standardized their configuration (Fig. 3).

Certain elements within the units were minimized rather than removed entirely due to cultural and practical considerations. For example, the act of removing one's shoes upon entering a private unit is deeply ingrained in Korean culture. Depending on whether individuals remove their shoes at a common entrance or at separate entrances, they are perceived as either living together or independently. Therefore, when multiple semi-basement units were legalized and arranged on a single floor, individual entrances with minimally sized shoe storage areas were planned for each unit. While this may seem less efficient in terms of space utilization, having individual entrances aligns with cultural norms and is considered essential.

Additionally, minimized windows and fans were installed to facilitate cross-ventilation within the units. Prior to legalization, most semi-basement units lacked windows other than those facing the street. However, with the systematic layout of multiple units, new elements such as windows and fans could be strategically installed on the side opposite the street. To maintain privacy, these elements were positioned higher than eye level, thus preventing visual intrusion from neighboring units. These adaptations reflect a balance between regulatory compliance, cultural norms, and practical considerations within the unique context of semi-basement living in South Korea.

The Evolution of Semi-basement Units

As a by-product of the military tension between South and North Korea, basement floors have evolved into a significant component of urban space in South Korean cities. Initially mandated for use as storage and shelters, these spaces could not remain unoccupied amidst the rapid population growth and urbanization. Consequently, they were re-purposed as residential units. Today, there are over 200,000 semi-basement or basement residential units in Seoul, comprising more than 5% of the city's total housing stock.[6]

The integration of these semi-basement units into urban development and daily life has rendered them almost invisible as defensive artifacts. Instead, they have become an essential housing type, particularly for marginalized populations. This transformation reflects the dynamic interplay between the exigencies of military preparedness and the pragmatic demands of urban living in Seoul.

Once the code mandating basement space was repealed in 1999, the legality of residential units on semi-basement floors was effectively nullified. Since then, semi-basement and basement levels have primarily been developed into large spaces intended for commercial use. Concurrently, many existing semi-basement residential units began to be converted into commercial spaces. As urban growth slowed, the demand to utilize every available space for residential purposes, including marginalized areas like semi-basements, diminished. Furthermore, in low-rise residential neighborhoods, where semi-basement units were prevalent, gentrification led to a shift toward mixed-use developments. This transformation saw commercial functions increasingly replacing residential uses on semi-basement floors.

Those elements of semi-basement units that were considered deficient for residential use have become advantageous for commercial purposes. For instance, the thin barrier between these units and the streets, which previously posed privacy and security issues, transforms into an excellent display window for commercial enterprises once elements like translucent sheets, window lattices, and flood protection panels are removed. In some cases, akin to the commercial streets in Back Bay, Boston, semi-basement units effectively double the commercial area on the street by adding another commercial space below the first floor.

This gentrification has enabled semi-basement units to be more responsive to street-level interactions and socioeconomic demands. Originally deemed unpleasant due to the lack of a buffer between public streets and private units, these units are now seen as ideal for commercial use. Consequently, these semi-basement units, initially constructed as defensive artifacts and intended to be the most secure spaces, have evolved into pseudo-public spaces accessible to anyone. This transformation has rendered the defensive nature of these structures virtually invisible in the urban landscape.

Conclusion

It has been over seven decades since the signing of the armistice agreement in 1953, which marked the end of the three-year conflict between South and North Korea. However, as the term "armistice" implies, it did not signify a formal end to the war, and since then, there have been over 200 provocations from North Korea directed toward South Korea. This staggering statistic equates to an average of one provocation every other week over the past 70 years. Consequently, it's not difficult to comprehend why South Koreans have grown accustomed to these provocations and threats from the North, leading to a sense of numbness.

This phenomenon of living with constant military threats, without experiencing actual fear, has resulted in the creation of invisible war artifacts. These artifacts are not invisible in the sense of being visually unseen in the city; rather, they are camouflaged within the urban landscape. They are integrated into the fabric of daily life, yet their significance is often overlooked or normalized due to the prolonged exposure to military tensions. This normalization of the threat landscape has shaped the collective psyche of South Koreans, contributing to a resilience and adaptability in the face of ongoing geopolitical challenges.

As anticipated, North Korea has also developed various defensive structures, particularly to protect against aerial bombings. Notably, Pyongyang, the capital of North Korea, boasts one of the deepest metro systems in the world, with tracks reportedly situated 110 meters underground. This metro system serves the daily transportation needs of Pyongyang's citizens but is also designed to function as an air-raid shelter in the event of war. By contrast, many of South Korea's defensive structures are intended to counter tank attacks, reflecting the distinct military experiences of the two nations during the Korean War. While South Korea faced invasions by North Korean tanks, North Korean cities suffered extensive bombing by the US Air Force. Regardless of their specific purposes, these wartime defensive structures in both Koreas have become seamlessly integrated into the urban landscape, rendering them invisible in the fabric of everyday life.

These invisible defensive artifacts for war are fundamentally distinct from more overt symbols, such as the Demilitarized Zone (DMZ), a four-kilometer-wide buffer zone stretching across the Korean Peninsula between North and South Korea. While the DMZ holds significant value as physical evidence of the Cold War and has often been leveraged in discussions of political geography, it has become mythologized due to its relative isolation from human activity over the past seventy years. In contrast, these invisible artifacts are seamlessly woven into the daily fabric of urban life.

The DMZ, characterized by its unique wilderness, serves as a geographical scar resulting from the war, yet it simultaneously symbolizes peace on the peninsula. Visiting the DMZ is often regarded as a ceremonial event, offering a solemn opportunity to reflect on the tragedy of the Korean Peninsula and the imperative of peace.

In contrast, the defensive artifacts for war in both countries have either been assimilated into the routines of city life or removed and repurposed. Unlike the pristine and symbolic nature of the DMZ, these artifacts have been absorbed into the urban landscape, their significance often overlooked or forgotten amidst the hustle and bustle of daily existence. Thus, while the DMZ serves as a ceremonial reminder of the past, the invisible war artifacts underscore the enduring legacy of conflict in the mundane realities of contemporary urban life.

In short, South Korea's cities bear the imprint of war and ongoing military threats through the construction of various artifacts, both above and below ground. Some were intentionally built as war-readiness projects, while others were mandated by legislative codes designed for the same purpose. Interestingly, during periods of peak military tension between North and South Korea, urban development accelerated, leading to widespread implementation of codes mandating the construction of war bracing artifacts, such as basement shelters.

These artifacts, as the result of preparative action in military, became ubiquitous in the urban landscape, evolving into invisible symbols of wartime preparation that most citizens are unaware of. As South Koreans gradually became desensitized to military threats, these artifacts lost their original significance, blending into the backdrop of peaceful daily life. Take, for example, semi-basement units, originally designed as shelters in emergencies, especially during wartime. Ironically, these spaces, intended to be the safest in buildings during crises, emerged as the most fragile and vulnerable aspects of daily life in peacetime. This raises questions about their effectiveness as shelters and bunkers in the event of war. Overall, these artifacts reflect the complex relationship between wartime preparations and the realities of peaceful urban living in South Korea.

Acknowledgments

This essay grew out of a talk I gave at the Lavender Festival in Oak Ridge, Tennessee, in June 2019. I want to thank the organizer, Barbara Ferrell, for the invitation and all the Oak Ridgers who shared their anecdotes about atomic gardening with me over lavender lemonade.

-----

[1] *The History of the United Nations Forces in the Korean War* (Republic of Korea, Ministry of National Defense, 1972).

[2] Jong xoo U and Vin Kim, " Yŏn-Kyŏl-Ŭi Sŏn Mun-Hwa-Ŭi Ch'uk [Connecting Lines, Cultural Axis]," *kŏn-ch'uk-kwa to-si-kong-kan* [Architecture and Urban Space] 32 (Winter 2018).

[3] Wonho Lee, "Chi-Ha-e Sa-Lam-i Sal-Ko Iss-Ta (지하에 사람이 살고 있다) [People Are Living in the Basement] ." 참여연대 ch'am-yŏ-yŏn-tae [People's Solidarity for Participatory Democracy], October 5, 2022, https://www.peoplepower21.org/magazine/1914005.

[4] "통계로 보는 서울 t'ong-Kye-Lo Po-Nŭn Sŏ-Ul [Seoul Statistics]," 서울정책아카이브 *Seoul Solution*, April 3, 2024, https://www.seoulsolution.kr/ko/seoul-stats

[5] Sangyoung Shin, Sungeun Kim, Hyunjung Nam, and Sangkyoon Kim. 서울시 반지하주택 유형과 침수위험 해소방안 (*sŏ-ul-si pan-chi-ha-chu-t'aek yu-hyŏng-kwa ch'im-su-wi-hŏm hae-so-pang-an* [Semi-Basement Units in Seoul and Their Flood Protection Plan] (Seoul: Seoul Institute, 2023).

[6] "서울의 반지하주택 얼마나 있나 (Sŏ-Ul-Ŭi Pan-Chi-Ha-Chu-t'aek Ŏl-Ma-Na Iss-Na. [How Many Semi-Basement Units Are There in Seoul]," 서울연구원 (Seoul Institute), September 13, 2022, https://www.si.re.kr/node/66309.

Forgotten Fire Control Towers in Plain Sight

Randy Crandon

At 291 Ocean Avenue in Marblehead Massachusetts, a seaside town just north of Boston, an ominous, vine covered concrete tower sits silently in the backyard of a cedar-shingled summer cottage. An old National Register of Historic Places application reveals that the parcel was sold to the United States of America in an urgent, but willing sale in 1943 to build a military observation tower. Just nine years later, the site was surplussed by the government and bought by a couple to resume living on. Other Massachusetts Historical Commission filings tell similar stories of nearby parcels being acquired (declarations of taking) from their owners beginning in 1941 for the same purpose, and then being sold off in the early 1950s. Just up the road at 310 Ocean Avenue, one can barely make out the top floor of a sister military observation tower; this one was designed to imitate a three-story residential cottage with clapboard siding. No historical designations or applications exist for this site; its history is invisible.

The auctioning of these towers marked the moment they lost all utilitarian value to the US Government, effectively reducing them to obsolete structures scattered across hundreds of miles of coastline. Many were sold back to the private sector, but with no coordinated preservation effort, the towers were cast into the periphery of everyday life. Because of their robust concrete construction, they were hard to tear down and continue to quietly exist; they are material

Fig. 1 A fire control tower in Brant Rock, Massachusetts. Photo by Randy Crandon.

deposits of rapid military urbanization.

The origin of these towers follows the history of defense in the United States. Before the advent of airplanes, most American adversaries could only approach by sea. Coastal fortifications were the logical alternative to maintaining a large standing army or navy, and they were built up over many decades to safeguard major harbors. The prospect of fortifying the totality of America's coastlines, however, was a frivolous one. By World War II, new German submarines had closed in on these unprotected waters and began attacking merchant ships off small American harbor towns and barrier beaches.

In response, the US War Department rapidly acquired sites along the Eastern Seaboard and erected Fire Control Towers (FCTs). They were typically five- to eight-story tall extrusions with small footprints and panoramic windows, and together they constituted a new coastal defense network along with nearby bunkers and artillery batteries. An extensive report published in 1945 by the US military, *Owned, Sponsored, and Leased Facilities*, states that over 11,000 acres of land was leased for harbor defense installations. FCTs were tasked with detecting and anticipating the trajectory of enemy surface vessels offshore by way of visual triangulation. Once targets were located, FCTs would direct coastal batteries to fire upon approaching ships. Upwards of a hundred towers were built as a part of this network, often sited in small coastal villages and abutting residential homes. Because the threat of

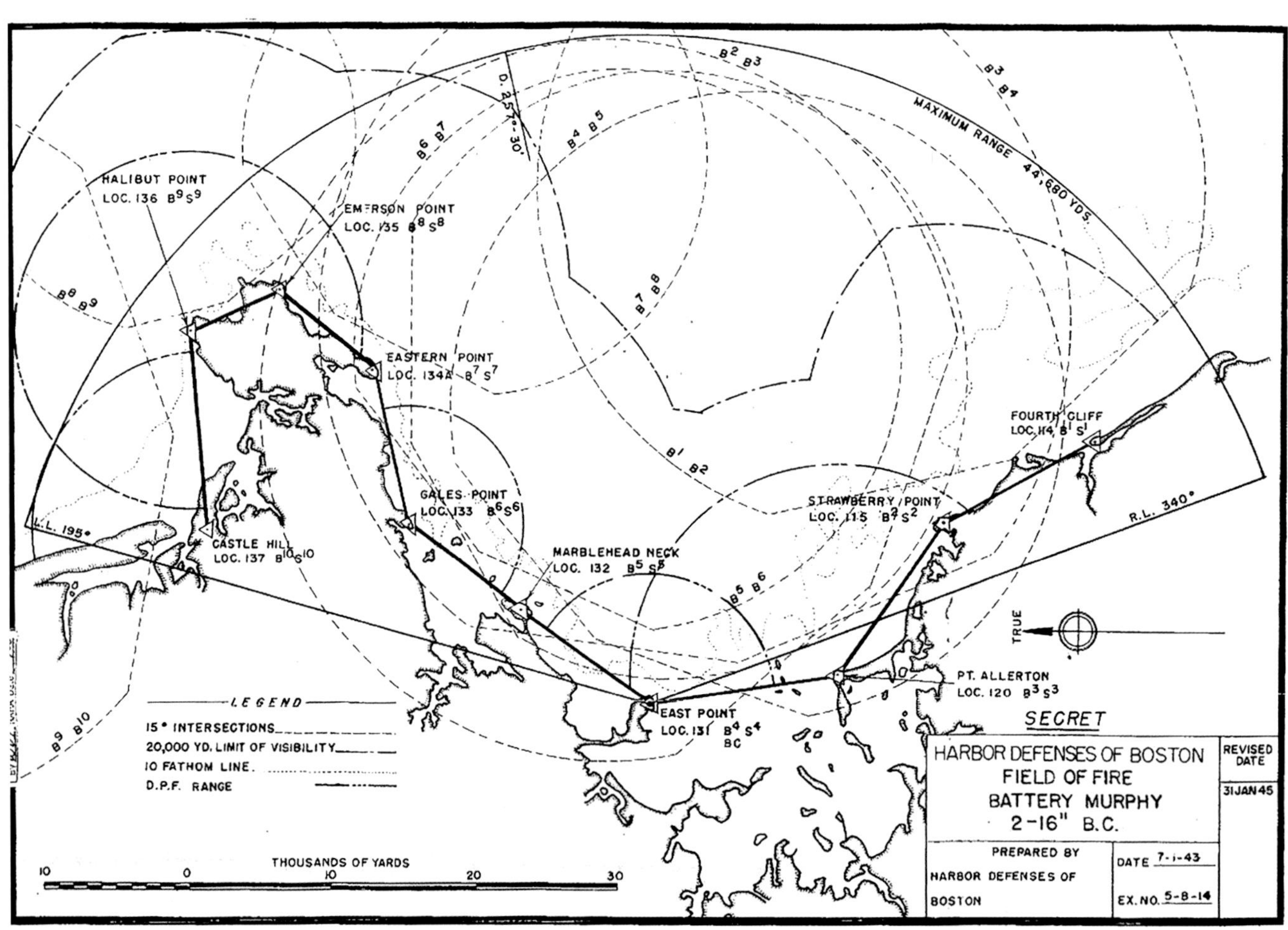

Fig. 2 Map of the fire control structures serving Battery Murphy in Boston Harbor. Public Domain Image.

attack quickly transitioned from naval to aerial actions, FCTs were quickly rendered obsolete. While many of the towers were decommissioned at the war's end, several were reactivated in 1952 to host long range anti-aircraft M33 radar. This, too, was short lived, and they were permanently decommissioned by 1958 because of technological obsolescence.[1]

Form and Materiality

Construction of concrete fire control towers began simultaneously in 1942. This was in tandem with the substantial seacoast fortification effort authorized by Congress in September 1940. It is not yet known which of these tower constructions came first, nor which architects were responsible for the design, but it is widely accepted that FCTs were international in style. Prototyping of these towers began as early as 1905, with the first being metal towers with steel clad wooden observation decks. Their form, height, and placement along the seacoast directly reflected the requirements of the optical instruments they housed to triangulate position, as well as the desire to keep them inconspicuous on the landscape.

Each concrete tower took around eight days to construct. They were one-foot-thick reinforced poured concrete construction, and beach sand was sometimes added to the aggregate mix. Designs typically ranged from 40 to 90 feet in height, or five to eight stories, and up to 17 feet in width.[2] Some were circular in plan to mimic tall water standpipes (those of the New Jersey and Delaware coasts), and others were square (typical of the Boston harbor defense network). FCTs typically hosted three upper levels of panoramic windows spanning three sides with visored concrete shading projections, and lower levels played host to small, punched openings at stair landings. While some towers were painted with green tree silhouettes to blend them in with their forested backdrops, others in more exposed areas featured faux wooden water towers or lighthouse lanterns on top to conceal them as infrastructure. Paul Grigorieff, author of coastdefense.com, highlights one of the most obscure designs, the Point Allerton FCT, located in Hull, Massachusetts: "the tower had a chamfered design, called 'ornamental' by the Army Engineers. . . The corners of the top two stories of the tower were carved away to give them a hexagonal plan. It is doubtful that this design flair did anything to 'camouflage' the tower."[3] Other towers, such

Fig. 3 Early fire control tower prototype (1905-1915) at Fort Monroe, Virginia. Photograph courtesy of the Coast Defense Study Group (CDSG).

Fig. 4 Point Allerton fire control tower in Hull, Massachusetts. Photo by Randy Crandon.

as the Marblehead-South FCT at 291 Ocean Avenue, commonly employed camouflage elements like faux double-hung windows with tacked-on window sashes. Some tower designs, like the Fort Ruckman station in Nahant, Massachusetts, featured attached plotting rooms on the ground level that were designed to look like residential cottages. Each tower was operated by six to 12 personnel, which is why many were directly adjacent or attached to residences.[4]

Exploring the towers' peculiar status today offers new insights into the history of militarization, coastal defense, and short-lived federal resources. The following passages seek to trace the development of FCTs by surveying the history of America's coastal defenses and fire control technology.

Coastal Defense and Fortifications

The geography of North America, like unified island nations, grew without the need for fortified cities. The United States has always needed to protect its coastlines and strategic ports, however, and except for an attack from Canada or Mexico, all adversaries would arrive by sea. T. McGovern and B. Smith offer a concise chronology of this topic in their 2006 book, *American Coastal Defenses* 1885–1950:

> While virtually every nation recognized the superiority of forts over ships and relied on fortifications to protect their harbors, America took to them with particular enthusiasm. They particularly suited the American character. It required little manpower except during time of war and did not threaten the liberties of a people raised to distrust standing armies.[5]

After gaining its independence in 1776, the United States appropriated funds to refortify its war-scarred harbors. This effort was coined the First and Second Systems of American seacoast fortification, and its projects were built mostly of earth with masonry backers. These structures were scarcely durable and uniform, and construction dropped off in parallel with a brief period of peace. Efforts were rekindled after the War of 1812 when Congress appropriated funds for a new fortification program in 1816. Coined as the Third System, this program was more ambitious in scope and uniformity. These projects were largely masonry structures that could house many guns behind their vertical faces and replaced earlier projects at strategic ports. A Board of Engineers for Fortifications was appointed by President James Madison in 1821, and an 1850 report recommended that upwards of 250 sites across coastal America be developed. The design and construction of these projects were overseen by the Army Corps of Engineers, an arrangement that would continue for decades. Of the hundreds of sites identified, only about 25% were built out.[6]

The urgency of the Civil War period, from 1861 to 1875, ushered in another rapid construction effort for Third System forts, both existing and new. The conflict also introduced underwater minefields as an element of seacoast defenses. By this time, however, advancements in heavy artillery had begun to outrun the pace of fortification design; in 1867, Third System fortifications projects stopped altogether as appropriations for masonry construction went dry.[7]

In subsequent years, longer-range guns and new weapons technologies were introduced. At the same time, America's navy had plunged into a neglected state, and its seacoast defenses were abandoned. In response, President Grover Cleveland initiated the Endicott Program in 1885 to strengthen coastal defenses. Also known as the Board of Fortifications, the group initiated one of the largest construction programs to date. With this came a shift in policy. The US naval fleet, now armed with more sophisticated weaponry, was to be used offensively. Therefore, a new system of coastal defense was required for greater self-sufficiency. Concrete was introduced as a primary building material for new, larger artillery batteries, and underwater minefields were electrified for increased control.[8] The Spanish-American War of 1898, intensified interest in the use of long-range coastal artillery. As McGovern and Smith explain, the "war caused panicked fear of a Spanish fleet descending on unprotected coastal cities. Appropriations surged, for both temporary and permanent works. At the same time, the army began to consider how to direct and control the new weapons, and the first fire control stations were constructed at the turn of the century."[9] These early fire control posts were more fragile in comparison to their concrete successors and were characterized by tall, open steel frameworks around a tubular steel tower with observation rooms on top. The upper volume of the tower was clad in corrugated metal, and floors were framed with wood. The distinguishing panoramic windows of later FCTs were present in this early design.[10]

President Theodore Roosevelt's administration commissioned another advisory board in 1905 to advance Endicott-era objectives. Led by then secretary of war William Taft, the board recommended technical improvements related to electrification, communications, optical range-finding, and illumination of strategic ports via networks of searchlights. The Taft board also recommended fortifying newly acquired territories of Hawaii, Cuba, Panama, and the Philippines. America's seacoasts and military borders have always been malleable and ever-changing. Recognizing this period's rapid technological development of artillery and surveillance techniques, Congress split Field Artillery and Coast Artillery into separate branches; in 1907, the US Army Coast Artillery Corps (CAC) was established. This group would remain busy in the development of new coastal fortifications for the next several decades, until dissolving in 1946. The group also recognized the introduction of the airplane as a formidable weapon and developed its own specialized branch to develop anti-aircraft artillery defenses.[11]

During World War I, progress by the CAC slowed as the focus shifted abroad. Existing seacoast gunnery was sent overseas to support artillery units. America's coastal fortifications became training areas for enlisted personnel preparing to deploy, and the threat of naval attack lessened during this period. By the war's end in 1918, many coastal fortifications were put into hibernation, or "caretaker" mode.[12] The subsequent years leading up to World War II were a time of continued development and experimentation across all military disciplines. In the late 1930s, coastal defenses were rearmed with long-range 16-inch weapons and designs for batteries, command centers, and fire control tower observation stations were standardized. This was a part of the 1940 program that Congress authorized, and construction efforts intensified in 1942.[13]

In his 1994 book *Alongshore*, John Stilgoe, professor in the history of landscape at Harvard University, reminds us how expansive the effort was to safeguard the totality of America's coastlines. During the first three months of 1942, for example, German U-boat submarines closed in on American waters and sank more than 100 ships off the Eastern Seaboard; many of these attacks were within eyeshot of coastlines.[14] Stilgoe writes:

> Submarines threatened shallow-water shipping, small harbor towns, and even barrier beach property owners not so much because they moved about underwater and fired torpedoes but because they made nonsense of established coast-defense thinking. No one expected the [fire control] towers to be of much use again German battleships like Bismark, which could destroy cities and harbor shipping from afar... but the towers did offer some hope of scanning inshore waters. In a time before radar, telescopes and binoculars provided the best bet of enhancing the time-honored utility of the keen-eyed lookout. From the towers the watchers might spot submarines, might spot clandestine landing operations, might spot air attack.[15]

Constructing Fields of Vision

In parallel to the development of America's coastal defenses, technological advancements were being made in the realm of fire control systems. These systems were the components that worked together to assist a ranged weapon in locating, tracking, and hitting a target. In England, many new techniques and instruments were being developed, and American inventors were quick to follow. It is during this frenzy that the first range-keepers (electromechanical analog computers for tracking moving targets) and gyrocompasses (rotor devices for maintaining true north) were introduced.

In his 1975 seminal text, *Bunker Archaeology,* Paul Virilio reminds us that "progress in topography has come since the sixteenth century from numerous European wars—as if progress in arms and maneuvers caused progress in territorial representation; as if the function of arms and the function of eye were identified as one and the same."[16] In a later text, *War and Cinema: The Logistics of Perception*, Virilio goes on to speculate that the ultimate weapon of the future would be an automated totality of vision: "The act of taking aim is a geometrification of looking... It's thoroughly objective, and the semantic loss involves a new obliviousness to the element of interpretative subjectivity that is always in play in the act of looking."[17] In this respect, fire control towers are one spatial manifestation of weaponized vision.

Fig.5 Soldiers using a DPF instrument in a fire control station. Personnel were trained to identify enemy ships by their silhouettes. Photo courtesy of the San Francisco History Center, San Francisco Public Library.

David Mindell provides a comprehensive account of this technological era in his 2002 book, *Between Human and Machine: Feedback, Control, and Computing before Cybernetics*, and highlights the tension between individual marksmanship and the newer, centralized systems of firing that instruments afforded. For long-range gunnery (shooting upwards of 20,000 yards), "director fire" was introduced, which "split apart the perception and articulation of continuous aim and put the guns under the control of a central location, or director." As Mindell explains, "Director fire effectively displaced aiming from sailors operating guns to officers with instruments." This was a tough sell, however, as "many officers still considered manual control heroic and more accurate."[18] But by 1905, this method was adopted as common practice in both England and the United States.

Fire control towers operated in pairs under the logic of director fire, and triangulation was the primary method of locating a given target. Within this system, towers were typically positioned within sight of two others, and the distance between any two was surveyed precisely. When an enemy surface craft was spotted, bearings to it were measured from each tower, also called "base end stations," at 15-30 second time intervals (announced by bells) using optical instruments like telescopes, depression range finders, and azimuth scopes. These figures were plugged into triangulation equations, and a location was computed. This information was then relayed to a corresponding artillery battery director, who gave an order to fire upon the target. The process was highly choreographed and involved constant communication and feedback between personnel and machine.

It is during this period that one of the most comprehensive texts on contemporary coastal defense and fire control, *Notes on Seacoast Fortification Construction by Colonel Eben Eveleth Winslow*, was published by the Army Corps of Engineers for use at its engineering school. In it, Colonel Winslow explains that there were three available systems for range finding: 1) the long horizontal-base system, 2) the self-contained short horizontal-base system, and 3) the vertical-base system. Each system had its merits and flaws.

The long horizontal-base system was the most accurate but required a sizable distance between any two towers. Colonel Winslow notes that finding suitable locations was a challenge. While distance increased accuracy, it also made it more difficult to confirm that the same target was being observed, especially in situations where multiple ships were in the field of view and smoke, fog, and other obstructions disrupted visibility. To assist in training the eye, the military published a field manual called *Ship Shapes, Anatomy and Types of Naval Vessels*, which offered a chart of enemy ship silhouette profiles to personnel operating FCTs. Archival photographs depict these charts pinned up within the observation rooms of the towers.

A large plotting board device, called the Whistler-Hearn board, was critical to the long horizontal-base system: it received position data and represented the geography of the harbor defense network in question. The board's mechanisms translated the relayed position data into firing data, which could then be manually adjusted. Upwards of a dozen soldiers were required to manage this system, and plotting rooms were often attached to FCTs.

The second self-contained short horizontal-base system presented an alternative to this first one and comprised several instruments—featuring optical glasses, prisms, and mirrors—that superimposed two images from a given point of view. The accuracy of this method relied solely on the reading and conversion of a very small angle into a distance, which demonstrated its limitations, particularly in determining long ranges.

The third vertical-base system, like the first two horizontal systems, relied on triangulation—but in the vertical plane. This method allowed ranges to be determined from a singular vantage point without the need for a corresponding tower station and a plotting room loop. The instrument used was called a depression range finder (DPF) because the only necessary measurement was the angle of depression from the center of the instrument to the waterline of the target in question. This, however, brought a host of complications, the first being that the vertical base line measurement, from instrument center to the water surface elevation, varied with the tide. The waterline of an enemy target itself was also hard to determine by sight because many warships were painted dark green and blended with the color of the water when seen at a distance, especially with heavier wave action. The second complication was refraction, which "is always present in the passage of light rays through the atmosphere and is due to the decreasing density of the air as one ascends."[19] Nonetheless, depression range finders accounted for these two variables in their mechanics, and field-testing experiments were deemed successful. Consequently, this method was adopted as the standard position-finding system, and a tower prototype (mentioned earlier) was rolled out around 1905. It was determined that a vertical base line of 60 feet long was sufficient for accurate readings of a certain range, and the tower prototype reflected this height. In *Notes on Seacoast Fortification Construction*, Colonel Winslow addresses this FCT prototype:

> At small forts only one or two of these were built, but at some of the larger ones as many as eight were constructed. . . Unfortunately, the harbor entrances at all of our South Atlantic and Gulf ports, and occasionally elsewhere, are bounded by low sandy shores. It was, therefore, thought that they were too vulnerable, and the type was abandoned. In fact, before many of them were actually completed they had been declared to be obsolete. . . Experiments were then made with lower stations, some having an instrumental height of 40 feet, some 30 feet, and some of 15 feet only. These were found not to be satisfactory and finally the idea of depending exclusively upon this depression position-finding system had to be given up except for localities where high sites were available, and even then for comparatively short ranges only.[20]

Ultimately, it was determined that the horizontal-base system, which was the most accurate, would be employed with a vertical-base system (depression range finder instrument) present in each tower base end station to provide redundancy and mitigate the limitations of each method. Of the upper three stories with panoramic windows, the top level of the tower housed a DPF instrument, and the lower two housed azimuth instruments.

Fire control systems would continue to be refined and transformed over the next several decades, surpassing the FCTs' short history and paving the way to the emergent field of cybernetics. The instability of technology has always been at odds with the immortality of material. This period of rapid technological development between human and machine also signaled a new era of seeing and making sense of the world.

A local newspaper describes that by the end of the war, no enemy crafts had been fired upon using the Boston Harbor Fire Control Tower system: "in 1945 all observation details were canceled, and in 1946 the guns of Fort Ruckman were tested for the final time with a warning to the residents of Nahant issued via a Lynn newspaper to close the windows and protect fine China 'from the percussive impact of the firing.'"[21]

Preservation and Obsolescence

In the years after their auctioning, some towers were destroyed, some were taken over by municipalities, and others got lost in overgrowth. The most well-known FCTs are in Delaware, where the state rehabilitated one for public access. Only a couple were consumed by coastal homes and converted to lofts. In one instance, a tower was used as an internal structural core for the construction of a large beachside resort hotel; today, one can just make out the top floor of the tower peeking above the hotel block's parapet. The FCTs of Maine, specifically those on remote islands and in forested lands, also stand out as quietly untouched. Collectively, the towers have become so embedded in the landscape that they have been rendered invisible to the public eye: a forgotten infrastructure now synonymous with coastal vernacular. Outside of their immediate surroundings, most people are unaware of the towers' history. Many incorrectly assume that they were intended as sites for spotting and shooting German U-boats.

FCTs may be most visible to sailors, who still use them as waypoints for coastal navigation. The adage is that, from the top of the northernmost FCT in Maine, one can see the next one south and so on to the Carolinas. Professor Stilgoe writes of the towers and their presence in *Alongshore*:

> So ugly, so charged with unsettling associations are the World War II observation towers that many tourists and many scenery photographers ignore them, even when the towers stand adjacent to accepted salty structures like lighthouses. . . War does not belong on the beach, does not belong on vacation. . . No one sees the tower. No one realizes it. . . No painter or photographer records it.[22]

Fire control towers were conceived to see from, rather than to be seen. Stilgoe reminds us of this in his comparison to lighthouses, heroic buildings that were always colorfully painted and maintained by the coast guard and preservations group alike. FCTs, in contrast, may be more like the nineteenth century Martello towers of the British Empire. These were circular stone defensive forts that were built along coastlines and became obsolete with the introduction of new artillery guns. Many still stand today and have gained preservation status and reuse as museums. In the realm of infrastructure, FCTs are similar to the forgotten concrete coaling towers of America's railroad lines that were built in the early twentieth century during the heyday of steam locomotion. Self-taught photographer Jeff Brouws has spent years documenting these now dormant structures, and like FCTs, they are "seemingly impervious to the vicissitudes of time, decay, or outright removal. . . They recall an earlier technological era most of us never witnessed."[23] FCTs also recall the old U.S. Coast Guard lifesaving stations that once lined the American seacoast and delimited hazardous coastal waters. But what makes the towers unique is their ominous wartime energy that nobody wants to think about while on vacation at the beach and while sailing alongshore.

Today, as homes along the coastline are being swept away by stronger storms and hurricanes, the fire control towers remain standing. Despite the dangers that climate change pose to critical infrastructure, an increasing number of Americans are still moving to the seacoast. Could these invisible monoliths be recast to be productive for coastal landscapes today?

Time, materiality, and technology are all agents that have shaped the towers' invisible status. Over the decades, many towers have become host to feral vegetation growth that has camouflaged them even more against a backdrop of summer greenery. The *Historic Fortification Preservation Handbook*, published by the Pacific Northwest Preservation Partnership in 2003, describes why fire control towers have faded into our periphery. The sheer abundance of the FCT typology across the Eastern Seaboard, as well as their different ownership structures, makes a cohesive preservation effort difficult to achieve. Their transition from military to civilian use was often made without any regard to the historic values the fortifications had. And out of close to a hundred tower sites, which ones were worth calling attention to? As the handbook reiterates:

> It is more difficult to identify fortifications built after 1890. . . This most recent period produced structures that are scattered widely, and related components of such fortifications might be separated by miles of land and water. In some instances, the structures may not be readily identifiable as belonging to a system of defense. The complexity is compounded by changes in land ownership. What was once a large military reservation may now be a group of smaller parcels owned privately or in a mix of public and private ownership. Often overlooked are the many

small auxiliary structures that made for the complete functioning of the defense. They are important pieces that complete the full picture of significance.

The history of fire control towers, and their peculiar status today, brings conversations of architectural obsolescence and preservation to the table. As Jorge Otero-Pailo, Director and Professor of Historic Preservation at Columbia University, affirms in *Experimental Preservation*, an object's lack of attention and cultural invisibility opens the possibility for public imagination, projection, and experimentation on the towers' future use.[24]

FCTs were constructed to last for only a decade, yet they still stand today as material deposits of rapid military territorialization. The towers exemplify how architectural form responded to the constraints of site and technology, and they were experiments in constructing the largest field of vision possible to tame a dangerous and ever-changing landscape. Today, the ocean continues to be the force that threatens the security of thousands of residents in coastal areas, and FCTs continue to delimit this otherwise invisible zone of hazard between land and sea.

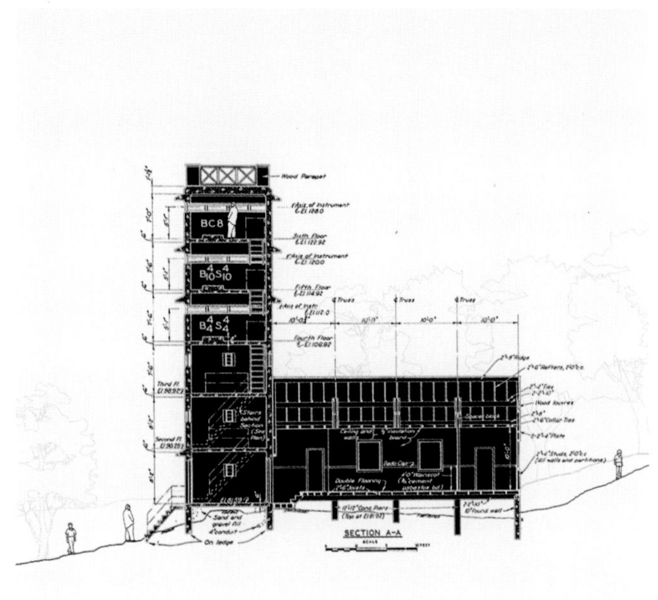

Fig. 6 Section drawing of a fire control tower with an attached plotting room designed to mimic a cottage. Image by Randy Crandon.

-----

[1] Oksana Kotkina, "Landmarks Tower over Nahant." *ItemLive*, June 7, 2022. https://itemlive.com/2022/07/07/landmarks-tower-over-nahant/.
[2] "Fire Control Towers," Division of Historical and Cultural Affairs, State of Delaware, April 5, 2021, https://history.delaware.gov/preservation/firetowers/.
[3] Paul Grigorieff, "Coast Defense," Pt. Allerton Tall FCT, https://coastdefense.com/allerton_tall.htm.
[4] "The Towers: Fire Control Stations in Nahant." *Nahant Harbor Review*. Accessed October 2024. https://www.nahant.com/harbor/2009-JUNE.pdf.
[5] Terrance C. McGovern and B. Smith, *American Coastal Defenses 1885–1950* (Osprey, 2006), 4.
[6] "U.S. Seacoast Defense Construction 1781–1948: A Brief History—Coast Defense Study Group." Coast Defense Study Group, April 1, 2021, https://cdsg.org/united-states-seacoast-defense-construction-1781-1948-a-brief-history/.
[7] "The Civil War Era, 1861–1865," Coast Defense Study Group, April 1, 2021, https://cdsg.org/united-states-seacoast-defense-construction-1781-1948-a-brief-history-the-civil-war-era-1861-1865/.
[8] "Modern U.S. Harbor Defense Construction 1886-1917: The Endicott and Taft," Coast Defense Study Group, April 1, 2021, https://cdsg.org/modern-u-s-harbor-defense-construction-1886-191-the-endicott-and-taft-boards/.
[9] McGovern and Smith, *American Coastal Defenses 1885–1950*, 13.
[10] "Fire Control Towers," FC-Towers, http://www.fortsaulsburyde.com/FC-Towers.html.
[11] Modern U.S. Harbor Defense Construction 1886-1917: The Endicott and Taft," Coast Defense Study Group, April 1, 2021, https://cdsg.org/modern-u-s-harbor-defense-construction-1886-191-the-endicott-and-taft-boards/.
[12] "Plans and Projects between the Wars, 1917–1940," Coast Defense Study Group, April 1, 2021, https://cdsg.org/plans-and-projects-between-the-wars-1917-1940/.
[13] "The World War II Era, 1940–1950," Coast Defense Study Group, March 17, 2022, https://cdsg.org/the-world-war-ii-era-1940-1950/.
[14] "Fighting U-Boats in American Waters," National Museum of the United States Air Force™, https://www.nationalmuseum.af.mil/Visit/Museum-Exhibits/Fact-Sheets/Display/Article/195991/fighting-u-boats-in-american-waters/.
[15] John R. Stilgoe, *Alongshore* (Yale University Press, 1994), 259–263.
[16] Paul Virilio, *Bunker Archeology* (Princeton Architectural Press, 2008), 17.
[17] Paul Virilio and Patrick Camiller, *War and Cinema: The Logistics of*

Perception (Verso, 1989), 2–3.

[18] David A. Mindell, *Between Human and Machine: Feedback, Control, and Computing before Cybernetics* (Johns Hopkins University Press, 2004), 26.

[19] Eben Eveleth Winslow, *Notes on Seacoast Fortification Construction* (Washington, DC: US GPO, 1920), 318.

[20] Ibid., 321.

[21] oksana@itemlive.com. "Landmarks Tower over Nahant." *ItemLive,* June 7, 2022. https://itemlive.com/2022/07/07/landmarks-tower-over-nahant/.

[22] John R. Stilgoe, *Alongshore* (Yale University Press, 1994), 241, 246.

[23] Jeff Brouws, *Silent Monoliths: The Coaling Tower Project* (Steidl GmbH & Co. OHG, 2019).

[24] Jorge Otero-Pailos, "Experimental Preservation," Places Journal, September 2016. Accessed 04 Oct 2024. https://doi.org/10.22269/160913

Carter Manny and the Design Industrial Complex

Charles Waldheim

"Contrary to what is suggested by most historical accounts, the Second World War was a key moment in the modernisation of architectural theory and practice." [1]
– Jean-Louis Cohen, 2011

This essay describes the education and professional formation of architect Carter Manny and American organizational methods of architectural practice derived from Manny's World War II experiences with industrial logistics. The emergence of a military-industrial complex in the post-World War II years has been well documented. The role of architects in the development of that complex has received less attention. Equally obscure has been the impact of the war years on the corporate organization and cultural formation of design culture. This essay proposes that a nearly invisible form of corporate architectural response emerged in response to the logics and structures of the war effort, a nascent design-industrial complex supported by new educational programs and new forms of architectural practice. Rather than an exception to or interruption of conventional architectural practice, the war years represented an acceleration of new forms of practice shaped by the experience of the architects engaged in the logics of logistics and military organizational methods.

In his canonical book *Architecture in Uniform*, of 2011, architectural historian Jean-Louis Cohen critiqued the conventional wisdom that World War II represented a gap or pause in the development of modern architecture. Rather than the interregnum typically described in histories of twentieth-century architecture, Cohen argued that the war years accelerated architectural practice worldwide.[2] Further, he found that architects were pressed into various forms of service on behalf of all nations and across all war fronts. The exhibition that accompanied *Architecture in Uniform* chronicled two dozen architects involved in all facets and fronts of the war, including Albert Speer,

Fig. 1 Carter H. Manny Jr., circa 1956. Courtesy Graham Foundation for Advanced Studies in the Fine Arts.

Myron Goldsmith, Dan Kiley, and Bruno Zevi, among many others.[3] This chapter presents Carter Manny as a late entry to Cohen's incomplete list of architects mobilizing for the war effort. Manny embodies a unique form of a modern architect in service of a nascent "military-industrial complex."[4] His Harvard undergraduate education in fine arts was leavened by encounters with three of the twentieth century's leading modernist architects: Walter Gropius, Frank Lloyd Wright, and Ludwig Mies van der Rohe. Manny was equally well-versed in the industrial logistics of military mobilization, completing a master's degree in industrial administration at Harvard Business School in the run-up to the US entry into the war. This unique combination of experiences prepared Manny for leadership as project architect of the most important airport in the history of jet-age aviation.

Carter Hugh Manny Jr. was born to a prosperous family in Michigan City, Indiana, in 1918. Manny did well in Michigan City's public schools and was accepted to Harvard University. In his final undergraduate year at Harvard, Manny took classes with Walter Gropius and Marcel Breuer in the Graduate School of Design, formed only three years prior. With the onset of the war, Manny enrolled in a war production program in industrial administration offered by the Harvard Graduate School of Business Administration. In 1942, Manny joined the war effort as a civilian member of the Aircraft Scheduling Unit as part of the War Production Board at Wright Field in Dayton, Ohio, where he worked through the war's end. After the war, Manny spent a year apprenticing with Frank Lloyd Wright at Taliesin West. He completed his extraordinary architectural education with two years of graduate work with Mies van der Rohe at the Illinois Institute of Technology in Chicago.[5] Manny's intellectual formation combined a classical humanist liberal education with the principles of modern architecture embodied by the twentieth century's leading lights. It was leavened through the multiple logics of data, administration, and organization. This unique set of experiences prepared Manny for leadership in the most extensive, expensive, and complex public works project in Chicago's history, O'Hare International Airport.

The Manny family had long-standing ties to the small Indiana town on the southern shore of Lake Michigan. Young Carter Manny was the third generation of his family to graduate from Michigan City's public high school.[6] His grandfather, who had graduated in the class of 1879, worked as a freight agent for the Monon Railroad while building a range of business interests, including a family business extracting sand from the nearby dunes of Lake Michigan. The sand was acquired by foundries and glass manufacturers across the Midwest for various industrial uses.[7] Manny's father (Carter Sr.) entered the family's thriving sand business, subsequently expanding into lumber and other enterprises in nearby Chicago. When these businesses

IN MERRIE ENGLAND

Fig. 2 Carter H. Manny, Jr. on a bicycle tour through Europe, 1936. Reprinted from *The Evening Dispatch* (Michigan City, IN), September 23, 1936.

failed to survive the economic crisis of the 1930s, he returned to Michigan City and the sand trade. Carter Manny's grandfather died in 1933 and left Carter Sr. some money and the still viable family sand business, which continued to prosper despite the Depression.[8]

While Carter Manny Jr. had no plans to study architecture, he was introduced to the fine arts at a young age, including painting and architecture. The Manny family enjoyed a modest collection of paintings, and the young Manny took up painting himself. His parents were also friendly with Catherine Baxter, daughter of Frank Lloyd Wright, who lived in Michigan City.[9] Manny would maintain an affection for Wright's unique form of modern American architecture throughout his education and apprenticeships.

In 1936, benefiting from his family's resources and cultural aspirations, a 17-year-old Manny spent the summer between his junior and senior years of high school on an extensive bicycle tour of Europe. This petit tour was described in the local newspaper, The Evening Dispatch, under the headline "Bicycle Tour Saga of Modern Pioneers in Europe: Carter H. Manny, Jr., Tells of Long Journey through Old Country during Summer Days."[10] The article featured a photograph of a thin and muscular Manny posed with his bicycle in front of a cottage in Stratford on Avon, England, that had been home to Anne Hathaway, William Shakespeare's wife. During his tour of Great Britain, Manny described his fascination and affection for the people and architecture of London and Edinburgh, among other cities.[11] Notably, Manny recalled the growing anti-German sentiment he encountered in London. Crossing the English Channel by boat, Manny arrived in Germany in the summer of 1936, traveled down the Rhine River through Nuremberg, and "arrived in Berlin only a few days after the opening of the Olympics." Over his five-day visit, he toured the famous flying field at Tempelhof and Manny found the German capital "plastered with Nazi flags."[12]

Upon his return to Michigan City, Manny considered applying to college to pursue a business career. His great-uncle Frank Manny encouraged him to apply to Harvard.[13] Manny was a good student, graduating eighth in his high school class, crucially, as the "top boy." [14] [Through] the strong endorsement of his high school principal, who praised his creativity, "thoroughness and initiative," Manny received acceptance to Harvard College's Class of 1941 with the support of a John Harvard Scholarship.[15]

Manny arrived in Cambridge that fall intending to pursue a career in business and take courses in government, economics, and history.[16] His freshman adviser, Dr. David Worcester, strongly advised against this course of study, as Manny's small-town midwestern public school education wouldn't enable him to keep up with such rigorous programs. Rather, his adviser recommended a less demanding survey course in fine art history.[17] This was not the only time that he would be dissuaded from joining the elite prep school culture of Harvard College. Manny never felt completely accepted by his East Coast prep school classmates, favoring the company of public high school graduates like himself.[18] Manny took his advice, and in Fall 1937, enrolled in a survey course in fine art history taught by Wilhelm Köhler. Manny thrived in the course and, by Spring 1938, decided to pursue an honors degree in the theory and practice of fine arts.[19] Manny was also inspired in this decision by a talk given by Harvard president James Bryant Conant, who had recently formed the new Harvard School of Design and appointed Joseph Hudnut as its first dean.[20] By his senior year at Harvard College, Manny committed to pursuing a career in architecture and enrolled in courses at the School of Design.

Manny was one of five undergraduate fine arts majors who took courses at the new design school. Among the incentives for such a course of study, Manny and his four colleagues replaced a written thesis requirement with architecture design projects, which would be critiqued by the likes of Marcel Breuer and Walter Gropius.[21] Indeed, during his final year as an undergraduate, Manny took courses with a range of design school faculty, including color theory with Arthur Pope, architectural history with Kenneth Conant, and design with George Holmes Perkins. Manny's classmates at Harvard Design School included Philip Johnson.[22] Johnson was a dozen years Manny's senior and already a prominent figure, but the two became close friends and Manny credits Johnson with elevating his taste in music, among other things.[23] Other classmates included architects John Holabird, Ben Thompson, and Edward Larrabee Barnes.[24]

Manny had a rare window into the origins of modern architecture education at Harvard. His undergraduate

U. S. Army Signal Corps

Trainees in Army Supply Officers School learn the intricacies of tabulating machines in the basement of Baker Library.

Harvard News Office

Members of Reserve Officers' Training Corps board truck, heading for practice bivouac. Chase Hall is in background.

Fig. 3 Army Supply Officers School, Reserve Officers' Training Corps, and Navy Supply Corps School students in uniform on Harvard campus, circa 1944. Courtesy Baker Library, Harvard Business School.

Fig. 4 Harvard wartime school students in formation in front of Baker Library, 1944. Courtesy Harvard University Archives.

experience spanned the formation of the design school through the appointments of Joseph Hudnut as dean and Walter Gropius as chair of architecture. His experiences in that final year of college confirmed his intellectual and professional commitments to the vocation of architecture. In Spring 1941, with Nazi Germany invading France and tensions rising in the Pacific, Manny graduated with an AB in fine arts magna cum laude and Phi Beta Kappa membership.

President Franklin Delano Roosevelt signed the Selective Training and Service Act in September 1940 to prepare for US entry into the war. This legislation instituted the first peacetime conscription for military service in the country's history and required men aged 21 to 35 to register with their local draft board. Graduating from college at 21 years of age in May 1941, Manny was therefore obliged to register with his local draft board. In May 1941, however, just before his graduation, Manny learned of a new graduate program recently announced by Harvard Business School as a "National Defense Plan of Training." This program offered a condensed and reoriented Master of Business Administration (MBA) focused on industrial administration to support the looming war effort.

> Current happenings in Europe have emphasized that in modern warfare industrial preparedness and production are of great importance and

> that any failure behind the lines will seriously affect the chances for military success. [25]

As graduates of this new program were preparing for roles in defense industries, candidates were eligible for deferments by their local draft boards. Manny enrolled in the Harvard Business School's new 12-month course in September 1941 , completing courses in accounting, marketing, industrial management, statistics, procurement, mobilization, governance, and economics.[26] Although both were still in Cambridge, Manny saw less of his friend Philip Johnson during his graduate studies as he courted Radcliffe graduate Mary Alice Kellet, his future wife.[27]

In May 1941, Harvard Business School announced the closure of its traditional two-year MBA program. Going forward, the school committed to the ongoing training of industrial administrators through its 12-month program in parallel support of the US Army Industrial College, which had trained military officers and civilians in war logistics since its inception in the 1920s.[28] The new Harvard curriculum in industrial administration was accompanied by the formation of a new Army Supply Officers School and a Navy Supply Corps School, established at Soldiers Field, the football field adjacent to the business school.[29] These programs complemented an expanded Reserve Officer Training Corps (ROTC) Program at Harvard that was first established in January 1916 in the context of the Great War. While Manny remained a civilian, his experience in the graduate program was shaped by the rapid mobilization of Harvard's educational capacities in service of the looming war and the arrival of various uniformed cohorts on campus. Campus and

Fig. 5 Reserve Officer Training Corps ROTC students marching in Harvard Yard, 1944. Courtesy Harvard University Archives.

Fig. 5 Reserve Officer Training Corps ROTC students drilling with rifles in Harvard Yard, 1944. Courtesy Harvard University Archives.

Fig. 7 Army Air Forces Statistical School graduates, Harvard Business School, 1942. Courtesy Harvard University Archives.

Cambridge life quickly came to emulate the national preparations for war, as Harvard graduates entered the military, ROTC officer candidates marched across Harvard Yard, and Harvard schools pivoted to prepare graduates for various roles in the war.

The relationships the Harvard Business School developed with the army and navy in the run-up to war were not simply improvised in response to national emergency; rather, these relationships stretched back to the US involvement in the Great War, 1917–1918. During those years, Harvard witnessed the depletion of its student body and attrition among the faculty. In the early 1920s, Assistant Secretary of War Dwight F. Davis called on the dean of Harvard Business School to inquire how officer training might effectively include instruction in industrial production. This conversation informed the establishment of the US Army Industrial College in 1924, to complement the long-standing US War College and also resulted in an annual program for army and navy officers to enter the Harvard Business School's two-year MBA program. By 1939, several hundred of these officers had graduated from Harvard, with several occupying positions of significant authority in the US military hierarchy.[30]

With the Japanese attack on Pearl Harbor in December 1941, Harvard's mobilization to a war footing accelerated and intensified. By June 1942, six months after the Japanese attack, Harvard had consolidated its contribution to the war effort as a primary training center for supply and logistics across all armed services branches.[31] Professor W. Arnold Hosmer described the school's contribution as "an instance of the art of administration in action, based on foresight and on another factor—that administration, whether in civilian or military fields, is essentially the same art. It is the art of getting things done in spite of difficulties."[32]

Following the entry of the US into the war in December 1941, Manny's draft number was called as the Selective Service conscripted a far larger number of young men than before. Upon his registration examination, Manny was found unfit for military service and declared IV-F (4F), due to a childhood bout with rheumatic fever.[33] Rather than a military commission, Manny pursued a meaningful contribution to the war effort as a civilian, accepting a job in the Aircraft Scheduling Unit of the War Production Board at Wright Field, Dayton, Ohio, only 250 miles from his boyhood home of Michigan City.[34] Manny remained in the Aircraft Scheduling Unit at Wright Field from his graduation in September 1942 through the war's end in September 1945. His primary responsibilities included procurement, production scheduling, and allocation of aircraft engine carburetors for army and navy aircraft.[35]

Following the US entry into the war, President Roosevelt authorized the establishment of War Production Boards in January 1942 to direct the conversion of industrial enterprises from peacetime operations to war production; the streams of materials, products, and services; and the rationing of essential materials, including gasoline, heating oil, metals, rubber, paper, and plastics.[36] These Boards deployed 120 field offices, including the one at Wright Field in Dayton, Ohio.[37]

During the war, Dayton was home to two major airfields, Patterson Field and Wright Field. In 1939, the two facilities employed a combined workforce of 3,700 civilian and military staff. During the war, that number ballooned to over 50,000 workers operating three shifts twenty-four hours a day.[38] The two airfields and their supporting infrastructure provided the US war effort with a major logistical center and supply hub, safely ensconced in the continent's midsection, remote from Axis incursions.[39] Wright Field managers administered the second-largest procurement division in the US military, supervising the production of nearly 300,000 military aircraft between 1942 and 1945. This extraordinary explosion in industrial production was accomplished through a range of innovative administrative and logistical techniques, including concurrent development processes and accelerated flight testing.[40]

Carter Manny was not on the flight line. He was not involved in flight testing. He arrived at Wright Field at the height of industrial mobilization for war in September 1942. He worked deep in the administrative apparatus of the Aircraft Scheduling Unit at Wright Field, working through the procurement, production, and deployment of advanced fuel-delivery systems for the most advanced aircraft engines of the era. In 1944, at the peak of US military-industrial production, Manny and his colleagues in the War Production Board procured and produced nearly 100,000 aircraft, doubling the ambitious target of 50,000 aircraft per year that President Roosevelt had set in May 1940.

Manny worked in the Power Plant section of the Aircraft Scheduling Unit, which was responsible for developing and deploying aircraft engines and their subcomponents. The efficient and reliable fuel delivery to aircraft engines became an increasingly significant challenge with the growth of larger, heavier aircraft capable of carrying heavier payloads over greater distances. Manny and his colleagues worked to advance carburetor technology and advocated for developing direct fuel-injection systems with industrial suppliers. This proved both innovative and effective, as fuel-injection systems developed with Bosch and Bendix contributed to the development of larger aircraft power plants.[41] Manny recalled that, during his visits to Bosch and Bendix headquarters, he often encountered colleagues from the Manhattan Engineer District, the group responsible for developing the Manhattan Project and the first atomic bomb.[42] Apparently, those Manhattan Project engineers were equally concerned about carburetors, as the engines of the aircraft delivering the first atomic bombs over Hiroshima and Nagasaki were fueled by direct-injection fuel systems.[43]

After the bombing of Hiroshima and Nagasaki and the Japanese surrender in September 1945, Manny resigned from his job at Wright Field. Longtime friend Philip Johnson urged Manny to study with Ludwig Mies van der Rohe at the Illinois Institute of Technology.[44] However, Manny still held a fondness for the work of his boyhood giant, Frank Lloyd Wright. Manny and Mary

Alice returned to Michigan City to live with his parents. The following year, Manny accepted a paid position as assistant to FLW at Wright's Taliesen West school in Arizona. FLW paid Manny 100 dollars per month, describing him condescendingly as "professor."[45] Manny spent three months in Fall 1946 working with Wright and his students, returning to Mary Alice upon the birth of their daughter, Elizabeth. Manny completed his extraordinary trifecta of apprenticeships with modern masters, finally accepting Philip Johnson's advice to pursue graduate studies with Mies van der Rohe at the Illinois Institute of Technology.[46] Manny completed his graduate work at IIT in spring 1948 and immediately joined Naess & Murphy, where he worked through his retirement in 1984.

In 1956, Chicago mayor Richard J. Daley awarded the commission for planning and design of O'Hare International Airport to architects Naess & Murphy.[47] Eight years after joining the Murphy firm, Carter Manny, who had recently supervised the design and construction of a temporary building for American Airlines at O'Hare, was appointed project architect and partner-in-charge of the O'Hare project, the largest public works project in the city's history. He was, more than anyone else at the Murphy firm, responsible for the team and the quality of design that the team produced.

Manny moved quickly to assemble a team of designers from within the Murphy firm, including several who had worked on the Central District Water Treatment Plant, as well as from the leading Chicago offices. He appointed critical design team members, including Stanislaw Gladych and Walter Metschke, who would make significant contributions to the conception and completion of O'Hare. Manny also recruited many architects who had worked with Walter Netsch and Skidmore, Owings, and Merrill on the US Air Force Academy campus near Colorado Springs, Colorado. These precedent projects informed the work at O'Hare and the firm's culture, which was characterized by the same systems of command and control used in the war years. It was also shaped by the corporate culture and organization of American business practices. Murphy himself had been trained in such an environment in the Burnham firm and its successors. These firms did not emulate the European fashion of an artist's atelier or design studio. Instead, the larger architectural firms practicing in Chicago and elsewhere in the US during the late nineteenth and first half of the twentieth centuries tended toward an organization that emulated their corporate clients. In this corporate structure, discrete aspects of the work, such as client acquisition, project management, conceptual design, detailing, specifications, and construction management, would be assigned to specifically trained and experienced individuals and teams. Rather than a synthetic artistic act, this form of practice greatly valued the Fordist division of labor into subcomponents and the optimization of various independent tasks throughout the project.

This organizational structure allowed a firm to simultaneously build and maintain a strong reputation for project management and delivery while allowing its design work to shift and evolve in response to cultural changes and client demands. It also had the profitable attribute of mirroring its largest clients' organization and corporate culture. In this mirroring, the commercial, government, or military client, a CEO, and a military general, or a director of public works was insulated from the artistic temperament of the project designers while being managed by a partner in charge of the project. This mirroring of corporate structure extended beyond military and government clients to include the US' largest private corporations and industries.

After the war, this organizational structure and its attendant top-down culture became known as the "American" organizational model. This new model for architectural practice was informed by the wartime experiences of architects across the country engaged in procurement, logistics, and wartime organizational structure. While many of the designers working on O'Hare were educated by leading European architects such as Walter Gropius at Harvard or Mies van der Rohe at IIT, those designers did not generally bring with them the collectivist impulse of Gropius or the master/apprentice model of Mies. Instead, they adapted their commitments to modern architecture to operate within the dominant culture of "American organization" they found at SOM and the Murphy firm. By the time of their postwar airport commissions, Naess & Murphy and Skidmore, Owings & Merrill embodied this American organizational structure inherited from Ernest Graham and Daniel Burnham. The 1950 Museum of Modern Art exhibition featuring the work of Skidmore, Owings & Merrill suggested as much when it described the work of the three partners and their staff as "animated by two disciplines which they all share—the discipline of modern architecture and the discipline of American organizational methods."[48]

Manny was named partner in 1957, after just nine years with the Murphy firm, to acknowledge his new responsibilities on the O'Hare project. He worked on various aspects of O'Hare's development for over a quarter-century until he retired from architectural practice in 1984.[49] In addition to O'Hare, Manny played a leadership role in several notable commissions, including the design of the Federal Bureau of Investigation's headquarters in Washington, DC, and the First National Bank in Chicago. In certain respects, Manny and the culture of the Murphy firm reflected the "organization man" ethos of the era through a deep commitment to the professional, political, and public institutions that ordered the postwar period. However, contrary to the stereotype, Manny demonstrated creativity, flexibility, and innovation working within and through those structures. He was an extraordinarily talented architect whose accomplishments remain relatively underreported. Despite his prominent role and the enormous success of his work on O'Hare, Manny retained an inherent modesty about his achievements in public and private, most often deflecting responsibility for his achievements and crediting individual team members for their contributions.

In a testament to the enduring quality of Carter Manny's modern architecture informed by the logics of military logistics, classmate Philip Johnson wrote to Manny in April 1962 as O'Hare opened to jet-age operations: "Stopped over one hour at your airport, and I think it is the best airport in the world."[50]

-----

[1] Jean-Louis Cohen, *Architecture in Uniform: Designing and Building for the Second World War* (Canadian Centre for Architecture, 2011), back cover.

[2] Cohen, *Architecture in Uniform*.

[3] Jean-Louis Cohen, curator, "Architecture in Uniform: Designing and Building for the Second World War," exhibition, Canadian Centre for Architecture, Montreal, April 13–September 18, 2011.

[4] The formulation "military-industrial complex" appears in the journal *International Affairs* in 1931. See *International Affairs* 10, no. 442 (1931). While the precise etymology of the concept remains contested, the idea was popularized by US President and former five-star general Dwight D. Eisenhower, who used the term in his farewell address in January 1961. See "military-industrial complex," *Oxford English Dictionary*; https://www.oed.com/dictionary/military-industrial-complex_n?tab=meaning_and_use.

[5] Carter Manny, "Oral History of Carter Manny;" and Carter Manny, personal correspondence with the author, April 25, 2014. See also Robert Bruegmann, "In Memoriam: Carter H. Manny Jr. (1918–2017)," *Journal of the Society of Architectural Historians*, 77, no. 3 (September 2018): 252-255.

[6] Carter Manny, "Oral History of Carter Manny," Interviewed by Franz Schulze (Art Institute of Chicago, 1995), 1.

[7] Manny, "Oral History," 1-2.

[8] Manny, "Oral History," 5.

[9] Manny, "Oral History," 31.

[10] "Bicycle Tour Saga of Modern Pioneers in Europe: Carter H. Manny, Jr., Tells of Long Journey through Old Country during Summer Days," *The Evening Dispatch* (Michigan City, Indiana), September 23, 1936.

[11] "Bicycle Tour Saga of Modern Pioneers in Europe."

[12] "Bicycle Tour Saga of Modern Pioneers in Europe."

[13] Manny, "Oral History," 5.

[14] Manny, "Oral History," 5-6. Harvard College did not accept women in 1937. While Harvard's School of Education enrolled women as early as 1920, and Harvard Medical School admitted women in 1936, Harvard College was a male only institution until its integration of Radcliffe Institute in the 1960s.

[15] Application of Carter H. Manny Jr., 1937, UA III 15.88.10, Box 3252, Harvard University Archives, Cambridge, MA.

[16] Plan of Study for Carter H. Manny Jr., 1938. Harvard University

Archives, Cambridge, MA.
[17] Manny, "Oral History," 6–7.
[18] Manny, "Oral History," 34.
[19] Manny, "Oral History," 7; and Plan of Study for Carter H. Manny Jr.
[20] Manny, "Oral History," 6–7.
[21] Manny, "Oral History," 9–10.
[22] Manny, "Oral History," 11.
[23] Manny, "Oral History," 33.
[24] Manny, "Oral History," 15.
[25] *Alumni Bulletin*, May 1941, Baker Library Special Collection and Archives at Harvard Business School, Cambridge, MA, 237–238.
[26] *Alumni Bulletin*, May 1941, Baker Library Special Collection and Archives at Harvard Business School, Cambridge, MA, 338.
[27] Manny, "Oral History," 38
[28] Everett N. Case, "The Business School and the War," *Alumni Bulletin*, Summer 1942. Baker Library Special Collection and Archives at Harvard Business School, Cambridge, MA, 215.
[29] *Alumni Bulletin*, May 1941, Baker Library Special Collection and Archives at Harvard Business School, Cambridge, MA, 338. See also Case, "The Business School and the War."
[30] Case "The Business School and the War," 215.
[31] Case, "The Business School and the War," 217.
[32] Hosmer, W. Arnold. "War Record of the Alumni and the Business School," *Alumni Bulletin*, Autumn 1946. Baker Library Special Collection and Archives at Harvard Business School, Cambridge, MA, 75.
[33] Carter Manny, "Oral History of Carter Manny," Interviewed by Franz Schulze (Chicago: Art Institute of Chicago, 1995), 38–39.
[34] Harvard College, Class of 1941, Sexennial Report. Harvard University Archives, Cambridge, MA, 1947.
[35] Manny, "Oral History of Carter Manny," 39.
[36] Thomas D. Morgan, "The Industrial Mobilization of World War II: America Goes to War." *Army History,* no. 30 (Spring 1994): 31–35.
[37] William D. Carey, "Central-Field Relationships in the War Production Board." *Public Administration review* 14, No. 1 (Winter 1944): 33.
[38] History Office Air Force Life Cycle Management Center Air Force Materiel Command Wright-Patterson Air Force Base, *Wright-Patterson Air Force Base: The First Century*. Dayton, OH, 2015.
[39] Alexander McSurely, "War in the Air: Dayton's Role Vital, Indispensable: Powerful Air Armada Created by Work at AAF Bases in Area." *Dayton Herald*, December 5, 1943. https://www.nps.gov/articles/000/-h-our-history-lesson-aviation-and-defense-industry-in-dayton-and-montgomery-county-ohio.htm; (accessed May 27, 2024); History Office Air Force Life Cycle Management Center Air Force Materiel Command Wright-Patterson Air Force Base, *Wright-Patterson Air Force Base,* 13.
[40] History Office Air Force Life Cycle Management Center Air Force Materiel Command Wright-Patterson Air Force Base, *Wright-Patterson Air Force Base*, 14.
[41] Manny, "Oral History of Carter Manny," 39–40.
[41] Ibid.
[43] Ibid.
[44] Manny, "Oral History of Carter Manny," 42.
[45] Manny, "Oral History of Carter Manny," 46.
[46] Manny, "Oral History of Carter Manny," 60, 63.
[47] Charles F. Murphy, "Oral History of Charles F. Murphy," interviewed by Carter H. Manny (Art Institute of Chicago, 1995), 48.
[48] "Skidmore, Owings & Merrill," *Museum of Modern Art Bulletin* 18, no. 1 (Fall 1950), 5; as cited in Sheri Olsen, "Skidmore, Owings & Merrill" The Project Team," *Modernism at Mid-Century: The Architecture of the United States Air Force Academy*, ed. Robert Bruegmann (University of Chicago Press, 1994), 36, note 13.
[49] Carter Manny, "Oral History of Carter Manny," and Carter Manny, personal correspondence with the author, April 25, 2014.
[50] Philip Johnson, letter to Carter Manny, April 11, 1962, private papers of Carter Manny.

{Excerpts}

Under the Cardboard Pines

Keaton Bruce

Images of the forest have been constructed as poignant symbols of planetary savior, yet most of the world's trees fall under the colonial gaze of capital extraction and corporate-ownership. As carbon sinks, the planet's lungs, as regenerative material factories, and biodiversity "hotspots," the world's forests are central to missions of sustainability and as such, have become intertwined with corporate and state-sponsored green objectives that expand the role of the forest far beyond its canopy of trees. In her book, *Designing the Forest and Other Mass Timber Futures*, Lindsey Wikstrom speaks to this technical complexity of forested land and its bountiful capital when writing "forest resources are slowly and incrementally being traded, shared, and negotiated below ground and above ground, above the canopy, across boundaries and borders and socioeconomic zones, by fungi and trees and humans." From a natured "other," the forest has evolved into a technical land, a process largely involved as a driving force of anthropogenic climate change. This commodification of timber resources and their conversion to infrastructural systems of capital is based on hundreds of years of what Wikstrom describes as the "Eurocentric conquest and its imaginaries of forests, nature, value, virtue, and personhood." In this imagination, the forest has been left vulnerable to the unfettered exploitation of capital interests.

Deforestation has become one of the primary drivers of anthropogenic climate change due to the inability of alternative ecosystems to sequester or filter carbon from the atmosphere. These very forests, however, are used as symbols of corporate initiatives for sustainable futures. Carbon credits and sustainable forestry represent moral justification for the utilization of natural resources as elements in a capitalist system of extraction and consumption. The forest is actively destroyed by the very interests which exploit its potential for ecological harmony – seeing a forest of timber renders the forest of ecological systems largely invisible. All that remains is the imagination of forestry as a sustainable actor, whilst the actual forest ecosystem is reduced to single species farming and wildfire kindling.

Forest ownership is dominated by private landholders—family and corporate holdings included. This private territorial occupation of extractive industries is not readily presented in claims of forest products and sustainability. Instead, an advertising campaign by 'sustainable' packaging giant Smurfit Kappa (owning 170,00 acres of forestland globally) presents a cardboard rocket ship which asks, "Where will you take us." The image positions the company in connection to global futures, sustainable forestry, and ultimately, human progress. At first the rocket ship seems like a playful image for a cardboard company to use. But an awareness of timber companies' utilization of private satellite imagery to monitor large swaths of timberland reveals a connection between cardboard production and extraterrestrial access. The forested terrestrial becomes an occupied farm actively managed for optimal harvest, an occupation so expansive it cannot be viewed on foot, nor from atop a tractor, but by satellites in atmospheric orbit.

Pigs and Plutonium

Carly Browngardt

Nuclear waste has left a long-lasting impact on places like the Savannah River Site in South Carolina. As depicted in Lindsey Freeman's memoir, *The Atom Bomb in Me* we can understand how the nuclear era has affected generations. From architects designing secret cities for the Manhattan Project to today trying to find innovative ways for architects to assist in determining the future land use of the Savannah River Site after it's done serving its purpose of storing the nuclear waste, while we figure out what to do with the nuclear waste long-term. Exploring the past, present, and future for the SRS, we can recognize the challenges we are faced with and figure out an effective solution that doesn't disrupt the future environment, people, and animals. The Savannah River Site, located in Aikens, South Carolina, spans 310 square miles and today serves as a nuclear waste clean-up site owned by the Department of Energy. Previously, the land was used to produce plutonium-239 and tritium, key elements used for the manufacturing of nuclear weapons from the 1950s until the end of the Cold War. The construction of SRS was approved by Harry S. Truman, to make room for the site; this caused six towns to have to relocate. During full production of the nuclear weapons at SRS the surrounding community in Aikens South Carolina was not pleased. Frequent protests occurred near the Savannah River Site, expressing their concerns about nuclear production.

The Savannah River Site and other regions in the South are struggling with a significant issue: a dense population of wild pigs. These animals not only pose a threat to the site's operations and a risk to workers at the SRS but also face the negative effects of nuclear waste. Studies have shown that pigs contain high levels of radioactive waste in their bodies. Places like the SRS are making efforts to manage the wild pig population, aiming to limit the population to around 500 pigs to help minimize ecological damage. This problem serves as a reminder of the lasting impact and consequences of nuclear activities on the environment, wildlife and human health. Showing us the need to plan and design our future as these challenges will not go away on their own and continue to get worse. If wild pigs and other animals continue to be radioactive due to their exposure to nuclear waste, it will continue to show an increase in negative consequences. Radioactive contamination can lead to genetic mutations, reproductive issues, and many other concerns. Additionally, consuming contaminated meat could cause serious health issues.

There would be an overall ecosystem imbalance. The biggest challenge will be determining ways to remove nuclear waste from the site or even the Earth safely. Additionally, there is an ongoing debate about whether moving the nuclear waste from the site is the best option, or if it's better to keep the waste where it is and avoid more land contamination. However, there are complications to leaving the nuclear waste in its current location, and concerns about it seeping deeper into the ground, which could lead to more negative effects. Over the next decade, there are plans to tackle the radioactive tank waste, which is the largest environmental risk on the site, through new waste treatment facilities.

Dredging Terra Nullius

Logan Paulukow

In a world of commodities, high speed interconnectedness has become the most valuable resource in the world. Data transferring subsea internet cables stretch the oceans to connect lands. We are swimming in a densely knit rhizomatic cloud of data and infrastructure. Unprecedented resources necessitate unprecedented extraction methods. No longer do we extract through taking of land. Instead, we make land. Identifying tangled infrastructural pinch points, manufactured land/territory can intercept, seize, and influence the streams of commodity that run between them. Vulnerability seized through a vulnerable process; the island, the Spratly Islands. With every effort to extract as much as we can from our world, we have spun together layers of invasive viaducts. Some lay empty, some fossilized, some maintained: all infrastructure. Scaffolding our environment, infrastructure has paved our landmasses together into a single traversable territory where resources mingle without boundaries. No longer does the island condition exist on earth. The entirety; a single neo-island. In observation of our infrastructural tendencies, a cycle is identified. The cycle is as follows: Establish territory, deplete resources in territory, colonize beyond territorial boundaries, extract foreign resources for territory, identify foreign infrastructure, seize resources, establish territory.

Rooted on a series of shallow coral reefs in the South China Sea, the Spratly Islands are manufactured islands. Fueled by the Peoples Republic of China, the Spraty islands solidify a piece of Chinas 9 dash line enveloping the most highly contested sea territory in the world. Technical lands are always strategically placed. The artificial islands sit at a crossroads of tangled infrastructural pathways. They sit along an oil shipping route, atop a speculated oil reserve, within arm's reach of neighboring territories and their resources, and they are an extension of surveillance and sign of power. The Spratly Islands impose a threat to the greater reaches of its immediate locale if they tap into the subsea cable lines bypassing their mainland.

Paradoxically, through the simple intricacies of the Spratly Islands, both visible and invisible, we can see the impact and importance of our infrastructure at a higher resolution. Although we can't necessarily understand infrastructures on a large scale, there are multiplicities of resolutions in which infrastructure can be observed. The Spratly islands are infrastructure in an almost pure form. Isolated, the islands' remoteness assists in ascending infrastructure from its invisible form into a physical observable node. Islands' remoteness is what gives them the paradoxical power that they have over non-islands. Islands produce vulnerable opportunity. Paradoxical in nature, they are isolated snags in the geographical fabric, that can be resown or patched, or torn larger. In the case of the Spratly Islands, the fabric of the ocean torn open and out pulled a thread from the fabric below. From a distance, the tiny incision is invisible. Once observed, it cannot be mistaken. They conceal through their isolation but are vulnerably revealed through the same isolated condition. From a distance, a clear boundary of containment.

Capitalism Cremated Centralia

Breana Haselbarth

In an empty landscape with only trees and overgrown roads lies an idle community. Once a vibrant mining community with entertainment, residents, and business, now only a few homes and the local firehouse remain. Beneath the barren landscape, a fire smolders, slowly working its way over the hillside and passing underneath the sleeping town. Centralia's story is not a new one. With a fire burning for over 60 years, the once vibrant mining town has disappeared. Many efforts have gone into remediating the areas, yet they have never been able to recover. The coal fire still burns beneath the landscape heating the soil and causing sinkholes. The land cannot be "saved" after it has been contaminated or abused by humans for profit. The idea that you can extract resources from the ground, possibly contaminate the land in the process, and then "put it all back" is a false one. The resource is still missing, the land has still been contaminated, and it cannot be put back to the way it was.

Centralia was officially founded in 1866, but mining had defined life for the decade prior. By the mid-1900s, the town was declining as the demand for anthracite coal also declined. In May of 1962, town firefighters were setting the local landfill on fire as they did every year on Memorial Day. The landfill sat on top of an old strip-mining pit unbeknownst to the firefighters. When they set the landfill on fire, fire seeped into the mine and caught the large coal vein below on fire. Efforts were made to extinguish the fire but it continued to spread under the town. Between 1962 and 1978 state and federal governments spent more than $3.3 million trying to extinguish the fire. The town continued to get hotter and hotter with some of the smoke being released from the mines reaching 900 degrees (f). Smoke filled basements and residents were required to share carbon monoxide detectors to make sure it was safe to be in their homes. In 1981 a 12-year-old boy fell into a sudden sinkhole that opened in his grandmother's yard causing calls for state help. By 1983 an OSM study estimated that it would cost $663 million to extinguish the fire completely. Instead, it was decided that $42 million would go toward the voluntary purchase and relocation of residents and businesses. In 1992 it was decided it was no longer safe for any residents to stay in Centralia, and the Centralia Task Force condemned the remaining properties.

Centralia had become a poor mining town with little support from the state government. In efforts to remediate their own town, they ended up bringing its end. The fire was then allowed to burn for 20 years without state governments stepping in to make a real change. How many more communities will be subjected to hazardous waste and further economic downturn because they are so easily ignored by governments, designers, and laws alike? When there is no wilderness left to escape to, will we finally look at what we have done to the environment of which we are a part? At that point, it will be too late. The damage will be done, and we won't be able to fix what we broke in the first place, all in the pursuit of money.

Exposing Externalities of Extraction

Victoria Betterly

Port of Barranquilla, namely is the largest port in Colombia and exports the most amount of oil of the county's ports. The port located on the Magdalena River is connected to the Caribbean Sea. It sits on a 2.94- acre terminal that includes a warehouse, lab, and office which will provide 50,000 barrels per day. This facility transfers and processes seven million barrels of petroleum products a year. From the ports, huge oil tanker ships export the product to receiving ports. America is the largest receiver of oil from Colombia and most of the ships dock at ports along the coast of Texas. Texas has 12 deepwater ports that have seen an increase in cargo from oil and chemical exports recently. From there, the oil is sent throughout the country, by waterways or highways. The oil eventually reaches its final location in its final state as the "product." The product takes many different forms, from the gas you put into your car to the makeup you put on your skin. Skincare products labeled as "moisturizing" or "hydrating" frequently contain ingredients derived from petroleum. These same components are commonly present in makeup, hair care, and nail care items as well. The product's origins can be traced back thousands of miles of externalities to an extraction site.

As technology advances and global economies expand, the mine is becoming more accessible than ever before, yet the mine remains hidden from the public eye. Externalities are linking the mine, to the port, to the refinery, and so on. These changes are being orchestrated behind a cloak of "remoteness" which allows these processes to unfold. Technical lands in Colombia that are created through extraction and ambiguity will be identified within this paper to demonstrate the expansiveness and impact of the mine.

In 2008, Total Energies held an advising campaign where they displayed photographs of a site of extraction, mirrored by how the extracted material or good was being consumed. What was missing from these images was the processes and technological systems for getting the extracted material from the mine to the consumer. The infrastructures that support these functions are often lost on society because they are designed to be in sparsely populated areas deemed to be remote. A concept that has its pros and cons. A remote place can be deemed the perfect wasteland because of the geographical isolation it has from the general population. It can also be seen as a haven of unregulated territory. Making a remote area the perfect location for externalities and or technical lands. Regardless of their legality, these areas of extraction in Colombia are all capitalist lead extraction practices resulting in technical lands that contribute to the deforestation of the Amazon Rainforests and surrounding ecosystems. The dense, sparsely occupied jungle of Colombia, where the Andes Mountain range and the Amazon Rainforest overlap, creates the crucial separation and invisibility needed for these extraction processes to be carried out. Corporations and illegal harvesting groups both use this to their advantage so there is less opposition surrounding their processes.

Contributors

Pedro Ignacio Alonso is an architect, educator, and curator and associate professor in the Theory of Architecture and Design at the Universidad Católica de Chile.

Ryan Bishop is professor of Global Art and Politics at Winchester School of Art, University of Southampton (UK).

Keaton Bruce is an interdisciplinary graduate student and research assistant pursuing his Master of Architecture at the Tyler School of Art and Architecture at Temple University.

Randy Crandon an architectural designer, photographer, artist, sailor graduate student at the Harvard University Graduate School of Design.

Lindsey Freeman is an associate professor of sociology and the graduate program chair in Sociology and Anthropology at Simon Fraser University.

Philip Glahn is a historian, theorist, and associate professor of Aesthetics and Critical Studies in the Tyler School of Art and Architecture at Temple University.

Gretchen Heefner is a military and environmental historian and the chair and professor of History in the College of Social Sciences and Humanities at Northeastern University.

Ghazal Jafari is a designer, spatial historian, territorial scholar in exile, and assistant professor of Urban and Environmental Planning in the School of Architecture at the University of Virginia.

Eliyahu (Eli) Keller is an architect, historian, and an assistant professor at the Technion Faculty of Architecture and Town Planning.

May Khalife is an architectural historian and assistant professor in Architecture and Interior Design at Miami University, Ohio.

César Lopez is a first-generation Mexican American architectural designer, researcher, educator, and assistant professor in the School of Architecture at the University of Virginia

Jeffrey S. Nesbit is an architect, urbanist, founder of Grounding Design, and assistant professor in History and Theory of Architecture and Urbanism in the Tyler School of Art and Architecture at Temple University.

Hugo Palmarola is an associate professor in the School of Design at the Pontificia Universidad Católica de Chile and holds a PhD in Latin American Studies from UNAM Mexico.

Victoria Sanger is a specialist in early modern architectural and urban history and adjunct assistant professor in the Graduate School of Architecture, Planning and Preservation at Columbia University.

Malkit Shoshan is the founder and director of the architectural think tank FAST (Foundation for Achieving Seamless Territory) and design critic in Urban Planning and Design at the Harvard University Graduate School of Design.

Mark Stanley is an assistant professor at the University of Tennessee College of Architecture and Design and co-founder of StudioMARS, a speculative design-research practice.

Charles Waldheim is an architect, urbanist, and John E. Irving Professor at the Harvard University Graduate School of Design where he directs the Office for Urbanization.

Kate Wingert-Playdon is an architectural and cultural historian and senior associate dean and director of Architecture in the Tyler School of Art and Architecture at Temple University.

Dongwoo Yim is an architect, researcher, educator, co-founder and principal of PRAUDarchitecture, and an assistant professor in Architecture at Hongik University in Seoul.

Image Credits

0.1 Keaton Bruce, "A Network of Infrastructure," cartographic detail, 2023.

0.2 Keaton Bruce, "A Territory of Militarization," cartographic detail, 2023.

0.3 Keaton Bruce, "A Geography of Extreme Environments," cartographic detail, 2023.

0.4 Nik Shuliahin, Smokestacks Rising Above Clouds, Kentucky, US, photo, 2018. Courtesy Nik Shuliahin / Unsplash.

0.5 Iewek Gnos, MERLIN Dish, Cambridge, UK, photo, 2021. Courtesy Iewek Gnos / Unsplash.

0.6 Clayton Malquist, USS Yorktown, Charleston, South Carolina, US, photo, 2021. Courtesy Clayton Malquiest / Unsplash.

0.7 Keith Hardy, Sand Dunes, Namib Desert, Namibia, photo, 2017. Courtesy Keith Hardy / Unsplash.

0.8 Collab Media, Landfill Fire, photo, date unknown. Courtesy Collab Media / Unsplash.

0.9 Ivan Bandura, Coal Ash Pond Sediment Delta, Alberta, Canada, photo, 2018. Courtesy Ivan Bandura / Unsplash.

0.10 Tony Stoddard, Mount Climie Track Comm Tower, New Zealand, photo, 2017. Courtesy Tony Stoddard / Unplash.

0.11 Sergey Omelchenko, Chernobyl Radar Duga, photo, date unknown. Courtesy Sergey Omelchenko / Unsplash.

0.12 Arian Hackbart, Radio Towers, Brazil, photo, 2016. Courtesy Arian Hackbart / Unsplash.

0.13 Getty Images, Oil Geyser Flare, photo, date unknown. Courtesy Getty Images / Unsplash.